Breakthroughs in Six Brief Psychotherapies

Breakthroughs in Six Brief Psychotherapies

George Carpetto, Ph.D.

Writers Club Press
San Jose New York Lincoln Shanghai

Breakthroughs in Six Brief Psychotherapies

All Rights Reserved © 2000 by George Carpetto

No part of this book may be reproduced or transmitted in any form or by any means, graphic, electronic, or mechanical, including photocopying, recording, taping, or by any information storage retrieval system, without the permission in writing from the publisher.

Writers Club Press
an imprint of iUniverse.com, Inc.

For information address:
iUniverse.com, Inc.
620 North 48th Street, Suite 201
Lincoln, NE 68504-3467
www.iuniverse.com

ISBN: 0-595-13326-6

Printed in the United States of America

To Diane,

my wife and best friend,
in gratitude for your support

Contents

Preface ix

Acknowledgments xiii

Introduction xv

Chapter 1

Brief Therapy as a Notion:Its Origins, Its Early Evolution 1

Chapter 2

The MRI Brief Therapy Project 47

Chapter 3

The Milan School's Circular Interviewing 107

Chapter 4

Steve de Shazer's Solution-Focused Therapy 141

Chapter 5

Solution-Oriented Therapy 177

Chapter 6

The Constructivist Model 225

Chapter 7

The Narrative Techniques of White & Epston 285

References 311

Index 327

About the Author 337

Preface

The intent of this book is to present an introduction to six specific brief psychotherapies that essentially have evolved out of systemic/family thinking. It also entails experiencing their distinct presence as major breakthroughs in psychotherapy's evolution. The text is directed toward professionals in the psychological services and to students who would like to learn more about these specific areas.

A considerably substantial introductory chapter offers the background of brief therapy's early notions, from Freud to the establishment of the Mental Research Institute in the 1950s. The ensuing chapters each depict the essentials of a specific working model whose strategies and techniques have proven to be useful and practical. Not purporting to be a critical text, this book presents extensive bibliographic references, indicating an ample list of writers whose works may elucidate problem areas or controversial topics.

Our immediate agenda involves illustrating the basic pathways of six models that have been tried and tested within the last four decades. Their origins are best described, collectively, as systemic/family inspired. Their more recent evolution has involved additional refinements and developments. Generally speaking, their collective trends have advocated, more and more, the fostering of a greater sense of empowerment in the client and, correspondingly, the advancement of a greater sense of "aesthetic" sensibility and "ecological" responsibility in the therapist.

This text is aimed at those readers who may have previously worked with a specific model or with an eclectic modality and may now feel it is time to explore systemic/family modalities. Collectively, the member modalities of the latter group have all corroborated their theories and abundantly documented their success in practice. Systemic/family thinking has grown heartily from its "grass roots" 1940s research and experimentation, focused mainly on schizophrenia in a family context, up to its more recent 1990s best-selling book, *Narrative Means to Therapeutic Ends*. Coauthored by Michael White and David Epston, it has become a worldwide classic text.

To readers who would like to augment their exposure beyond the purview of this systemic/family-oriented text, we recommend Bloom's *Planned Short-Term Psychotherapy*, which deals with psychodynamic, cognitive/behavioral and related integrated approaches. Bloom's book, a standard text regarding *short-term* therapy, traces its development from its psychodynamic origins whose intent involved a *planned* short-term treatment that would "accomplish a set of therapeutic objectives within a sharply limited time frame" up to a maximum of about twenty interviews (pp. 3–4).

Bloom points out that the beginning of short-term therapy was reflected in a series of large volumes in the 1960s (Bellak and Small, 1965; Malan, 1963; Phillips and Wiener, 1966; Wolberg, 1965). He goes on to elaborate that it was obviously no coincidence that so much concentrated literature on short-term therapy proliferated simultaneously with the phenomenon of the community mental health movement of the 1960s. Bloom's book succinctly accounts for the history and evaluation, not only of psychodynamic, but also of cognitive and behavioral short-term therapies. Other clinical short-term approaches are also included.

This book, instead, focuses on *brief* therapy, not *short-term* therapy. Brief therapy emanates from systemic/family thinking whose foundations were built in part by practicing psychiatrists such as Carl Whitaker, Milton Erickson, and Don Jackson, and in part by thinkers from other fields such as Gregory Bateson in anthropology and cybernetics, and Jay Haley in communications. While the specific brief therapy models that we elaborate may incorporate some elements from psychodynamic thinking as part of a systems integration, it would be safe to say that an incorporation of psychodynamic data is not very typical. Hence, to the interested reader, this book, in many ways, aptly contrasts and complements Bloom's text which has been described as essentially psychodynamic and cognitive/behavioral in nature.

The goal of this book involves presenting a synthesis of practical information, theoretical and philosophical developments, and relevant examples of specific practices of some of the major schools embracing the global term systemic/family thinking that has employed brief therapy approaches. This book does not claim to be exhaustive of all those brief psychotherapeutic schools that employ systemic/family thinking, but it does hope to present a useful and unified perspective of the major schools that are specifically discussed in the text.

In their thematic unfolding, there is a decisive chronological component in discussing their development. Our intention involves making the time dimension less abstract and more tangible. This takes place by working with specific time intervals and depicting specific developments within those intervals. Additionally, the book's ideological structure assumes the existence of a dialectic reality. Therefore, when a school's philosophy is discussed or when a significant innovation becomes illustrated, the book's exposition is ever mindful of antecedent modalities, conditions, and generally speaking, connections with prevailing or dominant past perspectives so that subsequent changes and innovations may be more clearly understood and visualized.

For example, well before the term "brief therapy" was coined, there was the noted historical presence of Ferenczi in the 1920s. He had experimented with new therapeutic applications, often for years at a time, in order to abbreviate the length of therapy while maintaining or improving therapeutic effectiveness. His many "experiments" could *not* have taken place in a therapeutic vacuum, nor were they isolated from the prior influences of psychoanalysis. On the contrary, Ferenczi's training and practice as a Freudian psychoanalyst were, in fact, preparatory and necessary as a staging area for his experiments to take place.

Certain aspects of the prevailing Freudian mode, which Ferenczi was obviously attempting to change, were necessarily involved in the crucible of his manipulations and modifications. Ferenczi's attempted changes and their movement in time, when studied historically, clearly represented a dialectical (Hegelian) dimension. The changes, or rather the attempted changes, surely implied the eventuality of the modifications to specific components of the *antecedent model.*

Since all history is process, the relevant components both from the past and the present must become the essential ingredients in the consideration of visualizing and understanding change. The dialectic approach allows one to see the links between the old and the new and, specifically, which elements in the past have moved forward and which elements have been left behind. This dialectic approach represents a major stylistic aspect in the infrastructure of this book's presentation. Historical developments are treated as important and critical to appreciating positive changes and not as if they were one huge, gray, amorphous narration not worth the trouble to decipher.

Acknowledgments

In writing this book, I owe much of my inspiration and moral support to my wife, Diane, who supplied the initial motivation and idea about three years ago. Her encouragement and support have proven to be invaluable. I thank her for having proofread the early versions of the manuscript.

Special thanks are in order for Dr. Sally A. Larson, editorial consultant, for proofreading and fine-tuning the crucially important last versions of the text. She helped me to clarify many of my thoughts and to make my writing achieve greater fluidity and specificity. Though she critiques with her pen, she has performed her craft in many ways like a dedicated artist, always ready with the flair of an extra fine brush, always concerned about improving the shape and quality of expression.

I would like to acknowledge all my colleagues at St. Leo University, particularly at its Gainesville campus, especially Gerald Roberson and Dr. Edward Petkus who have since retired from St. Leo University, and Dr. Christopher Cronin, the Chairman of Psychology at the main campus. I would also like to express my appreciation to the entire St. Leo administrative staff at the Gainesville campus.

Of course, my acknowledgments would not be complete without recognizing the importance of my many hard-working and dedicated students, both past and present. I would like to thank them for allowing me to videotape them in class practice sessions of therapeutic interviewing where respect, compassion, active listening, and effective counseling skills were emphasized.

I want to reiterate my gratitude to all the people mentioned, since in one way or another they provided me with the many special conditions that made this book possible.

Introduction

Modern brief therapy represents a fascinating craft. In some ways, it parallels the advent and growth of the modern computer. Both seem to have defied the establishment and its traditions that had once boldly defended how certain things were to be done. But while far from being iconoclastic, both developments maintained many specific links to their respective pasts. Upon examination, one can witness a certain continuity that shoulders the process of history and its complex workings.

Rarely does history work as most encyclopedic narratives would like one to believe. In its specifics, history represents serially complicated phenomena which we, as "expeditious" observers, often reduce to simple formulaic relationships. Similarly, in the field of psychology, we frequently do the same by reducing complex, dynamic, interactive processes to levels of inertia as if to suggest a narrative flatness and a two-dimensionality with our subsequent labeling and unintended stereotyping.

By contrast, history rarely offers a smooth excursion to the traveler. In reality, its terrain behaves more like an old, unpaved, bumpy road, winding into uncharted detours which, in turn, embraces irregular chronologies of its own, full of trial and error. History is, then, one huge, ongoing series of heuristic meanderings that are held together and unified by the historian's interpretative skill. From time to time, however, when certain occurrences seem important enough to remember to an historian and/or to a large collectivity of "observers," we punctuate them, noting time and place, assigning them memorable names and labels.

Essentially, we raise noteworthy occurrences to the status of historical events, such as the "attack on Pearl Harbor" or the "landing on the moon."

xvi • *Breakthroughs in Six Brief Psychotherapies*

Yet the process by which we punctuate, isolate, and identify historical events becomes all the more difficult when we choose to view the birth and growth of *ideas* as "events" too. Indeed, ideas in themselves represent events despite their ethereal nature. Their development in time's continuum usually becomes inextricably bound to physically perceptible occurrences when ideas are executed and fulfilled in actions and behaviors. To be sure, key ideas, paradigms, and ideologies, despite their inherently abstract nature, do develop, change, and evolve in time. And, paradoxically, in a deep metaphoric sense, they create and maintain a life of their own.

It is with this complexity and with this metaphoric reality of *ideas as events* that I present this study of six specific brief psychotherapies that share many common thematic threads. While these modalities do have some overlaps, both in theory and in practice, they contain notably different qualities that define their uniqueness. One of the book's goals is to mark both their uniqueness and commonalities within a clear timeline.

The study of the evolution of abbreviated therapies, when taken as a whole, is surely not the invention of one person. It is an aggregate development, and to this day, it represents an ongoing multi-faceted development with many variations emanating from competing schools of thought. Abbreviated therapy did, in fact, begin as a seminal idea with Freud himself. Later, its faint, conceptual glimmerings, nurtured by a number of pioneering people through many decades of varied experimentation in the first half of the twentieth century, eventually grew through time and acquired a physiognomy all its own. By the 1950s, the initially vague notion had finally acquired benchmark status in history as a clear idea. The prior scenario of brief therapy as a vague notion, lasting fifty years, is represented in Chapter 1.

Where specific brief therapy models are concerned, the establishment of the Mental Research Institute (MRI) in 1959 in Palo Alto, California represents the first significant major benchmark in brief therapy's subsequent and more recent trajectory. Surely, the MRI as an institution had its own history emanating from both the work of its prior researchers and its more recent thinkers. The MRI's originating group consisting of key figures Don D. Jackson and Jay Haley, and its prophetic personalities such as Gregory Bateson and Milton Erickson, created a complicated and powerful network of forces, all with the intent of making therapy briefer and better. While the term "brief therapy" had already been in use, it was in 1967 that the MRI would become responsible for introducing it as a *formal heading in systemic/family* therapy (Watzlawick et al., 1974, p. xiv).

While the MRI model, also called the problem-focused model, used terminology associated with the medical or "pathology" model, the former's use of some of the latter's medical terminology remained decidedly couched in the newly evolving family, strategic, communicational, cybernetics, and systemic foundations. In fact, for its time in the 1960s, the pathway taken by the MRI represented a major pivotal event in the history of psychotherapy. It was an innovative stance moving away from pathology-based thinking while shifting to significantly different non-pathological perspectives. Cybernetics and communication systems, which were two new areas of research in psychology, were beginning to confute the prevailing pathology-driven world of psychiatry and psychiatry's fledgling creation of its 1952 *Diagnostics and Statistical Manual of Mental Disorders* (DSM).

In addition to a long list of publications by the MRI's members, both jointly and individually, to date their three main originating texts are: *Pragmatics of Human Communication* (1967), *Change: Principles of Problem Formation and Problem Resolution* (1974), and *The Tactics of Change: Doing Therapy Briefly* (1982). Throughout its history, the MRI group would genuinely epitomize a deep and continuously refreshing wellspring of inspiration, well into the 1990s. For example, Watzlawick's 1990 book, *Münchhausen's Pigtail*, exemplifies the constant refinement of some very powerful ideas from the 1950s and 1960s. It was in those pristine and vigorous waters that many psychotherapists would seek inspiration in order to quench their thirst for innovation and creativity.

If we were to view the use of *reframing* and the development of *paradoxical interventions* as the only hallmarks of this school, we would be obviously missing a significant part of its essence. It was a school of thought that had implemented and effected a major shift in psychotherapeutic direction, inspiring newer therapies. Its movement helped depathologize mental problems on the one hand, and, on the other, helped further explore those uncharted territories recently discovered by a host of pioneers, especially Erickson, Bateson and Jackson. The MRI's interesting vagaries, innovations, and bold transformations that have made their mark in modern psychotherapy constitute the contents of Chapter 2.

The Milan Group, the second major school, emphasized *circular questioning* as its centerpiece. In witnessing the enactment of circular interviewing, one cannot help but detect some very significant influences from the MRI group. Yet, despite the apparently notable influences received, the Milan group had utilized those influences for creating a remarkably effective amalgam. By the late 1970s, the Milan group had, in fact, created an exemplary, comprehensive method of eliciting, reframing, and contextualizing client information. Their model based on recursive patterns, systemic notions, and strategic and communication thought created their own distinctive style.

Together with its behavioral-analysis approach of the problem, its use of interventions and especially its circular questioning, the Milan group generated an extraordinary therapeutic model. Its essential interviewing techniques, together with various creative modifications, are still with us today, especially in university training programs and psychotherapy institutes. The circular interview still represents not only a very significant marker in brief therapy's trajectory leading to the 1990s, but also a host of immediately useful and practical components adopted quite universally by many modern therapy models. That series of developments and discussions are the essence of Chapter 3.

In the late 1970s and in the 1980s, the therapeutic field, particularly in systems (family), witnessed a benign flood of new information, research, and phenomenal innovations. Despite the presence of established schools of family therapies, which no longer struggled for recognition as they had in the 1950s and 1960s, and despite the vitality of strategic therapies (MRI), many innovators still marched forward exploring other ways of practicing or implementing brief therapy. This new movement called itself solution-focused therapy. Despite some similarities to antecedent models, *solution*-focused thinking generated a new model that in many ways differed radically from the preceding *problem*-focused models (MRI). The solution-focused model creatively adapted and utilized components of certain strategies and techniques from the MRI group, the Milan group, and from the more "traditional" family therapy models. However, it had, in effect, developed its own unique model.

Steve de Shazer represents the leading figure in the *solutions* therapy movement. A significant landmark, both literal and metaphoric, in the evolution of this branch of brief therapy began in 1978 in Milwaukee. Under his leadership, de Shazer and his associates established the Brief Family Therapy Center, dedicated to *solutions* therapy. Through several published books and articles, de Shazer effected a change that might be described, in one major way, as diametrically opposed to the antecedent MRI model. It was a distinct directional change that decidedly moved from a focus on the "problem" to a focus on the "solution."

De Shazer's many writings, replete with long, arduous, philosophically-based arguments, proposed solution-thinking therapy as neither mere happenstance, nor as a simple reaction to prior theories. To the contrary, his philosophically grounded arguments reflected a great amount of analysis that questioned the very foundations of epistemology. He frequently quoted with apparent ease from a host of traditional philosophers, as well as from radical constructivist, postmodernist, and poststructuralist thinkers. Steve de Shazer is the principal figure in the discussion of solution-focused therapy in Chapter 4.

Solution-thinking, as a mindset, has remained as one of the characteristically strong movements of the 1980s that naturally evolved into the 1990s. It is no wonder that both contemporaneous, and, subsequent to de Shazer's thinking, many parallel developments were spawned, both at the philosophical and practical levels. William O'Hanlon and Michele Weiner-Davis, for instance, two writers and practitioners of solution-thinking, immediately come to the forefront. O'Hanlon and Weiner-Davis prefer to present a broader, more varied infrastructure to the solutions approaches. Their methods characteristically include de Shazer's work and philosophy (O'Hanlon & Weiner Davis, 1989, pp. 21–25). Yet because of the heterogeneity and the expansiveness of their perspective, they have aptly dubbed themselves "solution-*oriented*" therapists, thus suggesting a wider continuum of therapeutic options, while respectively acknowledging and including de Shazer's work and the work of others in the field.

O'Hanlon & Weiner-Davis devote a good deal of their time to examining strategies and approaches that necessarily include different ways of handling exception-thinking, the developments in languaging, and channeling, a term unique to their school of thought. Their methods essentially challenge and deconstruct what they identify cognitively as "unhelpful certainties" which clients have trained themselves to believe. Their therapeutic goal is to transform "unhelpful certainties" into "helpful" ones. Their methods include the use of a broad-based *channeling* and *languaging* that deal with the proper manipulation of language to effect a change in the direction of client empowerment. These themes which expand the range of solution approaches constitute Chapter 5.

Constructivism, a philosophical perspective that posits the observer as an active agent in deciphering both the inner and outer worlds, has motivated a good deal of psychotherapeutic thought. It has generated many forms of expression, both detailed and broad, in various modalities. In this text, we have chosen one specific model containing a broad-based systemic/family foundation. This model, based on Terry Real's integrating work, synthesizes five major therapeutic stances that together present a highly effective modular design. Real's constructivist model works very effectively and is a great foundational model for the beginning therapist.

This protean model, a cleverly designed modular composite, is not only self-sufficient, but also allows additional incorporation of other strategies and techniques from other models. It is a therapist-friendly model. It advocates no direct interventions and emphasizes a do-no-harm-to-the-client philosophy. It is based on therapeutic strategies that promote an ongoing expansion of the client's cosmos at the affective, behavioral, and cognitive levels through the therapist's effective use of in-depth circular questioning. The worthiness and effectiveness of this style of therapy, especially for the novice, is the heart of Chapter 6.

The narrative techniques, such as those developed by White and Epston, represent the last model discussed. They offer many highly effective strategies, including *externalization of the problem*. Like circular questioning, externalization of the problem is an original idea. It is a process by which client difficulties and rigidities, which are related to the client's very narrow and concentrated sense of causality, find a new *locus* of reference that is "external" to the client. In many cases where the traditional and even some of the more modern kinds of psychotherapy have faltered, the proper use of the externalization strategy will often succeed, precisely because it offers a boldly different angle of attack, thus yielding an undeniably liberating effect on the client with regard to his problem.

The whole notion of "double description" introduced by Bateson in the 1950s, in a sense finds its culmination in White and Epston's process of externalization. The client's "reauthoring" of his or her script through a more collaborative type of therapy becomes a new "retelling" of "old" materials in a framework inspired and guided by *relative influence questioning*, another productive innovation. The new retelling drives the client's mind-set toward a liberating view while moving away from the embeddedness of the old scripts. This powerful model developed by White and Epston is the subject matter of Chapter 7. It offers an appropriate conclusion to the brief therapies discussed because it represents the culmination of roughly fifty years of work of participants who sought more effective and abbreviated ways to help people with problems.

It is our desire that *brief therapy*, as derived from and depicted in family/systemic thinking, be perceived as one of the crowning achievements of psychotherapy's evolution in the latter portion of the twentieth century. Its evolution has revealed a richness of thought at the ideological level and a surprising heterogeneity of approaches at the practical level that contain an inherent intricacy in their presentation and discussion.

Today the term "brief therapy" and its psychodynamic counterpart, "short-term therapy," have nearly entered the class of common household words. They have become what we might wish to call "modern therapy." Recent research shows that the practice of these versions of abbreviated therapy has been expanding and flourishing at a nationwide level (Bloom, 1990, 1997).

Chapter 1

Brief Therapy as a Notion: Its Origins, Its Early Evolution

This book intends to examine six highly effective and distinct brief psychotherapies that have evolved out of systemic/family therapy. It emphasizes both the theory and the practice of these six therapeutic approaches. However, since reader response experience has shown that the appreciation of any given topic is usually enhanced by an appropriate introduction, the first chapter will serve as a prelude to the examination of these six brief psychotherapies.

Beginning with abbreviated therapy's early efforts, which not surprisingly began with Freud and his followers, many of those specific attempts at abbreviating therapy time and at simplifying the lengthiness of Freudian strategies were discussed. The timeline of those early efforts lasted over forty years until the 1950s. Toward the end of that decade the efforts at abbreviating therapy became more solidified and recognizable as a palpable approach, and Chapter 1 naturally draws to its conclusion.

Brief therapy has become one of the most fertile and creative avenues in psychotherapy today. It has achieved many successes where other forms of traditional therapy have failed or have shown to be ineffective (White & Epston, 1990; Bloom, 1990, 1992; Garfield, 1989). When the history of psychological therapy is written after we are well into the twenty-first century, historians will no doubt bestow laurels and a position of honor upon brief therapy and its achievements. Certainly, it will be recognized and appreciated as one of the finest accomplishments of psychological thought of the twentieth century.

Let us first describe what brief therapy is *not*. It is not a specific school, nor a specific technique, nor a specific strategy, nor a catchall phrase for crisis interventions or for abbreviated treatment programs due to insurance company time constraints. Brief therapy, instead, is a rich aggregate of approaches and techniques which have been supported by abundant literature and substantiated research. It is limited neither to one thinker nor to one group of thinkers, nor is it synonymous with terms emanating from pop-psychology's penchant for reductionism and the buzz words such as a "quick-fix" therapy and the like.

There presently exist many therapeutic schools of thought that are labeled "brief" and that, interestingly, embrace many distinct differences. Generally speaking, these differences represent positive attributes. They reflect the ongoing process of evolution and enrichment that encourages a healthy openness and diversity not usually found in closed systems of thought. This openness and diversity ultimately assumes, despite many different modalities, a broader perspective (Sluzki, 1985) that many practitioners and thinkers have named *ecological* (Keeney & Sprenkle, 1982, p. 9). Unfortunately, the phenomena of openness and diversity do not sufficiently describe the ingredients for creating a working definition of brief therapy that will meet everyone's satisfaction.

To compound this difficulty, there also exists an additional dimension. Within the various schools practicing brief therapy there are therapists who, admittedly, not only exercise their own variations on the thematic principles of their school, but also monitor their function in a self-evaluative, ongoing process of revision, change, and evolution. Furthermore, despite so many rich commonalities and unique innovations that dovetail into the "global" character in the schools of thought espousing brief therapy, the rate of change has been occurring so rapidly that there is no precise name for what has been evolving.

The label "brief therapy" was proven less than accurate as much as a decade ago, and it is more so today given the rapidity of change. There is no other agreed upon term to describe that phenomenon at this time.

When William Hudson O'Hanlon (1993) was discussing this situation, Tapani Ahola from Finland cleverly suggested that what is presently happening *might* be called psychotherapy's "Fourth Wave." Upon being asked for clarification, Ahola went on to say, "The First Wave in psychotherapy was pathology-based. The Second Wave was problem-focused or problem-solving therapy. The Third Wave was solution-focused or solution-oriented. The Fourth Wave is what is emerging now. Only no one has a good name for it yet" (p. 3).

To further complicate the issue, we might consider the fact that two decades ago it had been estimated that there were more than "250 different systems of psychotherapy" operating in the United States alone (Corsini, 1981). Therefore, as a broad-based working definition with a necessary host of disclaimers and exceptions, brief therapy might generally be described as what is being employed by those practitioners whose philosophies tend toward empowering the client, diminishing the upmanship of therapist "expertise," utilizing client strengths and resources in the session, and emphasizing collaborative efforts between therapist and client who remain engaged in briefer time frames while maintaining better therapeutic effectiveness.

A wide repertoire of brief therapy's approaches has evolved. Many practitioners tend to de-emphasize and, often, completely or benignly ignore the once "obligatory" maneuverings of Freudian "excavation" and the "working through process." Much of the brief therapy in the 1990s also contains a de-emphasis of the "teaching" and "expert" roles of the therapist. Yet there are many modern therapists who employ "teaching" and "expert" roles that are inextricably woven into their strategies. This is especially typical of therapies that are *not* in the area of systemic/family thinking, such as in psychodynamic, rational-emotive, cognitive, Gestalt, behavioral, transactional, multi-modal practices and, in fact, most therapies. Hence, we incur the paradox that while many of these aforementioned strategies have developed "short-term" or abbreviated versions of therapy, they still maintain, to varying degrees, a component of therapist "expertise" or "teaching" traits.

When employing our working definition of brief therapy (systemic/family), we incur an even greater paradox in areas where we recognize that many approaches still carry *some* of the traditions of therapist "expertise." This is found, for example, in many of the interventive strategies from Haley, the MRI group, and the Milan group. This facet of brief therapy can be quite intricate because it still contains elements that presume some therapist "expertise." A reasonable explanation for this apparent complication involves the fact that many interventive strategies presume therapist "expertise." For instance, in systemic/family interventions, practitioners strive for second-order change, a significant change in strategy, discussed later, which represents a radical shift from traditional interventions.

Dating back to the 1970s, the Milan School model used circular questioning, and it considered its unique use of *interventive* questions as deliberately designed to make the clients' effect change their lives. This strategy represents a process opting for a second-order change (i.e., a radical shift in resolving the problem), and it is indeed an integral part of its model. Admittedly, interventions by their very nature imply therapist "expertise" or directive control. Ultimately, this factor alone does not contradict the essential nature of most systemic/family brief modalities which actively seek client empowerment and accomplishing that in the least number of sessions possible.

The Milan School techniques still are valid and useful forms of brief therapy. Similarly, the same may be said of "solution-focused" therapy, which includes therapist-assigned "homework" tasks for the client such as recording specific changes in the time frame subsequent to the therapy session. This appears to contain the behavioristic flavor of journaling, and it tends to imply the notion of therapist teaching traits. Again, this is only part of the modality and not the essence of the modality.

While it is difficult to create a present-day operational definition of brief therapy in a succinct comprehensive manner, it is equally difficult on a time continuum to describe the exact beginning of the "spirit" of brief therapy, i.e., before its present, more common use of the term brief therapy. How far back do we go? Do we begin with the word "brief" which was first *formally* used in the 1960s at the Mental Research Institute (MRI) in Palo Alto, California? In 1967, the MRI group of researchers initiated the so-called *Brief* Therapy Project, a program of therapeutic interventions aimed at employing a *brief*, pragmatic, behaviorally-centered, nonhistorical approach, named at that time *strategic* or *problem-focused*. Their approach was based on the fundamental premise that people's failed "solutions" to their existing problems became *the problem*. Therefore, therapy was aimed at dissolving the "problem" through a variety of interventions which became the basis for handling the client's difficulties.

If that project represented the *formal* beginning of "brief therapy" insofar as systemic/family therapy is concerned, then what of the preparatory steps or the pioneering spirit that led to it? Certainly, the need for a briefer therapy, a therapy that obviously involved a shorter duration that did not compromise effectiveness, did not appear on the scene inadvertently or overnight.

Like most ideas, the concept behind brief therapy has its own history. In fact, it is an interesting *story* whose seminal aspects were derived from a host of unlikely sources. As often is the case in a "history of ideas" scenario, an idea's history frequently represents and exhibits an evolution from unusual and unexpected sources. It is therefore no surprise that brief therapy's beginnings may seem very primitive or disparate when compared to its more recently evolved, developmentalized ideology.

With the advantage of hindsight, it seems apparent today that brief therapy, when viewed as a whole, is an *evolving aggregate* of therapeutic techniques, stances, and approaches with related philosophies. Accordingly, if we take the theoretical leap backward in time from its present status to its supposed beginnings, who is to say where its exact initial demarcations are located? Indeed, the evolution of ideas can get complicated in its retelling.

Since all history is interpretational by nature (Collingwood, 1956), the connections may at times seem elusive and even tentative. Yet, with the persistence of documentation and with the spark of imagination, ideas are nonetheless traceable. The journey can be both dramatic and instructive.

The need for a briefer and more effective form of therapy developed for many decades, as far back as Freud. He had also experimented with finding abbreviated forms of therapy (Bloom, 1992). It is, therefore, particularly refreshing and assuring to note that Freud too had grappled with the problem of finding new ways to shorten therapy time. Additionally, there also exists an interesting, corresponding history of early disagreements and debates that Freud experienced with many of his followers, such as Rank and Ferenczi. These disputes dealt with attempts at manipulating the original Freudian psychoanalytic model in order to find more effective and abbreviated approaches.

While Rank began to experiment in the 1920s, Ferenczi had already begun as early as 1919 to modify Freudian strategies in order to shorten the duration prescribed by the lengthier psychoanalytic model. Later, in 1937, after a long series of disagreements and debates and the eventual fracturing of Freud's original group of followers, well beyond that of Rank and Ferenczi, Freud still maintained a bold adherence to the essentials of his basic psychoanalytic model. In fact, in written response to the detractors of his so-called lengthy method of doing therapy, Freud came to the final and adamant conclusion that "the best way to shorten analysis is to carry it out correctly" (*Analysis Terminable and Interminable*, p. 317).

If we were to exercise poetic license in our leap to the past for detecting those very early, often ephemeral, "roots" of brief therapy, we might go as far back as the aforementioned Hungarian psychoanalyst, Sandor Ferenczi (1873–1933). His concerns for developing more abbreviated methods in analysis (1920) were reflected in two major ways: first, in his "active" therapy approach and then later in his "permissive" therapy approach (*Encyclopedia of Psychology*, 1973, p. 98). Both attempts represented challenges and modifications to Freud's original theories and practices, especially regarding the area of transference Freud had defined and developed. There appears, no doubt, that Ferenczi's attempts were a deliberate drive toward shortening the length of treatment and improving its effectiveness (Bromberg, 1975, p. 242). They essentially involved a radical manipulation of Freud's concept of transference.

Ferenczi's "active" approach employed a pre-session *deprivation method,* involving patient limitations on food, sex, and excretory functions. Deprivation in these areas, Ferenczi opined, would serve the function of heightening client frustration and would, in turn, speed up the emergence of the client's pathological defenses. Transference would become manifest at a faster rate, thereby shortening therapy. Years later, however, after the failure of this method became clear, he then presented the sequel to this therapeutic scenario in 1927. Ferenczi dubbed it the "permissive" method. It suggested something radically different from his earlier deprivation attempt.

The permissive method sought to underline a loving and caring environment created and maintained by the therapist (Ferenczi, 1927). This served as a therapeutic counterbalancing maneuver to provide care and attention that were assumed as previously lacking. The earlier deprivation method had been aimed at eliciting an accelerated transference phenomenon, ostensibly through the deprivation of food, bodily functions, etc. By sharp contrast, when using the "permissive" method, Ferenczi expected the elicitation of transference through the dispensation of a caring therapeutic attitude and secure environment. Ferenczi's premise truly discovered a new notion. A therapist's kinder and more "permissive" attitude could be useful in therapy.

Ferenczi's permissive method did not go unnoticed. Bromberg (1975, p. 249) strongly suggested that the general influence of Ferenczi's permissive therapeutic component, perceived as caring and attentive, did expand into the techniques of many psychiatrists in the 1930s and 1940s, such as the work of Paul Federn (1943). In fact, Federn specifically referred to Ferenczi for proposing the permissive method as "nourishing the transference through sincerity and kindness." Interestingly, Federn in turn also altered the Freudian model by diminishing the role of free association that was deemed time consuming. Federn focused, instead, on the immediate therapeutic situation, "the *reality relationship* which lay behind the unconscious material" (Bromberg, p. 249).

Backtracking to Otto Rank (1884–1939), we discover more interesting developments. In addition to being a Freudian-trained psychotherapist like Ferenczi, Rank held a doctorate in anthropology. He wrote prolifically, and his writings illustrated how his Freudian training had vividly affected his studies related to work on birth trauma (Roback, 1961, p. 350). Rank's writings also indicate how he had struggled with time-management problems, hoping to make therapy briefer and more effective (Menaker, 1982). As Freud's employment of terminal treatment dates with patients, Rank's strategy involved the similar use. Naturally, like Freud, Rank adjusted terminal dates to reflect clients' individual differences and needs.

Rank's *reasons* for the assignment of terminal dates and his *attitude* towards the patient were very different from those of Freud. By establishing a terminal date, Freud sought to unearth insight more quickly from the patient. This constituted part of his quest into a cosmos that he qualified as essentially deterministic and patterned. By setting a terminal date, Rank, instead, hoped to achieve something more than an abbreviated treatment program. Rank's desired effect has been described by Menaker's studies (1982) as one that probably intended fostering an "ego autonomy" in the client. Menaker's critique, which is a positive interpretation of Rank's work, seems acceptable and justified in light of Rank's many other corroborative writings. Rank's stance, in fact, might be substantially translated today as clearly engendering an attempt at "empowerment" in the patient.

Rank's avowed desire to find an abbreviated and more effective form of therapy is also reflected elsewhere. His writings exhibited many other ideas that would easily associate his thoughts as precursors of many additional present-day perspectives. For instance, Rank's anthropological emphasis on social relativism, his "respect for the uniqueness of each individual" client

(Menaker, 1982), his anti-dogmatic and anti-deterministic ideology, his concept of therapy as *creative-interaction* between therapist and "patient," all represented bold ideas in the 1920s and 1930s (Menaker, 1982).

Rankian perspectives placed considerable emphasis on the presumed positive motivation of the patient, the patient's "will," the patient's *here-and-now* affect, cognition, and behavior. In a new and refreshing way, these therapeutic postures took precedence over the prescribed Freudian analysis which necessarily involved excavations into the patient's past patterns of behavior, patient trauma, and the patient's oedipal complex. Rank's focus on the immediate dynamics of the patient's world, vis-a-vis the analyst, far outweighed the importance of any psychiatric/psychoanalytic interpretations or probes into the patient's excavated past. This was a bold idea in the early attempts to abbreviate therapy. Devoting an entire book to studying the artist as a metaphor of creativity, Rank concluded that the therapeutic relationship between therapist and patient was categorically a "creative" process (Rank, 1932). Again, with the advantage of today's hindsight, it is clear that Rank was far ahead of his time. Many of the elements of the "conversation-based," "aesthetic," or "ecological" perspectives in psychotherapy that developed in the last two decades of the twentieth century, which we presently cherish, are easily relatable to Rankian theories espoused well over sixty years ago.

There is also good reason to consider the importance of the Austrian psychiatrist, Alfred Adler (1870–1937). Like Ferenczi and Rank, he also had concerns for modifying the Freudian model for the purposes of abbreviation and effectiveness. In fact, Adler was particularly responsible for beginning the early shift in de-pathologizing patient neurosis. In its stead, he created the positive-sounding doctrine of the *creative self.* He thereby established the possibility of patients re-inventing themselves if "trained" therapeutically in the correct manner by the therapist (1927).

Adler placed great emphasis on the importance of social relationships. He perceived *power* and *status* motives as more important in understanding patient behavior than the broad-based sexual motives proposed by

Freud. The Adlerian emphasis on non-sexually motivated behavior scuttled the once time-consuming, painstaking, intrapsychic methods of Freud (Becvar & Becvar, 1993).

The focus on these social influences, relative to the downplaying of neurosis, eventually led Adler to develop his own approach, *individual psychology*, whose strategies assumed a clearly recognizable empowerment component. The net effect of Adler's approach, which had avoided the necessity of the "patient couch," tended to consider the treatment process as a *dialogue* between equals. Adler's innovative approaches all had the effect of tending to shorten therapy time (Bromberg, p. 246).

Karen Horney (1885–1952) immigrated to the United States in 1932 and had studied in Berlin as a student of Karl Abraham, an immediate follower of Freud. She not only spoke out against some of the rigidities of Freudian theory and practice, but also wrote extensively, (1936, 1939, 1945) attributing more importance to family and social roles and socially-informed influences. Widely read, she downplayed the emphasis that Freud had placed on childhood experiences centered on oedipal conflicts, on biology, and on instinctual drives (1939, p. 10). She chose, instead, to place more emphasis on the patients' current problems and on the prevailing neurotic behaviors. She believed in the use of methods of patient empowerment where the patient would assume an immediate sense of responsibility. This perspective contradicted the longer trajectory inherently demanded by the Freudian psychoanalytic search for the "old patterns" that would assist in establishing "insight." In addition to abbreviating time spent in therapy searching for certain parts of a patient's past, she helped establish, in the newly emerging crucible of psychotherapy, the importance of "environmental" factors such as family and societal relationships and cultural relativism.

By establishing the importance of environmental factors, Horney diminished the time-consuming role of free association, especially in the search for oedipally-based patterns. While downplaying childhood psychological "excavation" as in the traditional model, she emphasized, in its stead, a greater social role between mother and child. Similarly, she saw a broader social context in an individual's development, especially in the influence of societal pressures on an individual's neurotic behavior (1937, p. 284). In sum, she deemed these social aspects as more immediately pressing in the treatment of patients than the traditionally long reconstruction of a patient's childhood emotional past (Bromberg, 1975, p. 245).

Harry Stack Sullivan (1892–1949), an American psychiatrist, in a way similar to that of Adler and Horney in their reactions to Freudian thought, also played an important role in downplaying the search for Freudian intrapsychic excavation and its related patterns. Much of Adler's emphasis lay in the social aspects of the client, thus abbreviating the normally long course of traditional therapy. In similar ways, Sullivan focused on personality growth and development which he viewed as based on the individual's cumulative series of interpersonal relationships from infancy to adulthood (1953). The dynamic and interactive social features of growth and change were key factors in Sullivan's perspective. The significance of his influence becomes more relevant when one considers that Sullivan had trained both Murray Bowen and Don Jackson. They became two leading figures in the early development of systemic/family theory, developing the foundation and the infrastructure of family therapy, much of its nomenclature, and a host of fundamental ideas such as "redundant family interactive patterns" (Goldenberg & Goldenberg, pp. 59–60).

In summary, the socially-informed components in the therapies discussed, both as philosophical postures and as recognizable interactive processes, as a group represents one of the major factors in the foundation of family therapy which essentially had started in the 1950s and blossomed throughout the 1960s. Both as ideology and as practice, family therapy vividly represented a 180-degree turn from the more traditional therapeutic focus on the individual patient toward a marked emphasis on the multiplicity of therapeutic relationships classified as family therapy, group therapy, couples therapy, and later on, intergenerational therapy.

In an attempt to better understand family therapy, its very early development, and later its relationship to the development of systemic/family therapy, we again return to the 1930s. In that period, Nathan Ackerman, M.D., a child psychiatrist, created, according to Foley (1974), the first "family" publication. His article, "The Family as a Social and Emotional Unit," published in 1937, remains the first milestone in *family therapy* (Ackerman). With that article, we begin to see the focus shifting from the individual to the family.

Later, in the early 1940s, in attempting to improve the effectiveness of therapy and shorten its duration, Ackerman had his staff regularly experiment with conjoint therapy. Thus, a therapist would interview both mother and child *together*. As a fairly common deliberate procedure in Ackerman's method of supervision, this represented something quite new in psychotherapy. His treatment program dealt with patient populations defined as "non-psychotic" in nature (Ackerman, 1967). Ackerman's approaches were precursory to a more non-pathologically-driven form of therapy to which many therapists subscribe today.

The more immediate roots of family therapy became apparent in the late 1940s and early 1950s. During this period the once isolated experimentation of the psychiatric trailblazers suddenly became active movements in various sectors of the country. An ever-growing number had theoretical beliefs and practices that clearly demonstrated distinct reactions not only to the traditionally long Freudian insight-based modality, but also to its pathology-based foundations. However, as the mid-1950s evolved toward the end of the decade, the precursory reactions to the psychoanalytic model quickly accelerated.

Carl Whitaker is our first example. His work began in the late 1940s and attracted much attention in the 1950s. His methods involved therapeutic interactions with schizophrenics in non-traditional ways. He encouraged a deliberate stance in the shift to family and ultimately to abbreviated forms of therapy; in short, to more modern forms of therapy (Neill & Kniskern, 1982). We now recognize his innovative introduction of a cotherapist in a therapy session as significant for his time. Moreover, his introduction of the use of conjoint and intergenerational therapeutic settings *with schizophrenics*, and his use of in-depth metaphoric amplification methods that focus on affect and empathy in the interviewing process cannot help but impress us fifty years later. Their connection with today's use of team therapy, multigenerational interviewing, and with today's study and use of metaphor in therapist-client interactions are apparent. Much of Whitaker's pioneering work permeates many brief therapy approaches, particularly those "conversational" styles of Andersen (1991) and Anderson & Goolishian (1988).

Additionally, from another perspective there are elements of Whitaker's style that have much in common with many other contemporary family therapists. These elements are better identified under the heading of aesthetic stances. For instance, Whitaker demonstrated great ability in empathetically identifying with the client's metaphorical statements and following their implied or suggested flow. A contemporary therapist, employing constructivist theory, could easily identify the present day therapeutic stance called "matching" with much of Whitaker's therapeutic postures. In both cases, the strategies serve very effectively in unveiling and discovering what might have remained simply a neglected or overlooked source of information. In this very determined and highly focused context, there is the explicit refusal to accept the traditional Freudian term of client "resistance," which had been viewed by Freud as holding back therapy. By sharp contrast, "going with the client's resistance," and not necessarily confronting contradictory client statements were both openly practiced by Whitaker over fifty years ago. Today, these therapeutic postures have become standard practice for many therapists.

In essence, therapy has become more a matter of the therapist asking better "conversation-based" questions with genuine curiosity as the guiding spirit and totally bypassing potential entanglements caused by what Freud *considered* client resistance. Many of today's therapists have made full use of *amplification* of client metaphoric statements (Napier, 1988) and *matching*, or empathy with client's metaphoric statements, as major tools in entering the client's cosmos. Whitaker spearheaded the development of these approaches in the early evolution of brief therapy.

Similarly, Carl Rogers' work also began in the 1940s. He published his first book in 1942, *Counseling and Psychotherapy*, which contained many of his most basic notions, including the use of the nondirective approach. However, he remains most associated as the espouser of "client-centered" therapy in 1951 through his book *Client-Centered Therapy*. Unlike Whitaker, Rogers did not hail from the world of psychiatry, but from totally different areas, education and psychology. He brought numerous rich ideas to psychotherapy. In many ways, his presence represented a paradox. While his focus was on the client, *and not the family*, the old psychoanalytic mechanisms were all gone.

In Roger's method, the therapist essentially attends and listens to the client. The therapist mirrors what the client says in a continual and highly focused dialogue that sharpens the affect and the cognition that the client is experiencing at that moment. How that process may be related, in a useful manner, to the client's reasons for seeking therapy to resolve the problem becomes an integral part of the therapeutic artistry attributed to Rogerian therapy.

Roger's many innovative ideas, particularly in the 1940s and 1950s, must have seemed very radical. Today, of course, many of those ideas have become subsumed and integrated as standard elements of good interviewing. His concepts of empathy or accurate understanding at the affective level, positive regard or respect, and genuineness or congruence when applied consistently in the interviewing process involving reflection and clarification, inherently shortened the course of the therapy practiced by the establishment at that time. Roger's unique style which focused on the client's "here-and-now" affect and cognition had bypassed the whole phenomenon of psychoanalysis, its Freudian "excavation," psychological determinism, and instinct theories.

Although Rogers does not seem to allude anywhere in his writings to Ferenczi's work of the 1920s, specifically the latter's "permissive" method, Rogers does capture and refine to perfection those same care and attention factors Ferenczi had originally proposed and pioneered, the so-called "permissiveness." However, Rogers attributes his aesthetic sensibilities in creating a non-threatening environment to Otto Rank (*Art and Artist*, 1932). Rogers openly states that the "roots of client-centered therapy [are] to be found in the therapy of Rank..." (*Client-Centered Therapy*, p. 4).

When searching for the general beginnings of more modern forms of therapy, their relationship to family therapy, and ultimately to brief therapy throughout the fertile environment of the 1950's, even in the presence of such imposing figures such as Whitaker and Rogers, Milton Erickson comes to mind as being at the forefront. He represents the person most often identified with the more *immediate roots* of brief therapy as we know it today (Haley, 1973). Not only from a theoretical point of view, but also from a practical perspective, metaphorically he represents the "grandfather" of relationally and uniquely conceived strategies that are more immediately called *brief* therapeutic approaches. In fact, the word *immediacy* might very well be one of the key words in understanding his style.

In the 1950s, which was well before Erickson's involvement with the Mental Research Institute and their development of the Brief Therapy Project, he had already proposed two new pivotal "brief therapy" approaches, the "utilization strategy" (Erickson & Rossi, 1979) and "pseudo-orientation in time" (Erickson, 1954). To date, they represent two very significant general strategies that have survived, relatively speaking, the test of time.

Erickson's foundational strategies have been both useful and effective in bringing about *change* in the client. In the "pseudo-orientation in time" strategy, Erickson capitalized on two things, the use of hypnosis and Freud's "condensation" (a component in dream analysis). However, before discussing Erickson's unique and brilliant interpretation in handling these two ideas, a few words about the Freudian background.

When time is viewed in non-dream everyday phenomena, it is referred to as "mechanical time" (Bergson, 1911). In contrast to mechanical time, in *The Interpretation of Dreams* (Freud, 1900) Freud discussed *psychological time* where affect and intuition do not follow the same rules of mechanical time. This holds true particularly in the phenomena of spatial and time distortion in dreams, which he called *condensation*. Freud called the dream processes and their content *dream-work*. Condensation, one of its major processes, occurs when space (meaning geography or location) and time (real or imagined flow of events) are "fluid" and not mechanically sequential as one might expect. The psyche manipulates time and space so that dream components are re-arranged, distorted, and compressed in the dream-work.

In dreams, time intervals easily become *achronological*. Situations, which are historically-based, imagined occurrences or even desired or anticipated events, form amalgams. Their components, which may at first seem in apparent contradiction, form amalgams of sorts. Upon analysis, any given amalgam has a particular unity of its own which has been orchestrated by the subconscious. In any given moment then, the dream represents a mosaic of many elemental components of time, place, and situation in a new contextual relationship which conveys rich content and meaning for a probing Freudian analyst. In dream-work, the future, present, and past often form a new unity that, according to Freud, reflects a subconscious purpose. Interestingly, Freud's trailblazing dream-analysis and his use of hypnosis set the stage for Erickson's equally remarkable therapeutic innovations.

From the world of Freudian dream-work, Erickson re-invented the concept of "time distortion" and, assumptively, the "distortion" of place and situation. After hypnotizing the client, he would apply his own unique strategy of "time distortion." He would put a client in a trance which would then allow the client to mentally move back and forth in time so as to "release" or better "dislodge" the client from being "stuck" in the present and its time-specific problem. Once this was accomplished and the client had hypnotically been "freed" from the "shackles" of the present, the client was then asked by Erickson how he or she would resolve the problem. This constituted a radically new approach used in therapy to assist the client in the process of change.

For Freud, "time distortion" had been an analytical tool for understanding dream components and acquiring *insight* into the patterns of the subconscious. For Erickson, however, it became an *immediate therapeutic strategy*. Erickson's twist of cleverly anticipating an immediate solution *from the client* was based on a relatively new and ingenious therapeutic assumption. Erickson believed that once a client felt liberated from the shackles of time, place, and the embeddedness of a situation, the client could propose and advance reasonable solutions to the problem without the necessity of therapist-insight or without therapist "coaching." This therapeutic scenario involves what might be called "creative anachronisms." In fact, humanity's early creative use of anachronisms is identifiable in mythology. *Mythos* in classical Greek simply meant "short story." It was in those tales that storytellers employed creative narrations by anachronistically venturing back and forth in time. It was indeed in those very stories that people found meaning to their ethnic, cultural, and religious origins and to the existential challenges in their lives.

Erickson's innovative strategy of "pseudo-orientation in time," unlike mythology, usually dealt with the client's personal history and narrative, but like mythology had purpose. When Erickson combined hypnosis with the concept of "time distortion," it was referred to as the "crystal ball" technique (Erickson, 1954). However, when implemented without the use of hypnosis, Erickson's abbreviated use of "time distortion" was simply referred to as the "crystal ball question." In time, the latter would inspire newer versions such as Steve de Shazer's present-day technique called the "miracle question" (de Shazer, 1985) and Peggy Penn's "feed-forward" technique (1985), a "video" metaphor, which ultimately involves the use of the Ericksonian innovation.

Similarly, Erickson's "utilization strategy" provided another key therapeutic tool. Since its inception, it has had a major impact on thinking, not only for the practical applications suggested, but also for the theoretical issues it raised. On a practical level, it meant that in a creative manner the therapist could utilize whatever the client disclosed in therapy. This would include, but was not limited to, the client's interpersonal and experiential resources, strengths, beliefs, and special talents. For instance, a client, who presents himself as being depressed and who also alludes to being artistically endowed, clearly offers the therapist a therapeutic opportunity to explore and glean any immediate possible benefits from the client's artistic talents.

On a theoretical level, the "utilization strategy" implied a philosophically necessitated re-examination and redefinition of the traditionally held roles of therapist as "expert" and the client as essentially dependent, and in some cases, unalterably dependent on the therapist. The "utilization strategy" instead suggested a diminution of therapist/client role polarities and dichotomies. It implied, instead, fostering a more collaborative relationship between client and therapist, where client *empowerment* would become the focus of therapy. In Erickson, we clearly witness the concrete beginnings of an active "wellness" and "health-oriented" thinking.

Besides the "utilization" strategy and "pseudo-orientation in time" strategies, Erickson also advanced the use of storytelling and humor. His storytelling objective usually involved a *quest for meaning* and the motivation for change. He creatively merged interesting story lines, rich metaphors, and embedded commands (Rosen, 1982). His cleverly narrated stories and use of hypnotism were purposely rendered to "seed the client unconscious" with new possibilities. Questions and statements were posed to suggest positive action through the use of embedded commands.

Similarly, Erickson also practiced therapist humor in his sessions, specifically to encourage clients to take risks and dare to face unpleasant situations. The elements of playfulness and humor in therapy were designed to help promote not only client interest in change, but also empathically-generated "healing" powers particularly in painful situations (Rosen, 1982). Humor, like storytelling, was innovatively presented and developed by Erickson in abbreviating and rendering effective the therapeutic relationship.

To return to the question in point, if the 1960s' Brief Therapy Project represents the *formal* beginning of brief therapy in a systemic/family modality, taking numerous cues from the many aforementioned personalities, then what did it achieve in a broad sense? What is its importance for the present and the future? What were its contributions? How have they been useful to us? In order to broach these questions, it is important to first review some of the preparatory work that took place in the 1950s and early 1960s which ultimately and specifically had an impact on the Mental Research Institute's beginnings.

It was Whitaker who forged the trailblazing efforts in the late 1940s while working differently with a host of schizophrenics. In effect, the 1950s went on to produce, nationwide, a growing number of clinicians interested in this broader-based study of schizophrenia. Much of the interest was grounded on the enigmatic effects and challenges that schizophrenia posed to clinicians and also on the fact that through Whitaker's efforts conjoint therapy, cotherapy, and multigenerational therapy offered some rather impressive beginnings ripe for development. In the 1950s, along with this concentrated curiosity in schizophrenia, *family therapy* was spawned at a nationwide level (Guerin, 1976).

Simultaneous to the 1950s efforts of Whitaker and other psychiatrists working on schizophrenia and on the family as a psychotherapeutic unit, Ackerman arranged and led the first session on "family" at the American Orthopsychiatry Association meeting in New York City in 1955 (Nichols, 1984). His involvement with this association and with the American Psychiatric Association, together with his seminal articles on family, led him to the eventual publication of *The Psychodynamics of Family Life* (1958). This book, like Ackerman's pioneering 1937 article, and like Whitaker's experiments with non-traditional treatment of schizophrenics, represented still another major landmark for family therapy's early incursions into a psychoanalytically dominated therapeutic world. Despite the book's heavy intrapsychic tendencies, its uniqueness was attributable to the fact that Ackerman had produced "the first full-length study combining theory and practice, in which he emphasized the importance of *role relations* within the family" (Foley, 1974, p. 6).

Generally speaking, interest had grown sufficiently in family therapy, both in dealing with "schizophrenia" and without its presence, that it prompted seminars and other professional meetings. Ackerman and his followers, who tended to deal with family problems with non-psychotic features, had no particularly immediate or pressing interest in schizophrenia per se. However, a number of psychiatrists who had followed Whitaker's lead, and that of other psychiatrists, produced many articles on schizophrenia vis-a-vis the family.

In 1960, Don Jackson, a psychiatrist, examined and edited a series of articles on schizophrenia and published them in *The Etiology of Schizophrenia*. Despite Jackson's untimely death in 1968, he had edited and published more extensively in the area of family therapy than most others in the field (Foley, 1974, p. 70). Jackson was not only an important theoretician in family therapy's foundational era, but also a trailblazing administrative leader in the 1950s and 1960s. Ultimately, his initiatives in establishing the Mental Research Institute and its Brief Therapy Project would represent two bold landmarks in the continuation of family therapy's historical development and in the early trajectory of brief therapy in the latter half of the twentieth century.

A trend in the 1950s was obviously emerging from the many "family" articles and from conferences and seminars that were including "family" papers. That trend was asserting the existence of the growth and development of family therapy that traveled beyond its new frontier image just a few years earlier. That growth was in part philosophically based on a central idea that was emerging: a deleterious family *environment*, dubbed at that time as the "pathogenic family," was perceived as being involved not only with schizophrenia, but also with other disorders as well (Zuk & Rubenstein, 1965). With these substantial factors as background, the desire grew to do more research and practice based on what was being learned from all those studies, seminars and conferences. The thrust of the "family" movement, together with bold administrative personalities, became responsible for the realization and establishment of two major centers of research and practice. They influenced the growth and development of family therapy for the next four decades and, ultimately, brief therapy itself.

One such establishment was the *Mental Research Institute* (MRI) in Palo Alto, California. In 1959, Don Jackson, founded the MRI and invited Jules Riskin and Virginia Satir to join this new enterprise. At a later date, his program expanded, and it welcomed many notables including Jay Haley, John Weakland, Paul Watzlawick, Arthur Bodin, and Richard Fisch. In New York City, Nathan Ackerman similarly founded the *Family Institute* in 1960, a few years after establishing a clinic in 1957 called the Family Mental Health Clinic of Jewish Family Services. Furthermore, both leaders combined their efforts and talents in establishing the first "family" journal, publishing articles obviously related to this new area of "family therapy." In 1962, Jackson and Ackerman started this publication entitled *Family Process*. Jay Haley became its first editor. It soon became the key journal in family therapy. Today it still remains among the most influential and prestigious journals in the field.

The fledgling boldness of this relatively new area called family therapy, in many ways still cognizant of its novice position in a dominantly and intrapsychically-based nationwide psychiatric establishment, brought not only novel ideas to the field of therapy, but also contrasting views and often ideological conflict. This was similarly true within the ranks of those thinkers developing family therapy philosophies.

One major ideological battle that brewed regarded the differences in the relative influence between the established intrapsychic model and the newly emerging systemic/family approaches. Ackerman, who still leaned heavily toward the importance of intrapsychic factors, had nonetheless tempered his conspicuous penchant for intrapsychic by considering and including the importance of social roles and the relevance of "homeostasis," a process of self-regulation, both at the family and social levels. However, his relatively broad perspective was still nowhere near the new importance posited by the theories regarding *interactional sequences* that the systems-oriented family therapists, in sharp contrast, were espousing (Nichols, 1984).

With Ackerman's death in 1971, the Family Institute was renamed the Ackerman Family Institute in his honor. This was recognition of his lifetime efforts and achievements in developing family therapy. His contributions to psychotherapy were many. His practical contributions included the Family Services Clinic, the Family Institute, and *Family Process* journal. His theoretical foresight as one of the early thinkers effected some of the initial connections between the dominant intrapsychic perspective with the early cybernetic, systemic approaches. With his passing, some of the strong ideological divisions and tensions that once existed between these two camps and their followers began to wane, and family therapy developments clearly found it easier to proceed in a more *systemic approach.*

The systemic approach itself, however, has its own story line which also began years earlier. Gregory Bateson was the key figure who actively brought the systemic perspective into therapy and who fostered the growth of family therapy within systems theory perspective. First, his interests in social sequences of interactions went back to 1936 when he published a study dealing with tribal behavior in New Guinea. He became interested in the phenomena of *complementarity* and *symmetrical escalation* in tribal communication. These two terms, which are now standard terms in family therapy glossaries, were originally coined as concepts by Bateson under the label "schismogenesis" (Pentony, 1981). In other words, Bateson was convinced that there existed a principle of *reciprocal influence* in the phenomenon called communication. To what degree and what kinds of influences could be established, constituted the nature of the inquiries it suggested. Bateson hoped that these inquiries would be couched in the nature of scientific exploration so that relationships revealed in the communication process would be studied at length and eventually serve as a foundation for both sociological and psychological purposes.

In New York in 1941 and in 1942, Bateson attended two related conferences where Milton Erickson presented many of his ideas and, in particular, demonstrated the therapeutic use of hypnosis. Erickson's application of hypnosis had the effect of opening up further new perspectives for Bateson in the realm of communication sequences. Hypnosis now posed for Bateson, more enticing questions and issues regarding logic and thought processing not only for the individual, but also for culturally-defined units such as the family and society. In a communication perspective, Bateson wondered how to rationally explain hypnosis in the wake of over 2,000 years of Aristotelian tradition in Western logic (Bateson & Mead, 1976). Many epistemological questions with communicational implications were therefore raised with no immediate answers offered.

Bateson in 1942 also became acquainted with the emerging world of cybernetics. It whetted his appetite to learn much more about cybernetics and how it might be useful, but the ongoing war overseas redirected him to Southeast Asia. At the end of the war, however, Bateson returned to the U.S. and he eagerly re-engaged his efforts to learn more about cybernetics. His immediate goals included finding a framework for interpreting data more effectively in human behavioral contexts. He hoped that cybernetics would resolve some of the questions in his search. Until then, cybernetics had been employed in the military as essentially an engineering tool in electronics weaponry and guidance systems such as in radar and sonar. Cybernetics had been shaped and developed by the mathematicians Norbert Weiner (1894–1964) and John Von Neumann (1903–1957) during World War II. However, since cybernetics dealt with communication, information processing, and feedback and control mechanisms in electronics, Bateson wondered about its theoretical translation from the world of mathematics and engineering to a possible application in the study of the behavioral sciences (Heims, 1977).

In 1946 in New York City, at the Josiah Macy Foundation lectures, the mathematicians and scientists who had developed cybernetics for war-related research and weapons applications were presenting their ideas for other possible uses, not necessarily related to the military. What had been considered as exclusive information for defense research, surveillance, and weaponry now became information available for civilian use. Engineers and social scientists alike attended the conferences. Bateson, an anthropologist by training, now began fulfilling his long-awaited dream to obtain fresh ideas for establishing a framework that contained feedback mechanisms that would help explain social structures, their apparent stability as socially-informed structures, and their use for facilitating human change and motivation in future scenarios. His search for the delineation of scientific behavioral foundations based on the "translation" of cybernetics played a crucial role in connecting the communication knowledge of the physical, as applied in the military, with the foundations for family therapy.

After teaching at the New School for Social Research in New York City (1946–47) and at Harvard University (1947–48), Bateson became a research assistant, joining Juergen Ruesch at the Langley Porter Institute in the Department of Psychiatry at the University of California Medical School. After two years of full-time work at the Institute, he changed his status to part-time and began an association with the Veteran's Administration Hospital in Palo Alto, California. In 1951, Ruesch and Bateson coauthored a book, *The Social Matrix of Psychiatry*, where they discussed the issues dealing with the "role of feedback and information theory in communication" (Foley, 1974, p. 5). The cybernetic revolution in psychology had officially begun.

Cybernetics became a tool for studying *communication dynamics* in human interactions. For many, particularly those in family-oriented therapeutic modalities, this implied that researchers and practitioners could conceptualize how "systems" maintained their stability by self-regulation through the use of "reinserting the results of past performance" into current behavior. Understanding cybernetics' application to human communication patterns has often been compared to the operation and function of the household thermostat. In the world of physiology, it has been compared to the body's self-regulation of its temperature and metabolism called *homeostasis*.

Psychosis, especially schizophrenia, as well as non-psychotic disorders, and mental behavior in general, could now be approached methodically in newer and perhaps more useful and creative ways. This could be done by observing and recording transactional sequences of behavior, speech, paralinguistics, and kinesics, between individuals ostensibly communicating or attempting to communicate. This could be applied even ethnically or culturally, but more importantly, it seemed to have an immediate psychological and psychiatric importance to Bateson.

In 1952, after receiving a grant from the Rockefeller Foundation, Bateson started a research project dealing with the role of paradoxes of abstractions in communication and understanding the different levels of communication. In 1953, Jay Haley, John Weakland, and William Fry became members of his research team. Each one had a different background. Haley had been a communications specialist. Weakland had been a chemical engineer and had developed cultural anthropological interests. Fry was a psychiatrist interested in studying humor. They conducted behavioral research on animals as well as on humans. The team studied communication behavior in otters and in guide-dog training, as well as in the language of schizophrenics (Nichols, 1984).

Bateson received a two-year Macy Foundation grant in 1954 to direct more research on schizophrenic communication. This effectively extended the life of his original research program. Don Jackson joined the group as a clinical consultant and supervised the therapy with schizophrenic patients. The research goals were changed. The study, which originally focused on the contrast and conflicts between different levels of communication, was transformed into the search for a general theory of communication that might explain both schizophrenia in general and the contextual relationships of the schizophrenic's family.

The whole traditional notion of schizophrenia as a psychiatrically-defined "illness" came into question as they focused more and more on the communication aspects of schizophrenics (Heims, 1977, p. 153). By 1954, Bateson, who had already been developing this idea of studying schizophrenia from a non-pathological, communication perspective, presented the now celebrated *double-bind hypothesis*. After more research, Bateson, together with Jackson, Haley, and Weakland, wrote and published a landmark article that has had an indelible effect on family therapy as it attempted to de-pathologize schizophrenia. The article was entitled "Toward a Theory of Schizophrenia" and was published in *Behavioral Science* in 1956.

In essence, the article represented a major theoretical breakthrough, especially for those researchers studying schizophrenia. It had the overall effect of shifting the nature of both the theoretical and practical focus. Instead of asking the "why" kinds of questions that tended to focus on the patient's past, the new inquiry focused on the "what" kinds of questions regarding an individual's behavioral and communicational patterns in the interpersonal exchange and processing of information. In short, schizophrenia, which had been traditionally defined and examined in the context of an intrapsychically-based disease, could also be examined as a process based on relational, interpersonal and communicational phenomena.

This revolutionary approach was all the more remarkable considering that the traditional psychodynamic approach continued as the dominant model of inquiry and treatment. The psychiatric establishment still perceived *insight*, a specific term as defined by Freud, as essentially the only means of therapeutic change (Simon, 1982). However, the bold consequence of Bateson's innovative cybernetic perspective offered, in effect, a new rationale and foundation for studying the embeddedness of schizophrenia and other psychological problems in general.

At the theoretical end of the spectrum, Bateson's original double-bind presentation had the effect of philosophically justifying systems thinking. At the practical end (Bateson et al., 1956), it meant that researchers and therapists could now avail themselves of a new "road map" that could explore and examine the *system* of familial interpersonal relations and communication, including their nonverbal components. This constituted a major step in family therapy's early formation.

Bateson's studies showed that in cases of schizophrenia, for instance, communication between family members demonstrated contradictions or a serious lack of congruence in the overall messages exchanged between family members. More specifically, the "double-bind" situation, as the name implies, represented a condition wherein an emotional and perceptual deadlock resided. This impasse where the "patient" found himself was due to the disconcerting state in which the "patient" consistently received conflicting and contradictory messages from parents. Thus, for example, apparent assertions of parental love for the identified patient are also countered by nonverbal communication which seemed to indicate the opposite affect. This and similar kinds of ongoing and sustained modes of *miscommunication*, coupled with emotional and developmental learning trajectories, were viewed as very significant in the study of mental problems and disorders in general.

In short, the double-bind theory had paved a new way for studying psychological problems as communicational and relational in nature, thus creating the beginnings of a cybernetically-informed epistemology. This foundational thinking was based not only on the study of communicational sequences and feedback mechanisms, but also on the employment of those feedback mechanisms to effect change. Cybernetics, understood as feedback mechanisms as applied to psychotherapy, obviously implied systems-thinking. This, to be sure, encouraged the growth of more systems-oriented thinking. Both at a metaphoric level and at a literal level (de Shazer, 1991,

1994), the family was beginning to be viewed more and more as a cybernetic system and also as a system in general.

The 1950s, therefore, represented a very powerful and pivotal prelude that would permit the next decade of family therapy and systems ideology to flourish. The 1950s contained many significant changes and activities both in research and therapeutic practice. This accumulation of achievements necessitates a summary of ideas with some absorbing and ironic commentary.

First, with few exceptions such as Ackerman's treatment of nonpsychotic patient families in conjoint therapy, family therapy as a whole, ironically, received its most significant backing from the intense interest in the study and treatment of schizophrenia by members of psychiatry. Traditionally as a group, they did not allow the practice of conjoint therapy. But, psychiatry's usual conservatism based on scientific foundations nonetheless allowed conjoint treatment in this instance where ordinarily family members previously would *not* have been interviewed together in the treatment process (Goldenberg & Goldenberg, 1991).

Secondly, the 1950s witnessed many serendipitous developments that helped shaped the basis of family therapy and eventually its offspring, brief therapy. Often, many psychotherapy researchers and practitioners were investigating and practicing the same new family therapy approaches, independently, not knowing of the others' work (Briggs & Peat, 1984). For example, John Bell (1975), like Ackerman (1937), had independently experimented extensively in meeting with the entire family in nonpsychotic-oriented therapy settings. This was a relatively new phenomenon, and it illustrates how in science there are often "independent and parallel" developments.

Thirdly, cybernetics, originally conceived and developed as a mathematically-informed military medium, became a critical tool in schizophrenia research. Ironically, this occurred through the efforts of Bateson, an anthropologist. This, in turn, became the foundation for the development of Bateson's double-bind hypothesis, the cornerstone of systemics in family therapy. The importance of cybernetics as a catalyst in this "family" movement cannot be emphasized enough as an immense impact on family therapy's foundation, its growth and development. Subsequently, family therapy would exercise far-reaching bridging effects in the development and proliferation of brief therapy techniques and approaches which are with us today. Naturally, since theories cannot always explain everything, they are subject to modification.

With the hindsight of the 1990s and the most recent research conducted by thinkers like de Shazer (1991, 1994), we are beginning to understand some of the limitations of traditionally-informed family therapy which began in the 1950s and 1960s. Today we can assert with greater clarity that systemic/family thinking, as a result of the influence of cybernetics systems in the "electronic sense" and in a "somatic self-regulatory sense," represented "metaphoric" explanations of far more complicated phenomena than had been imagined. Cybernetics systems represented thinking that attempted to understand a very complicated reality whose ultimate connections as phenomena could have only been integrated by the metaphoric "family resemblance" concept (de Shazer, 1991, p. 15). This criticism, of course, in no way mitigates the monumentally historical importance of systemic/family thinking and its many contributions to the field of psychotherapy.

Fourthly, the 1950s witnessed a vital growth of interest in family-related therapy. This pivotal decade of intensified interest represented a significant, or at least the beginning, of a major therapeutic shift from an individually-based psychotherapy to one that would be *relationally-focused*. It also represented the era in which the birth of social psychology took place. To be sure, the family became the centerpiece, the basic unit of human relationships. Additionally, societal, ethnic, and cultural issues received renewed and emphatic attention.

The growth of interest in family and family-related areas was in great part a reflection of the increase in research and papers delivered at seminars and conferences. Don Jackson's establishment of the Mental Research

Institute in 1959 highlighted these phenomena. Much of the "family" progress achieved at conferences in that decade proved to be significant. The grants that Bateson received were also critically significant. Those efforts became all the more meaningful and concrete with the establishment of a facility dedicated to mental research in a new spirit based on inquiry into communication dynamics, social relationships, cybernetics, and systemic/family foundations.

At this point, the question is raised regarding reasons for the time devoted particularly to family therapy's beginnings, to systems thinking and to their implied relevance for brief therapy, the topic of this text. The present status of family therapy and its offspring, brief therapy, understood in their broadest perspective, may be likened to a "works in progress" scenario. Family therapy started with many bold and challenging innovations in the 1950s. It has since grown by adapting and changing to reflect the benefits of new research and assimilation and integration of more recent innovations. Although de Shazer (1991) has correctly called into question the notions of *what is family* and *what is family therapy* (pp. 3–16), and many other related issues, few can deny family therapy's obvious importance and its catalytic impact on the ultimate development of brief therapy approaches.

Today many would agree that family therapy, as a term, has clearly become a misnomer. In fact, "relationship therapy" might be a more appropriate term since the latter term would easily accommodate and reflect the changing fabric of modern society. However, that change in terminology seems highly unlikely to occur. To further describe the perplexity, it is important to note that the rich aggregate of brief therapies (systemic/family) that evolved in the last three decades have obviously evolved from the foundational family thinking of the 1950s. It is for these reasons that reiteration of the origins and development of family therapy become crucial in improving our fuller appreciation and understanding of the development of brief therapy. For instance, the present-day ecologically inspired models, the constructivist orientations, the various solution-oriented models, the narrative techniques of White and Epston, and the "conversation-based" approaches, which epitomize the 1990s' cutting-edge approaches, will be better understood and appreciated if one takes note of their precursory stages exemplifying the evolutionary struggles and stages.

Similarly, in the reiteration of the trials and tribulations of systemic/family developments, family therapy also means that one might profit philosophically by understanding its original shift from therapy based on individual psychoanalysis and from pathologically-based perspectives *to* relationally-focused perspectives, systemics, and cybernetics. Furthermore, one might better appreciate the present-day shift to *ecologically-based perspective*, i.e., studying systems within larger systems and their respective interactions.

An ecologically-based ideology means conducting psychotherapy in which therapy is not limited to a "system" such as family *systems*, which has been shown to be a semantically and philosophically inadequate term (de Shazer, 1994). It also means that therapists do not limit their effectiveness as therapists by *preconceived psychiatrically-informed notions* of categories, diagnoses, medical, and negative labeling which often serve as hindrances to a more effective flow of the therapeutic process and thus undermine client empowerment.

An ecological perspective therefore means calling into question all systems that may be relevant to the immediacy of the all-important "system" imminently created by the presence of the client, or clients, and therapist present in a session. This is reminiscent of Whitaker's thoughts (1976) regarding the act or process of doing therapy. Even before the use of the term "ecological" approach, Whitaker had already presented the *paradox* that the therapist should not become hindered by the theory of the model employed. He suggested that whenever a certain therapy does not seem to be working effectively, the uniqueness of the client situation should become the focus, acting as a new starting point.

In many ways, this also represents a reminder of the Rankian notion that the relationship between client and therapist is a creative one. The relationship transcends the limitations of any therapeutic method or modality (1932). The truly effective therapeutic session represents a "creative" relationship between therapist and client where there is the development of a meaningful and high-quality "conversation" that truly seems to matter, regardless of the quantity of techniques at one's disposal. It emphasizes empathetic listening and the creation of incisive questions that draw forth the conversation to liberating ends.

This brings us to the concept of "therapeutic flexibility." A therapist may become aware, especially at the beginning of the course of treatment, that the immediate approach being employed may not be working well. Upon scrutiny, the therapist may find that this may be partially attributable to the fact that many "constraints" that might have needed processing in therapy were omitted, cut short, or ignored by the therapist (Breunlin, Schwartz, & MacKune-Karrer, 1992). Additionally, perhaps too much focus on the in-session cognitive aspects may have undermined the importance of affective and behavioral data that the client may have needed to express. The spirit of therapeutic flexibility, therefore, presents a clear caveat, especially in dealing with cases of chronicity and trauma. The therapist must be on the alert and not ignore the special needs of an individual client or those of an entire family. Those needs may ultimately involve spending significant segments of session time in listening to the clients' re-telling of painful incidents and negative experiences. This rather significant procedural consideration may often be overlooked when psychotherapeutic models (especially, brief therapy models) are executed in a formulaic or in a perfunctory manner.

The general direction of the therapy session obviously depends on the style and strategy of the therapist, but it should *mostly depend* on the needs of the client. Indeed, what the last four decades of ideological maneuvering, conflict, and adaptations have taught us involves one key point. We should neither be self-complacent with our personal style nor dogmatic with our "models," our techniques, our modalities. Both the extant approaches and newer strategies are many in number, but they should be

Brief Therapy as a Notion: Its Origins, Its Early Evolution • 35

employed as useful tools and not become, as Whitaker would agree, ideological straightjackets.

The following case illustrates that point. A therapist, well-intentioned and dedicated to the ideal that empowerment will be the by-word of his or her approach, may conceivably miss the needs of a client who ostensibly wants and, perhaps needs, to "vent" or emote. By deliberately arresting the client's initiatives at venting and by proceeding instead with the initial "steps" outlined by a prescribed brief therapy model, the therapist may do a disservice to the client. For that particular client the initial session of therapy may represent the first time that client may have felt sufficiently safe and confident enough to unload the pain of his or her trauma. From another perspective, the client's apparent need to vent may have been media-driven or culturally-informed, and those influences share in the client's expectations in wanting to vent. Regardless of the motivation, a therapist's insensitivity to a client's need, such as a client wanting to vent, would be a therapist's violation of professional therapeutic flexibility.

An ecologically-informed approach also suggests that therapeutic sensitivity does involve the position that, once organicity is not viewed as a likely probability, those clients that present their problems to the therapist as marital, parenting, anxiety, depression, phobia, or somatization, should not be negatively labeled as such, especially at the outset. This form of labeling represents a detriment to the development of a more open and less prejudiced process of therapy. A therapist might be inspired to follow, instead, the lead of de Shazer and several other contemporary writers and practitioners who ask the client what he or she precisely means by depression, marital conflict, anxiety, and the like (de Shazer, 1991).

An ecologically-inspired therapy also means that the therapeutic process, especially in the beginning, focuses on eliciting relevant and ample client information in a manner that, in turn, characteristically enhances and encourages the flow of information *from the client*. The focus should be based not only on relevant and ample information, but also on the significance and meaning that the client ascribes to that information. In essence, it represents a "conversation" by which the therapist attempts to understand and to enter the client's cosmos. In many ways reminiscent of some of the traditions of existential and humanistic therapists such as Frankl and the client-centered philosophy of Rogers, the therapist's ecological approach attempts to enter the client's world of personal meaning and its implications.

The overt purpose of eliciting is summoning meaningful responses, ostensibly generated by therapist's good questions, based on genuine curiosity, concern, and relevance to the problem. This allows the client to view an expanded meaning of his personally constructed cosmos, unlocking or disclosing key beliefs from both the past and the present, revealing his affect and behavioral experiences. This approach, effected and encouraged by the therapist's genuine sense of curiosity and relevant questions, should also contain a corresponding posture strongly espoused by the Houston-Galveston School, the posture of "not knowing." In a style reminiscent of the Socratic tradition of "not knowing" in regard to the acquisition of knowledge, the process of therapy should not be hampered by a therapist's preconceived notions. A therapist's premature conclusions, or worse, the therapist's "zeal to heal," because he or she thinks or "knows" what's best for the client, will generally hamper the therapeutic process.

Hence, embracing these useful philosophies and the practices of these newer "ecological" strategies and their variations makes more holistic sense and bears more validity *if* a therapist understands these strategies because of the historical reasons that went into their existence. Acknowledgment and avoidance of easy pitfalls and all well-intentioned but unproductive approaches, will result in performing better quality therapy. Ultimately, a strong working relationship between a therapist's own therapeutic "belief system" and its effective practice represents the essential factor for conducting good therapy.

Thomas Kuhn (1970), a scientific historian, described the historical transition from old scientific paradigms to new ones. He showed how the constant build-up of anomalies and crisis situations within a given system

Brief Therapy as a Notion: Its Origins, Its Early Evolution • 37

of thought eventually yields to one of the competing interpretations that offers a greater and a more meaningful consistency. When this transition does eventually take place, the new paradigm becomes considered and employed and that phenomenon is called "scientific revolution" (p. 90). This timely idea was proposed at about the same period when much of family therapy was formulating its basic notions. Many family therapy thinkers grasped this opportune notion and thus designated the switch from individual (intrapsychic) therapy to a cybernetic epistemology as the now famous "paradigm shift" in the psychotherapeutic perspective. The cybernetic, relationally-based therapy, which had gathered momentum and acquired more concreteness in the 1960s, had matured in the 1970s. Thinkers like Haley (1971) and other contemporaries asserted that a clear break had been effected away from past therapeutic methodologies and that family therapy's new approaches had effected that shift.

They brandished this perspective presented by family therapy as a new set of premises and approaches for gathering and processing therapeutic data. This new perspective went beyond the individual, beyond the individual's personality and behavior, and beyond what happens between individuals, even when one of the individuals still appeared to remain the "center of attention" in a therapeutic session. Indeed, the focus of therapy had changed, and the new paradigm viewed the family unit as central. This became the designated arena whereby individuals in a family setting operated as members of a larger entity called the family system.

Being a relationally-based system, the family, as a system, was now being described by its founders as an entity that was "greater" than the algebraic sum of the available data from its components (i.e., the individual members). In short, the family system replaced the individual psyche, and the family replaced the individual (de Shazer, 1991, p. 22). Understanding systemic relationships had replaced the Freudian necessity to achieve "insight." Hence, whether a family as a whole presented itself for therapy, or an individual came for therapy, the system, i.e., the family system, was essentially the theoretical focus, the model through which to perform therapy.

With the advent of family therapy, a problem redefined and viewed as relating to the interactive set of family relationships would also have to find its resolution or its solution through the same set of relationships. That was both the connotative and denotative logic. The Mental Research Institute (MRI), which was instrumental in the family therapy movement during the 1960s and 1970s, developed its own model called the problem-oriented therapy model. It did not confine itself to just those families that had experienced schizophrenia (Bodin, 1981) as it extended its ongoing research and practice to families that had presented psychological problems in general. The MRI began to work with families with problem behaviors in areas such as marital conflicts, psychosomatic disorders, depression, sexual dysfunction and drug and alcohol dependence (Fisch, Weakland, & Segal, 1982). Their approaches and specific interventions represented, to a significant degree, clinical applications of the theories and practices of Erickson, Bateson, Jackson, and Haley.

Additionally, in 1964, Virginia Satir published *Conjoint Family Therapy*, a foundational text for that decade's growth in family therapeutic strategies. While at the MRI, she did much to popularize the family therapy model both through her publications and her many workshops throughout the United States and overseas. For a variety of reasons, the MRI achieved much acclaim as it became well publicized for its pioneering activity in the decade of the 1960s. However, many changes took place to alter its composition by the end of that decade. Satir left to become director of the Esalen Institute in the Big Sur, California. Haley moved back to Philadelphia, and Jackson died in an untimely manner in 1968.

The MRI group continued its interests in family communication and interactional patterns, but the Brief Therapy Project begun in 1967, just a year before Jackson's death, assumed the main focus and became the major ongoing enterprise. The original interests in schizophrenia had burgeoned into a wider range of interests which were well beyond its initial intentions.

The MRI had become a major focal point in research, practice, and development of new ideas. Many of their ideas had great relevance for the early application of brief therapy philosophies.

By the late 1960s, the MRI had been responsible for developing two major approaches to family therapy, the communications approach and the strategic approach. While there is obvious overlap between these two broad categories, the former approach has been most often associated with Virginia Satir, and the latter both with Haley's model and the one developed by the MRI group of Weakland, Jackson, Watzlawick, and Fisch (Fisch et al., 1982; Watzlawick et al., 1974). This partition, particularly in the strategic groups, is also very arbitrary because of the wide overlap of influences and variations.

The MRI group's brief therapy model has been described as *problem-focused therapy*, or often strategic therapy. It was time limited, usually lasting no more than ten one-hour sessions. Unlike the traditional psychoanalytic sessions which often were more than once a week, the MRI group's meetings took place on multi-weekly or monthly schedules to allow the client, or clients, time to effect change in their lives. Therapy was based on the notion that the client's continued inability to solve specific problems, presently identified and named as the "attempted solutions," had in fact now become the *problem.* It would therefore be crucial for the client to discontinue the seemingly usual, self-perpetuating and self-defeating failed attempts (Segal, 1982). The so-called solution was to be found in necessarily dropping old "attempted solutions" and creating in each individual case the conditions for a new solution to emerge. First, the strategically oriented therapist would study both the failed solutions as well as the current behavior that seemed to maintain the failed solutions. Then the therapist would create an intervention to break the cycle by changing those aspects that sustained the problem (Segal, 1987).

In the dominant form of psychotherapy, psychoanalysis, the methodology usually identified the individual as the unit of analysis. Its clinical theories, therefore, emphasized personal history and trauma in the search for intrapsychic conflict, explanations that ultimately would yield *insight*. Its time line was essentially retrospective. Then, with the help of insight, the client would perhaps be better able to connect the old, original, negative patterns of the past with the present-day problem. From start to finish, the focus was on the individual despite Freud's own avowal of the fact that trauma often had originated at a locus external to the client (Karpel, 1986). Hence, this individually-based, intrapsychic and pathology-driven scenario precluded, to a considerable degree, any potentially positive prospects from family relationships or supports.

Family-oriented therapists, however, by shifting the focus onto the family as the unit of analysis, even if the entire family was not present in therapy, allowed the relational and interactive factors of an individual within that unit a broader perspective. Problems could be recast and shifted from conflicting forces within the individual (psychoanalysis) to those struggles between family members (Haley, 1963). Psychopathology, or simply symptomatic behavior, could be viewed as a tangible indication of dysfunctional transactional sequences of behavior within the context of the family unit. For many therapists, especially family-oriented therapists, the taxing and painstaking search for an illusive pattern of behavior within the psyche of the individual now became, literally, a thing of the past.

Through this major change in focus, referred to as the *paradigm shift* (Haley, 1971), the family unit was categorically viewed as a system. Since the family was observed and treated *as a system*, that perspective implied that its member components' behaviors could be both examined and re-orchestrated for the purpose of positive change. The paradigm shift represented the change from therapeutic inferential probes of the individual's mind to the study of observable manifestations in a behavioral context of interpersonal relationships. The new, smaller establishment constituted by family therapists deemed the results of the paradigm shift as more useful, efficient, and realistic.

The systems perspective in therapy then allowed the formation of new principles and approaches for the treatment of therapeutic problems and the management of psychotherapeutic processes which were believed to be more efficiently and scientifically grounded. Murray Bowen, who had worked with schizophrenics in the 1950s, is recognized as the foremost developer of *family systems theory* which is still very much alive today, especially in the realm of terminology. The perception of doing therapy *as system* was truly a revolution, and it embodied "a whole new way of conceptualizing human problems" (Sluzki, 1978, p. 366).

Many family theorists and practitioners learned of the philosophical background in systems from Ludwig von Bertalanffy, a biologist who wrote much about general systems theory as early as 1945 (Foley, 1974, p. 40). As a scientist, his thinking reflected the position of a grand overview of living systems in a holistic and comprehensive way. He showed how smaller organic systems inevitably functioned as part of larger organic systems. Metaphorically, he viewed organic systems as a continuous and concentric overlay, much like the layers of an onion.

Much of Bertalanffy's unique thinking emphasizes a dialectical reality that encompasses not only a quantitative interaction of forces but also a qualitative interaction. Thus, a system is clearly more than an arithmetic sum of its parts or a simple total of its quantitative transactions. It is, more importantly, an ongoing process that includes an interaction of qualitative factors, characterized more by circular and multi-causal phenomena than by simple linear causation. His now famous *General Systems Theory* (1968) is one of the major theoretical markers in understanding the basis for those 1960s and 1970s versions of brief therapy that focused on second order cybernetics change.

The use of systems thinking, particularly the utilization of second-order change and cybernetics, as employed by the Mental Research Institute (MRI), are major areas discussed more fully in the next chapter, which is entirely devoted to the MRI. Thus, the MRI's powerful launch of Bateson's cybernetically-inspired agenda, Jackson's administrative dynamics of a research and practice-oriented program, Erickson's innovations, and Bertalanffy's system theories taken together made the MRI aggressive pioneers in the field of family therapy. Their influence persisted for decades as they also inspired, in varying degrees, different schools of brief therapy.

Historically, the Mental Research Institute has been described as going through three major developmental periods: its original interactional perspective, the strategic therapy as espoused by Haley and the MRI group itself, and its period of influence on other schools, such as the Milan School consisting of Selvini-Palazzoli, Prata, Boscolo and Cecchin of Milan, Italy (Goldenberg & Goldenberg, 1991, pp. 184–210). The commonality of these three periods involves their methodologies which focus on the *problem and its dissolution* through the analysis of behavioral data. An integral part of their behavioral analysis approach also involves the use of interventions. They view this combination as efficient and highly effective in bringing about good therapeutic results. Together with the influence of Milton Erickson, Gregory Bateson, and the theories offered by systems/communication, the MRI group and Jay Haley indubitably commanded a significantly large segment of the early portion of the continuum that today we commonly call brief therapy.

The first developmental period, described as interactional, more generally as systems and communication theory, dealt with the use and development of the seminal ideas of the 1950s and 1960s that permeated the initial fabric of family therapy. Cybernetic influences, information theory, systemics, homeostasis, the double-bind theory, relabeling, reframing, metacommunication, and paradoxical interventions were some of the major ideas that shaped the way psychotherapy would be discussed and practiced for decades to come. Key figures in the beginning were Don Jackson, Virginia Satir, Jay Haley, Paul Watzlawick, Richard Fisch, John Weakland, Arthur Bodin, and Lynn Segal.

Haley and the MRI group generated the second perspective, strategic therapy. Generally speaking, it constituted a more succinct form of their modalities from the 1950s and early 1960s. Just as important as their models is their influence. It cannot be emphasized enough that the MRI group represents the most important early group of theoreticians and practitioners in the growth and development of brief therapy. Both as a group and as individuals, their writings, practices, seminars, and influence have touched many areas of modern psychotherapy.

Haley, the first editor of *Family Process*, was a driving force in promulgating the major epistemological shift that took place. In the context of conceptual shift, he clearly delineated what he meant by his style of therapy (1973). He emphasized that the *strategic* clinician "initiates what happens during the therapy and designs a particular approach for each problem" (p. 17). While to some, he adds, this may seem "manipulative," the previous more "passive forms" of therapy were too reflective and time-consuming as the therapist would merely "reflect back to a patient what he was saying and doing" (p. 17). Obviously referring to the client-centered model and its reflective stance and in general to psychoanalysis, Haley viewed his form of therapy as more active and more efficient. On a more comprehensive level, Haley specified that "strategic therapy, however, is not a particular approach or theory but a name for those kinds of therapy where the therapist takes responsibility for directly influencing people" (p. 17). Eventually, of course, the term "strategic therapy" became permanent, despite Jay Haley's original dictum urging that it was not a particular theory.

Again, many of the innovations exhibited in the ingenious interventions devised in a problem-solving approach had much of their foundation in the works and ideas of Milton Erickson. He had been experimenting with their use as far back as the early 1940s. Indeed, it was the MRI's members, especially Haley (1973), who elucidated much of the Ericksonian research and practices which received much recognition and appreciation after years of relatively benign neglect. Many fascinatingly rich ideas fill the pages of Haley's books. The deliberate encouragement of client resistance, the analysis of power structures in family units (1963), and the use of therapeutic directives and paradoxical interventions are but a few topics of interest (1973).

The third perspective, which reflects the MRI's direct influence, is represented by Milan systemic family therapy. It has been recognized as the most *systemically* consistent of the three perspectives discussed. It was distinguished not only by the systematic and systemic search for the *differences* in family members' behaviors, but also by the emphasis placed on the way other members perceived and interpreted one another's behaviors. Its interests lay at an interactional or behavioral level and also at a semantic level, i.e., the "meanings," both familial and idiosyncratic, ascribed by family members in therapy to their behaviors.

Mara Selvini-Palazzoli established the Institute for Family Studies in Milan, Italy in 1967. Later, she and her colleagues became particularly inspired by Watzlawick, Beavin & Jackson (1967) and by Haley's strategic therapy (1963). The Milan School went on to develop its own unique therapeutic program. However, it did not present its major contributions, innovations, and influence until well into the 1970s. They published their first book in 1978, *Paradox and Counterparadox: A New Model in the Therapy of the Family in Schizophrenic Transaction*, which delineated their ideas. Perhaps their greatest contribution is the now celebrated *circular questioning* approach. With this technique, the therapist employs a well-selected, steady stream of contextualized questions related to the presenting problem. Generally speaking, the theoretical overview of this technique might be best described metaphorically as a grid of circular questioning that evokes not only discussion of family behavioral sequences in different time designations, but also the "differences" of family members' interpretations and their meanings of those sequences.

Theoretically, the circular-questioning layout involves the conceptualization of three vertical categories of time, past, present, and future, versus four horizontal areas of "contextual" questioning. While the vertical categories of time are easy to appreciate, the four contextual areas are more complicated as they deal with what relevant questions the therapist might ask regarding the problem definition, interactional sequences, comparison and classification of family members' affect, behaviors, and cognition, and interventions (Fleuridas et al., 1986, p. 116–119).

Through the strategic use of circular questioning, useful data is elicited regarding family members' behaviors. This is based, again, on focusing on the *differences* in events, relationships, and most importantly on the personal interpretation of their meaning. Adhering to a strategic orientation, the Milan School also uses positive connotation, a form of *reframing* which involves the "symptom," interventions, and "rituals." The Milan School effected not only an immediate sphere of influence in Europe, but also a major influence in therapeutic schools in the United States.

Admittedly, the Milan School is a major example of a school influenced by the MRI, but the MRI's influence was emphatically widespread throughout the United States and abroad. In sum, the practitioners and researchers at the Mental Research Institute, their strategic therapy, communications-oriented approaches, and problem-oriented approaches significantly influenced the initial progression of brief therapy both at home and abroad. Since its inception, the MRI has become synonymous with the term brief therapy, even though the group itself was, interestingly enough, not comfortable with that term (Watzlawick et al., 1974, p. xiv). Having boldly influenced psychotherapy for four decades, the MRI remains today as a living symbol of innovation and effectiveness in psychotherapeutic approaches. It is the major starting point for appreciating the many bold and exciting changes effected in the last forty years in the realm of family systems called brief therapy.

Chapter 2

The MRI Brief Therapy Project

Most historians of family therapy agree that the 1950s were its founding decade (Broderick & Schrader, 1981). The general acceptance and presentation of "family" papers at seminars and at annual conferences during that decade clearly indicated the significant headway that this fledgling movement had made. It remains, however, historically ironic that the family therapy movement owed much of its initial existence and "justification" to its immediate work on schizophrenia under the aegis of dauntless psychiatrists who had dared to differ with the establishment. It began, in part, with Carl Whitaker's pioneering work in the 1940s and, in part, with the work of many other psychiatrists who either followed that path into the 1950s or who were experimenting simultaneously with Whitaker's work in the late 1940s.

Many other pioneering figures emerged and their orientation and justification for newer forms of clinical treatment did not necessarily include patients with schizophrenia. Included was one of the Menninger Clinic's most outstanding psychiatrists, Nathan Ackerman. His foresight and lengthy efforts in developing the use of *conjoint therapy* dated as far back as the 1930s. Those client families in treatment had typically presented clinical problems that covered a wide range of difficulties dealing with familial situations. Ackerman's 1937 article, "The Family as a Social and Emotional Unit," became the first milestone in family therapy's early literature.

The "Child Guidance Movement" that began in the 1920s influenced Ackerman. The spirit and intent of the child guidance clinics involved "a setting for the study and treatment of childhood psychological problems, and of the complex social and family forces contributing to these problems" (Nichols, 1984, p. 18). Ackerman's work was preceded by John Bowlby's trailblazing work at the Tavistock Clinic. His sustained experimentation with conjoint therapy remains historically influential. Bowlby, as late as 1949, published his prior pioneering accounts in the area of conjoint therapy in *Human Relations*. He had begun, in effect, the essential historical "transition from what had been individual therapy to what would become family therapy" (Nichols, p. 20).

However, it was Ackerman who took the lead from Bowlby as early as the 1930s and carried out the latter's pioneering experimentation into actual practice. Ackerman made conjoint therapy "the major form of treatment in child guidance clinics" (Nichols, p. 20). For almost three decades, he had fervently implemented a prototypic form of "family therapy," which, for its time, represented a truly innovative procedure. Ackerman's writings culminated in his historically significant 1958 text, *The Psychodynamics of Family Life*.

Prominent figures including Christian Midelfort and his timely 1957 text, *The Family in Psychotherapy*, and other pioneering professionals developed clinical innovations and proposed new theoretical approaches to family therapy. In many cases, as in that of Carl Whitaker, much of their work began in the 1940s. Such figures included, but were not limited to John Bell, Murray Bowen, Theodore Lidz, R.W. Lidz, Lyman Wynne, and Ivan Boszormenyi-Nagy. In effect, they helped set the stage for family therapy's foundation, growth, and substantial development in the 1950s (Nichols, 1984, pp. 3–78).

In particular, Gregory Bateson historically remains as one of the most crucially important figures of this early period of family therapy's growth. An anthropologist by profession, he savored an extensive interest in communications research. Bateson's curiosity and his pursuits in those areas were evident; first, in his published doctoral dissertation in 1936, and then later, in his interests in Erickson's use of hypnosis in psychotherapy, and most importantly, in his study of cybernetics in the 1940s. Bateson's utilization of these three component areas presented a significant impact on family therapy's early formation in the 1950s. Particularly because of his introduction and use of cybernetic thought and its application to family therapy and because of his scrutiny of traditional epistemology, Bateson created a new perspective in the understanding and, ultimately, the treatment of clinical problems in familial situations. Cybernetics theory, once a tool in the development of military instruments in WWII, was for Bateson the key instrument for studying behavioral and communication patterns and their "deviations," and for offering the means to help clients in therapy.

Similarly by the mid-1950s, Milton Erickson's relatively long and unique legacy in psychotherapy had already provided almost two decades of trailblazing work. Both with and without the use of hypnosis, he presented a vast repertoire of psychotherapeutic experimentation, introducing an impressive array of innovative techniques in non-traditional, prototypic approaches. In an unassuming way, Erickson helped change the way many therapists would perform their craft in the coming decades. His immediate influence on Bateson and on the MRI researchers was just the beginning of his influence. In the 1990s it was no surprise that accolades to his historic importance flourished more than ever, as for example in *An Uncommon Casebook: The Complete Clinical Work of Milton H. Erickson*. Bill O'Hanlon spares no superlatives when stating that Erickson's legacy unequivocally reflects "the clinical work of one of the most unusual and innovative psychotherapists who ever lived" (1990, p. ix).

When Bateson's and Erickson's various influences are pooled together with Don Jackson's research and writing on family therapy in the area of schizophrenia and his clinical and administrative talents, we begin to see an intensely vigorous formation taking place. In the background, Bateson and Erickson were a powerful amalgam of influential forces supporting the theoretical and practical foundations of family therapy. Don Jackson channeled his energies into clinical research and administrative leadership. He spearheaded the activities that ultimately generated the emergence and early development of the Mental Research Institute (MRI), which materialized under his aegis in 1959 in Palo Alto, California. Before his untimely death in 1968, Jackson was lauded as the person who had "perhaps published more material on family therapy than any other theorist" (Foley, 1974, p. 70).

The Institute, which metaphorically had been in the making for almost a decade, had its origins in an ideal sense in the late 1940s and early 1950s when interests in the area of schizophrenia proliferated. Generally speaking, in addition to the numerous questions raised by the pioneering efforts of Carl Whitaker, many of the professional debates of that time centered on the etiology of schizophrenia, particularly on the cognitive and behavioral connections with familial relationships. There was special attention given to the relationship between the "pathogenic mother," schizophrenogenic mother, and the male schizophrenic child (Fromm-Reichmann, 1948, 1950).

The hotly contested perspective regarding the causes of schizophrenia (Lidz & Lidz, 1949) seemed to have effected the impetus in launching the study of the family, its structure, its environment, and its intrinsic and fundamental behavioral relationships (Waxler, 1975). These major developments were realized simultaneously with the steady ongoing progress that was already generated by Ackerman's work and influence in the area of conjoint therapy. Again, there were scores of other therapists experimenting and creating the foundations for family therapy, which was inherently characterized as a maneuver moving away from the traditional one-on-one Freudian modality.

The year 1951 might be a significant starting point for a discussion of the early "origins" of the Mental Research Institute and ultimately its Brief Therapy Project. In that year Bateson, who had been associated with the Palo Alto Veterans Administration Hospital in California, coauthored a critically important book with Juergen Ruesch. It was entitled *The Social Matrix of Psychiatry*. Cybernetically inspired, its contents dealt with the character and function of communication feedback and its relationship with "information theory in communication" (Foley, 1974, p. 5). In essence, it represented a major shift away from the questions raised by the analytical "whyness" of traditional psychiatry to the questions posed by the observational "whatness" of mental problems. In short, new emphasis was placed on the behavioral context and on a new cybernetic terminology hitherto never employed by therapists.

Instead of asking *why* a person behaved irrationally by the traditional psychoanalytic template of intrapsychic "determining factors," Bateson was more inclined to ask questions about the "nature of the present interpersonal context" and what specific behavioral adjustment existed regarding that context of the problem. Bateson might also ask if that adjustment would constitute "the only possible reaction" for the client (Watzlawick, 1990, p. 7). In other words, what makes the problem exist in the present? And more importantly, what makes the problem *persist* in the present? What is it, specifically, in the present context that contains the ingredients that allow the problem to continue into the future despite obvious attempts to the contrary?

The investigative focus would be placed clearly on the behavioral aspects, particularly in the exchange of communication data, the major component examined in the relationship between people. This shift was realized by the therapist's focus *moving away* from psychoanalytic scenarios that would have included childhood experiences, and particularly, childhood trauma, dream analysis, and transference. Traditionally, from these related areas, the psychoanalytic process was supposed to effect therapeutically an eventual integration or bridge between past and present pathologies, a "working-through process" which was to achieve "insight" for the client. Insight would represent, then, the liberating pathway leading away from mental problems.

The new cybernetic method replaced the psychoanalytic scenario through therapeutic inquiry that focused on interactional and behavioral patterns in the present with particular emphasis on communication patterns. The "royal road" of this new orientation did not lead to the subconscious, nor did it necessarily lead to the client's past, but mainly to the client's behavioral and communication patterns in the present. If the MRI therapist did delve into the client's past, this would have constituted only *part* of the new therapeutic effort to obtain sufficient past information to verify, confirm, and compare to *present family patterns of behavior*. Again, the new model's emphasis was on the behavioral aspects and on their patterns as opposed to Freud's model which was clearly based on the biological or medical model of his time. The new 1950s' cybernetics model, as developed by Gregory Bateson and associates, represented the study of behavioral and communication patterns, together with their so-called "deviations," understood, analyzed, and compared through negative or positive feedback.

As an integral part of the cybernetic model, the recognition of the social dynamics of reciprocal relationships and influence became important. In other words, the client's rather convenient fiction of employing linear causality, simple cause and effect as in stimulus-response manner to explain away psychological and social phenomena, became a thing of the past. This was replaced by a more sophisticated *circular causality* whereby the therapeutic emphasis lay in questioning the interactional sequences between the people involved with the problem in question. The difference between linear and circular causality might be described as a marked difference in the quality of description. For example, a stark unqualified statement like "My mother always makes me angry" is essentially linear in nature. By contrast, circular causality involves ascertaining through therapeutic questioning longer and specific descriptions that *depict the behavioral and communication sequences* in the interactional relationships, including, of course, the expression of anger between client and his mother.

It might be reasonably presumed in retrospect that it was through *The Social Matrix of Psychiatry* that the seeds were planted for the eventual creation of a research facility that could study and create a working model. A year later, in the fall of 1952, Bateson became the recipient of a grant from the Rockefeller Foundation. He became the director of research for the program entitled "Project for the Study of Schizophrenia," often referred to as simply the Palo Alto Project. Unlike most schizophrenia studies of that period, Bateson's was different. It was patently behavioral and non-psychoanalytic, and it was uniquely built atop a cybernetics foundation.

The Palo Alto project also involved a proposal to examine the levels of communication using the *Theory of Logical Types* as the framework (Simon et al., 1985, pp. 214–216). Bateson's more immediate influence had emanated, of course, from the application of 1940s cybernetics feedback mechanisms whose mathematical foundations, in turn, were based on the Theory of Logical Types. For these immediate influences and their source of enlightenment, he credited Nobert Wiener and Warren McCulloch whose cybernetics work was based on the original work of Whitehead (1861–1947) and Russell (1872–1970) and their lengthy work entitled *Principia Mathematica* (1910–13). The philosophical and mathematical work of Whitehead and Russell, consisting of three volumes, had broad interests. Among its many topics were the delineation of the *Theory of Logical Types* and its relationship to their uniquely conceived "process" philosophy. They termed their philosophy as *organism*, which in many ways exemplified "process" or systems thinking.

Bateson's writings indicated that his immediate behavioral communications interests combined with the theory of logical types would become a scientifically acceptable basis for studying the different hierarchical levels of abstractions. Since logical types inherently pertain to the broad communicational matrix in human expression, he argued that they also could be used in the study of communication patterns of clients diagnosed as schizophrenic. This implied studying the major differences, the differentiations, and nuances between the concept of *class* and that of *member*. Then, one could apply that knowledge as it pertained to differences in behavioral and communication data with schizophrenic patients.

In the world of logical types a *member*, by definition, is part of a *class*. It is the characteristic mark of a member that a certain commonality allows it to be associated with other members of a given class. Its philosophical corollaries involve two conditions: a class cannot be a member of itself and a member cannot be a class of itself. For example, the term that defines a class of cars cannot be identified as a specific car, nor can the term that defines a specific car be a class of cars. In sum, a class is a collection, and a member is an individual within a given collection. Thus, the statement, "My '56 Chevrolet is in a class all by itself," is a logical paradox, an error. The transgressions in defying and in disregarding these logical differences were identified as possible sources of confusion not only in logic itself, but also, and especially, in everyday communications between people in their various interactional sequences.

These seemingly abstract differentiations have much relevance for Bateson's theories and their practical application to psychotherapy. Abstractions, poorly handled, such as in the case of the disregard for the differences between class and member present themselves as logical paradoxes, i.e., errors in logic. These errors may be discernible, for instance, when a client in expressing his or her problem confuses a class such as depression, which is a global term, with that class' membership, i.e., the many different kinds of depression that range from situational to chronic. Errors in this area of logical types yields even greater relevance in understanding a client, especially when one considers the idiosyncrasies in "logical" meanings that each client brings to his or to her explanations regarding behavior, perceptions, and personal values. This is generally referred to as the "observer's" self-reference, the inevitable coloration and influence that the individual's own epistemological premises possess over one's perceptions which may range from minutiae to worldviews.

There is also another area in logical types, a phenomenon called *discontinuity*, which psychotherapy can employ in a positive way to bring about change in the client. At first glance, the term *discontinuity* may convey a negative affect as if something is lacking. In actuality, discontinuity deals with the so-called *gaps* that arise in the hierarchical levels between a logical "class" and its "members." The gaps which are the "space" in the vertical order from the most abstract to the least abstract levels allow for "second order" change to take place. How discontinuity lends itself to effecting serious change, second-order change, is a topic discussed later in this chapter. For now, discontinuity is the metaphoric "space" between different concept levels which, utilized imaginatively and creatively, can generate new perspectives in the mind of the client. The utilization of this phenomenon assists in the therapeutic process as it liberates areas that might otherwise remain in a psychological deadlock.

Interestingly, an unexpected boon precipitated from the philosophy of Whitehead and Russell. Systems thinkers, such as Bateson, found allies in these two philosophers who had proposed a special interpretation of *Nature*, the universe as *organism*. Whitehead's and Russell's work served as a truly convenient "touchstone," both as models of thought and as models of inspiration because their philosophy was one dealing with *process*. Serendipitously, this major aspect of their work functioned in tandem with the emergence of "family thinkers" whose shifts in thought moved precisely towards *process-based*, interactive, behavioral formations. The new cybernetics shift was in stark contrast to the dominant psychotherapeutic therapy of "insight" whose framework focused more on the "retrospective" examination of psychological excavation where pathological causality was viewed at its sources, as originating and then developmental determinants.

Whitehead and Russell had characterized Nature as a "*patterned process of events*" in continuous, interactive change. This was part of their "process" philosophy. These notions, deemed useful and timely for the "family" thinkers of the 1950s such as Bateson, delineated the idea of *process* as accurately describing the workings of the universe both at the material level of the physical workings of the universe, and at the idea level, human thinking. This perspective could and would allow a fresh application of the study of logical types dating back to the Greeks. It represented one specific way to understand the intricate qualities of human communication, behavior, and ultimately thinking. These notions regarding *process* helped elucidate psychologically related communication problems and the contextual relationships in social interaction. This could be useful on a practical everyday basis regarding behavior and on more abstract or intellectual matters.

As envisioned by Whitehead and Russell, Nature's underlying process involved an ongoing continuity in time. By definition, it is continuous and it stops for no one. Therefore, when we, as observers, for purposes of examination, description, and categorization, "stop" time in order to study an aspect of Nature, our observations ultimately get reduced to abstractions through the medium of human language. Whitehead views this as necessary and expeditious; yet, he points out that the fact remains that the study is delimiting because of the inherent limitations of human language and its concepts. Despite the great worth of language and logic, they are still unable to fully fathom the complexity of Nature, much less express it completely. Echoing some of Kant's thoughts, Whitehead suggests that we can only approach the truth of Nature, and only in *non-absolute terms*.

Thus, in an attempt to study the world around us, we create rather frequently and unwittingly, *logical paradoxes*, violations of the rules of logic. For example, we often simplify observations of social, psychological, or physical data for reasons of expediency, employing a kind of intellectual "cut and paste" approach to reality, often violating the logical distinctions between class and member. These "shortcuts" in communication represent errors in accounting for Nature's most complicated processes. Yet, these shortcuts in thinking become justifiably employed, nonetheless, in the hope that it will make sense.

To Whitehead, *Nature* is an all-encompassing term, not just the physical characteristics of the universe. It also includes the thought processes which we, as part of the universe, employ. Obviously then, since people communicate with one another about *Nature*, which is inherently inclusive of people themselves and how they communicate with one another, then the study of logical types becomes crucial in the communication processes. In short, the theory of logical types, well over 2,000 years old and dating back to the formal logic proposed and developed by the

The MRI Brief Therapy Project • 59

ancient Greeks, acquired new life and new meaning in light of a modern philosophy and communications theory that emphasized process, interactional and reciprocal influences, or systemics.

It is relatively easy to appreciate that modern process-based philosophies, as they are focused on change, would inevitably spawn old philosophical conflicts dressed in new clothing. Many of these philosophical conflicts were particularly manifest in the area of logical types. The potential for conflict was realized in the age-old battle between the ostensibly *static* quality of concepts and the inescapably *changing*, dynamic, and shifting movement of Nature in which we constitute a part and, paradoxically, become its observers at the same time.

To implement this study of logical types in communication for its applicability in psychology, Bateson initiated a research program to examine communication patterns and paradoxes. His studies planned to include working with animals as well as human beings. Cybernetics and the related theory of logical types served as the framework. Jay Haley and John Weakland joined Bateson in early 1953. At that time, Jay Haley was a graduate student in communications while Weakland, a chemical engineer by training, became interested in cultural anthropology. Later that year, the group increased in number with the inclusion of two consultants: William Fry, a psychiatrist, interested in studying humor, and Don Jackson, also a psychiatrist, who was interested in family therapy and schizophrenia.

This diverse group had many interests, but their commonality involved communications and cybernetics. The varied topics of study ranged from animal behavior in otters, to guide-dog training, humor, and schizophrenia (Nichols, 1984). In 1954, Bateson received another two-year grant, this time, from the Macy Foundation to direct a study on schizophrenic communication. The original research group grew as Don Jackson, M.D., again joined them as a clinical consultant in the supervision of the group's clinical work with schizophrenics. The project's emphasis switched from its original, more varied themes of communication to developing a theory of communication that would focus on schizophrenia, particularly its relation to family context. In the substratum of this research lay the strong desire to severely question, and perhaps set limits, or change the traditional definitions of psychosis, paying particular attention to schizophrenia.

Two years later in September 1956, as the result of Bateson's earlier work, an historic joint paper was produced introducing the *double-bind hypothesis* to help explain the development of schizophrenia in family members (Bateson et al.). Based on communication research, their thesis involved the idea that much of schizophrenia could be explained behaviorally through the study of the deleterious repetitiveness of so-called "double-bind" situations in the family interactions. This involves, for example, a child's habitual exposure to receiving contradictory messages from an authority figure. These contradictory messages are typically couched in such a way that the child feels inevitably trapped in a lose-lose situation and doomed to failure, despite any action or non-action in responding to persistent contradictory situations.

This study was heavily documented, listing the necessary conditions and sequential order of events leading to double-bind situations. It rigorously depicted specific qualifying scenarios that described the "ingredients" for double-bind conditions. Once these essential conditions were established, Bateson and his associates argued that their hypothesis clearly showed that there is "a breakdown in any individual's ability to discriminate between Logical Types whenever a double-bind situation occurs" (Bateson, p. 208). This study left such a significant impact on the literature of the time that it became, in fact, one of the theoretical cornerstones of family therapy in the 1950s.

The hypothesis seemed to confirm the existence of the deep interactive and communicational nature of people's clinical problems. Many family-oriented practitioners and thinkers had surmised this conclusion all along. Now, with some relative certainty established in this area, many practitioners assumed they had serious research in hand and a theory on which to support their claims and beliefs. The research and publication of this study also had the effect of establishing the groundwork for the justification of a major shift in psychotherapeutic theory and practice. Since then, many systemic thinkers consistently refer to this change as the "paradigm shift" in psychotherapy.

In essence, the double-bind hypothesis and the subsequent discussions regarding a "paradigm shift" served both to cement the growing ranks of "family" oriented therapists and to justify emerging philosophies advocating psychotherapeutic change in an age still dominated by traditional psychiatry, its medical model, and psychoanalysis. The steadily growing influence derived from the double-bind theory was loud and clear. This tool offered new explanations for therapeutic change since change could and would be seen through a new lens. It meant seeing clinical problems as resolvable, less through the traditional lens of intrapsychic modalities and more through the lens of *behavioral and communicational patterns*. The focus on here-and-now behavioral and communicational patterns in an interactive network in familial relationships became the bywords and the buzzwords of this growing area of psychotherapy.

Bateson's communications project at the Veterans Hospital in Palo Alto eventually terminated in 1962. A year later, he moved to Hawaii and worked there until his death in 1980, studying communication in animals at the Oceanographic Institute. The communications work which he had so boldly begun in the early 1950s had already found its natural progression. Bateson's associates bridged the gap between the original trailblazing cybernetics work and its growth and application in the future. Bateson's work proceeded unharmed.

Interestingly, that bridging was already initiated three years prior to Bateson's 1963 departure to Hawaii. On March 19, 1959, Don Jackson, who had been a consultant in Bateson's Palo Alto second two-year project, took the bold move to initiate and establish the Mental Research Institute (MRI) in Palo Alto. Jackson invited Jules Riskin and Virginia Satir to join him.

The Institute dedicated itself to the study of family patterns and relationships, their etiology, development, and resolution. The Institute, in many ways a continuance and parallel development of what Jackson had experienced in Bateson's project, began its early work with the ongoing research in schizophrenia. The group soon expanded its therapeutic interests into other fields of problem behaviors such as marital conflict, school-related issues, and psychosomatic disorders (Bodin, 1981).

The Mental Research Institute's initial staff of three increased with the addition of Richard Fisch, M.D. and Paul Watzlawick, Ph.D. Two researchers from Bateson's group, Jay Haley and John Weakland, also joined the ranks of the MRI. From this group, an important trend-setting family journal, *Family Process* in 1962 did much to popularize and disseminate the latest available literature and research relating to family, and specifically to interactive, communications approaches in therapy. Virginia Satir was responsible for initiating much of the use of family therapy workshops. Don Jackson together with Nathan Ackerman of the Family Mental Health Clinic of Jewish Family Services of New York City were the founders of *Family Process*. Jay Haley was its first editor.

The promulgation of family theories received renewed impetus, and so the movement and growth in family thinking intensified with each passing year in the second half of the 1950s and increased into the 1960s. To reflect the new perspectives and needs derived from this interactively-driven communicational and behavioral perspective in familial organization and relationships, family and family-oriented terminology were created (Jackson, 1965a).

By the late 1960s, the MRI group established the basic "theoretical foundation for a communication/ interaction approach to the family" (Goldenberg & Goldenberg, p. 185). Many of its ideas and its framework had been derived from "general systems theory, cybernetics, and information theory" (p. 185). As Goldenberg & Goldenberg stated:

The concept of family rules, family homeostasis, marital quid pro quo, the redundancy principle (according to which a family interacts within a limited range of repetitive behavioral sequences), punctuation, symmetrical and complementary relationships, and circular causality, in addition to prototypic work on the double bind in schizophrenia, are all attributable to the seminal thinking of the MRI researchers. (p. 185)

Generally speaking, the rich and exciting background of the 1950s and early 1960s served to inspire the creation of the Mental Research Institute's most important vehicle the Brief Therapy Project. Merely an idea at first, proposed by Richard Fisch in 1966 (Watzlawick et al., 1974, p. xiv), the Project's creation and sustained presence influenced many psychotherapeutic schools both at home and abroad. To date, the MRI still endures and continues its research activities. From its inception, its Project began by developing a number of innovative systems-related tactics in a wide range of clinical problem areas. This included, but was not limited to, marital conflict, sexual dysfunction, family discord, anxiety, depression, and drug and alcohol dependency (Fisch, Weakland & Segal, 1982; Watzlawick, Weakland & Fisch, 1974).

The MRI brief therapy model rested on some very important assumptions. It was based in great part on systems, cybernetics, and communications thought. The MRI group clearly assimilated Bateson's suppositions about behavior and communications: a person "cannot *not* behave" and a person "cannot *not* communicate." Communication was found everywhere and had become a key operational term. In fact, all behavior represented a form of communication. Even behaviors that involved both *not* talking and *not* doing anything represented choices which were significant and subject to interpretation according to their context. The important result of these developments was the crucial and liberating fact that therapists now had new therapeutic tools for addressing client problems, perhaps to accomplish better and briefer therapy.

Whenever clients presented outright "confusion" in their conversational patterns, contradictions or incongruities between the overt message of their spoken message and the message suggested by the paralinguistics and nonverbals, the therapists had specific new ways of handling them. The broad term used to describe these contradictions and incongruities is designated as *paradoxical communication*. Bateson and associates had discussed in detail the extreme case of paradoxical communication when they studied schizophrenia as exemplifying the form of double-bind messages.

Indeed, a speaker engaged in paradoxical expressions may say one thing and mean something entirely different because his or her assumptions or meanings are different from those of the listener. In effect, what has been expressed verbally inevitably becomes contradicted by a host of telltale inconsistencies and disparities that follow. As presented earlier (Bateson et al., 1956), exacerbated scenarios of paradoxical communication can and often do lead to a varying number of clinical problems as suggested by studies of schizophrenia. Yet in a totally different context, paradoxical communication can also become the object of jokes or one-line gags such as when a boss might smile at a worker and say, "Take your time and hurry up!"

The research conducted by Bateson's associates in his two projects (Bateson et al., 1956) and the research later completed by the MRI group (Watzlawick et al., 1967) consistently endorsed the new idea that communication invariably takes place at two levels. One level was based on the notion that the more ostensible message, usually the verbal one, was considered the *surface* or *content level message*. The other, less ostensible message, called *metacommunication*, operated differently and had the effect of qualifying the surface or content level message, acting as a "comment" on the first. If both messages matched, they were considered congruent and presented no apparent problem. If they did not match, the incongruence might justifiably serve as the basis for further inquiry into the meaning of the contradiction.

For instance, when friends meet, they usually ask each other how they are doing. Often, the verbal response, the content level, is, "I'm fine." Yet, the body language, especially the facial expressions or the metacommunication, may indicate that something else stands in contradiction to the content level. An inquiry, if it were possible, might reveal that the person is perhaps thinking: "I'm really not feeling well, but I'd rather not get into a discussion about why I'm not feeling well." A host of other explanations might also exist to explain the contradiction.

In another example, a man holding an open box of candy might extend his hand and simultaneously ask a female friend if she would like a candy. However, before the woman could even react to the question, the man bearing the candy retracts his hand with the candy all too quickly. An inquiry into this obvious contradiction in behavior might reveal that he really didn't want to share his candy with her so that his invitation was apparently quite perfunctory. Or, he may have suddenly realized that his apparently kind gesture wasn't such a good idea, especially since she had mentioned to him that she had been recently diagnosed as diabetic, and admittedly had spoken of her poor self-control in regard to eating sweets.

From a related perspective, the combined research reconfirmed much of the prior work completed jointly by Bateson and Ruesch (*Communication: The Social Matrix of Psychiatry*, 1951). Their research had shown that communication not only relates data or information called the *report*, but also contains another level of meaning called the *command*. Depending on what a speaker chooses to say, selective inclusion, or what a speaker omits saying, selective omission, communication conveys more than just the ostensible information. A communication sequence also makes a qualitative statement with an *implicit* directive named the *command*. It represents a desideratum of sorts which is usually expressed within the "rules" of the communicants. The so-called command informs, without a necessary overt explanation, the desires, wants, and needs of the speaker.

After a day's work, for instance, a wife telling her husband, "I really feel extremely tired tonight," might indicate many things. Given their "family rules" (i.e., what they as a couple have both tacitly understood or expressly stated in the course of their marriage), and given their general experiences and knowledge of one another, that statement contains two levels of communication which could indicate many things within the range of their "family rules." There is ostensibly the sense that she is indicating having had a difficult day at work (*report*), but there is also another sense that, as far as that night is concerned, she may *not* be terribly disposed to doing any activities, including going out, entertaining, or engaging in sexual intimacy (*command*).

This theory, espousing the idea that communication has two levels, also advocates the idea that the metacommunication or command portion also serves a dual purpose in a systemic, regulatory manner. First, the command informs the listener of the immediate implications, the conditions surrounding the present context. It also serves as a general, ongoing homeostatic device, a regulatory and stabilizing function, operating within the "family rules." The command acts to preserve and maintain the family balance, or homeostasis, as Jackson described (1965b).

Two major terms, *symmetrical* and *complementary relationships* (Watzlawick et al., 1967), and their related implications were derived from interactional/communications terminology. Despite the fact that these two terms have been challenged in varying degrees since their original 1960s development, their basic notions are still useful today. They have become useful in conceptualizing role behavior of marital pairs and catalytic in sparking a discussion on the role of "power structures" within the family unit, the communication patterns between family members, and between husband and wife. Particularly the "power" element in relationships, as defined and described by the individuals and/or by society in a relationship, has become an area of intense interest and debate.

Jackson developed these two terms, symmetrical and complementary relationships, for the field of family therapy; however Bateson originated them in a prototypic form as early as 1936 (*Naven*) and they were encapsulated in the term *schismogenesis*. It was a communicational term which generally referred to interactive influences, their properties, and their characteristics between two individuals (Pentomy, 1981, p. 147). If a relationship is characteristically based on a fundamental notion of equality between a husband and wife, then their "patterns of communication" will be essentially *symmetrical*. While they tend to mirror one another's behaviors, they also typically behave with a component of one-upmanship. Their communication patterns will therefore reflect a certain *competitiveness*.

By contrast, in a *complementary* relationship, the power structure assumes a superior position and an inferior position. The complementary relationship usually presents a typical scenario where there is less likelihood for the two individuals to haggle. Correspondingly, there is more of an effort on behalf of the person assuming the inferior power position to dovetail his or her actions into those of the partner's agenda. For instance, in a *symmetrical* relationship, a husband and wife might agree to get out early to the latest first-run movie to insure seating. But they also might haggle over a relatively minor point of a few minutes difference about when to leave for the movies. One might suggest leaving home 20 minutes before the movie starts while the other feels 25 minutes is much better. The relatively minor difference of five minutes illustrates the competitiveness. By contrast, in a *complementary* relationship, this scenario of haggling over a few minutes would not be a typical reality.

Returning to our major theme then, the Brief Therapy Project represented a unique chronological event. For the first time in history it employed a *brief family therapy* model whose terminology, methods, and theories were orchestrated to reflect the concomitant use of cybernetics theory, communications/interactive theory, systems-based thinking, and Ericksonian approaches. The new modality was called the *problem-focused model*.

The varied components became integrated for the express purpose of *resolving problems* and relieving symptoms more effectively and efficiently than prior modalities, hence, the term "brief therapy." The model programmatically de-emphasized the traditional roles of the medical model and its pathology-driven nomenclature and ideology. This remains true despite the Brief Therapy Project therapists' persistent use of the word "symptom."

The new definitions and approaches genuinely reflected the intense formation that had taken place in family therapy in the 1950s and culminating in the 1960s. Family therapy became a distinct, self-contained *corpus* of knowledge offering a new way to conduct therapy. Based only minimally on medical terminology such as symptom and symptomology, but essentially based on cybernetic and communications and behavioral theories, the MRI model of family therapy offered new pathways hitherto unavailable.

With a fresh capacity to integrate and assimilate new research, new theories, and new information from related fields, the MRI version of family therapy in its broadest sense contained a healthy capacity and appreciation for bolstering its self-changing mechanisms for growth, refinement, and for reshaping theories and practices. Its revolutionary character, typical of its 1950s' phase, became more typically its evolutionary nature. This was confirmed by the openness reflected in the useful practices of the many "family" schools of thought that came about in future decades.

The *MRI brief problem-focused model* represents a foundational model for the infrastructure of the first stage of brief therapy. It would be difficult to appreciate fully the more recent achievements of 1990s family therapy without first examining and understanding the revolutionary fundamentals encapsulated in the MRI model. For many therapists seeking a more effective way to do therapy, the MRI model not only offered a concrete set of working strategies, but also served as a starting point that inspired newer models to emerge and develop.

Weakland, Jackson, Watzlawick, and Fisch (Fisch, Weakland, & Segal, 1982; Watzlawick, Beavin, & Jackson, 1967; Watzlawick, Weakland, & Fisch, 1974) developed the MRI model. In terms of contact hours, it was conceived as a time-limited therapy program. Ten one-hour sessions represented the upper limit. Since the sessions were not weekly, the treatment time could theoretically range for as long as one year if deemed necessary. The model evolved from much of the thinking and research of the 1950s and the early 1960s. Its major components indisputably reflected the immense influence of Bateson's theories, Erickson's innovations, and Jackson's research and clinical experience.

The model involves a four-step procedure (Watzlawick et al., 1974, pp. 110–115). First, it becomes crucial to ascertain a "clear *definition* of the problem in concrete terms." Second, the interview process involves an in-depth view and thorough examination of all those *failed attempted solutions* that ostensibly have been employed to resolve the problem so far. Third, it requires a very clear and specific definition of the *concrete change desired* by the client. Fourth and finally, it requires that the therapeutic team carefully devise an intervention which includes the "*formulation and the implementation of a plan* to produce this change" (p. 110).

From the MRI model's inception, the core philosophy was based on a rather simple systemic and cybernetic notion regarding the nature of the clinical problems. From sustained observations, the MRI group consistently reconfirmed the notion that a client's attempted solutions to resolving a problem and the repeated failures became *the problem*. This was true because the repeated failures served to make matters worse, creating a newly entrenched self-defeating pattern (Watzlawick et al., 1974, pp. 31–39). This might be compared to troughs of snow on a mountainside which by themselves present potential problems to a skier, but become patently more dangerous when they create newly emerging formations leading to an avalanche.

The model's pragmatic, strategic approach also presented its theoretical obverse as true, i.e., the old failed solutions had a flip side. Since the resolution was found in a here-and-now behaviorally-based context, that meant that its focus on the nonhistorical present time challenged the necessity for psychoanalysis' excavation of the past. The MRI model sought a resolution *in the present* through the use of an intervention once the prevailing *system of interaction,* or behaviors, was changed. Again, the problem could and would be resolved despite the non-use of any Freudian-based etiology or history. Knowing the client's past history became significantly less important than it had been in psychoanalysis. The only essential items from the client's past consisted of clear and vivid descriptions of the "failed solutions" themselves, not a psychoanalytic etiology.

The therapy team's goals were geared to assist the client in describing the behavioral aspects of the problem by implementing strategies which would investigate the old, "failed solutions" thoroughly. They also involved assisting the client in defining the desired therapeutic change or the specific goal desired. Finally, they formulated an intervention and supported the client in the execution of the intervention.

It is of crucial importance that the intervention be designed to effect or alter the system as defined by the problem, its structure, its function, and its rules. The intervention must decidedly involve the behavioral knowledge of the "system" that has been defined and created by the problem. The intervention, based on systems-thinking, cybernetics, and communications theory, must ultimately effect a second-order change, i.e., a change that effects the very nature of the system itself, not just a portion or a part of the system. From the beginning of the therapeutic process, prerequisite attitudes and practices become critical.

MRI brief therapy practitioners typically "go with the resistance" of the client family. The therapists aptly avoid the pitfalls caused by entering into confrontation with the individual client or by entering into family power issues and struggles. The interviewing process does not focus on the content of client scripts, their rhetorical aspects, their digressions away from behavioral sequences, or their minutiae from the past. The therapists neither challenge the individual members' scripts, nor do they offer interpretations of those scripts. Instead, their immediate objectives involve the conceptualizing of the present problem in its most concrete behavioral aspects. The focus remains on the *process*, particularly on the behaviors that maintain the problem in the present.

The therapist conducting the session, however, is usually not operating alone. The MRI brief therapy model routinely involves a team effort. While the principal therapist conducts the interview, other therapists observe from an adjacent room behind a one-way mirror, often telephoning the principal therapist with questions directly addressed to the family or simply asking the therapist to seek clarifications of client statements. The team members meet, both before and after each session, to discuss the therapeutic issues by pooling their information, and offering reactions and discussing future strategies.

According to the model's theory, therapy really begins when the therapists determine from the interview that the clients are ready and able to replace their old "failed solutions" with something new. It involves the clients' willingness to explore a different way to approach how the clients have perceived and behaved in the "system" that has been defined by their problem.

On the surface, the MRI group's approach may sound relatively easy to perform, ostensibly due to the therapists' obviously strong, directive role. To the contrary, this model requires great interviewing skills. It means being able to ascertain the exact behavioral sequences and to understand the client's *position*, i.e., the client's general beliefs and values that obviously influence his or her perceptions and behaviors.

Attentive therapeutic inquiry necessitates not only grasping the behavioral specificity of the problem, but also learning the cognitive particulars that have apparently sustained those behaviors. In other words, it means specifically knowing what things have managed to perpetuate the problem into the present and similarly, which things currently act as reinforcers in perpetuating the problem's future recurrence. It is therefore important that to insure the success of the intervention that its creation requires great skill and talent by the therapeutic team. They must take into account the all-important factors of client safety and client idiosyncracies.

The creativity and experience of the therapist team obviously become crucial in effecting change through intervention. For the novice therapist using this model, perhaps without the use of a team, there may be many pitfalls along the way. For instance, suggesting to a shy person an intervention such as going out and programmatically interacting with more people than usual can become, in the long run, patently ineffectual. Fostering unwittingly an interventive scenario that replicates a mere first-order change, an intervention which involves the client simply doing the opposite of an unwanted behavior, despite initial successes, this tactic can become quickly ineffective and even puerile, easily rendering the therapeutic efforts frustrating.

Accordingly, the advocates of MRI strategic therapy believe that an intervention that entails merely "doing the opposite" typically will invite "more of the same" failed behavior in the long run. That kind of "oppositional" approach is considered simplistic and ineffective because it has, in effect, benignly ignored the system as defined by the problem. Therefore, that kind of simplistic intervention will not really effect or change the "system" of interaction, i.e., the overall pattern that has encompassed the problem (Watzlawick et al., 1974, p. 22).

For truly effective change to take place then, the therapist team must devise a strategy that effects the system at a circular, interactive level. This crucial strategy must be capable of effecting a second-order change whereby the *system* functions differently from before. The disarmingly simple notion that failed solutions have now become the problem has its complications. Interventions must be individualized in great detail according to the client problem because the specificity of the impasse and the idiosyncrasies of any given "system" presented by the client or by the client family vary (Watzlawick et al., 1974, p. 114).

Variations can come from many avenues. On the one hand, there is client *cognition* that may perceive the problem differently from any given norm. On the other hand, there are different client *behaviors* that act to support that problem. Moreover, in defining the problem, it becomes

The MRI Brief Therapy Project • 73

crucially important to ascertain not only the client's perceptions, but also his or her beliefs and the semantic structures and patterns that represent the "reasoning" behind the cognition. As mentioned earlier, the MRI refers to this as the client's *position* (Fisch et al., 1982).

In investigating "failed solutions," the general strategy becomes one of ascertaining both the "position" and the specific behavioral sequences between family members. In essence, the goal of the model's strategy is to discover how a specific kind of self-defeating, reciprocal interplay between cognition and behaviors of the family group constantly reinforce one another. This is precisely where effective change needs to take place. The MRI researchers have recognized that the proposed intervention must be an activity that can *make a difference at a second-order level* (i.e., be able to change the system that the problem has defined) in order to break the vicious cycle whose repetitions have been described as an endless "dance."

This "dance," described behaviorally as mutual reinforcement, becomes the main target of the MRI brief problem-focused model. In order to resolve the problem then, *interventive measures* have to effect strategically the beliefs/perceptions and the behavioral patterns so that the *system* in question is effected. However, different contexts involve the existence of different systems. If a marital problem involves in-laws in addition to the husband and wife, then the "system" is composed not only of the husband and wife, but also of the in-laws who together define the problem's unique nature.

Resolving clinical problems by investigating the behavioral relationships between individuals has to employ means other than those of traditional psychoanalysis, by and large based on childhood experiences, trauma, dream analysis, and transference. The MRI group chose the course that Bateson and Jackson had taken. Their therapeutic orientation reflects a focus on "process rather than content, and at the here and now rather than the past" (*Change*, p. xiv). This implied the template of systemic thinking, communications, and cybernetics. This orientation also meant employing "direct interventions" (p. xv) in the therapeutic process

74 • *Breakthroughs in Six Brief Psychotherapies*

which, because of Erickson's trailblazing efforts, made the transition smoother and more feasible.

In essence, the MRI group focused on two foundational approaches, *reframing* and *paradoxical interventions*. While these represented its core of therapeutic strengths, the components that made up these strategies inspired many thinkers to develop new and different models in the 70s and 80s. The MRI's influence was felt for many generations to come, exercising much influence even abroad. What is of particular interest at the moment are the ways that the MRI group incorporated the available 50s and 60s theories and research, of which many of its own members were responsible, into a unique amalgam referred to as the *problem-focused model*. To appreciate more fully this major accomplishment necessitates backtracking into those areas that afforded the means for problem-focused phenomenon to take place.

Cybernetics represented one major area. As a branch of electronics communication, cybernetics had functioned in the military in WWII as a scientific means of collecting, monitoring, and processing data electronically. For example, in the case of radar or sonar, the constant, recursive bleep on the screen represented the end result of ongoing, high-speed monitoring of information through the use of an electronic beam directed at a "target" and then feeding back information about the target. The updated, instantaneous results of the target's location or change in location, called "feedback," reflected the target's starting position plus any other movement. A target's change in position would, in turn, be called "deviation." Thus, understood as a scientific term, deviation simply indicated a change in position, and it would be reflected on the radar or sonar screen.

Putting aside the electronic aspect of cybernetics, and transferring the same principles to the realm of psychotherapy, one can begin to appreciate from a communications standpoint the theoretical opportunities that Bateson and associates and, ultimately the MRI group, had utilized for the creation of the problem-focused model. In fact, cybernetics, as interpreted by Bateson's group and other groups in the 50s, offered the theoretical basis for systematically studying socially-based and psychologically-based interactive patterns between people.

There is an analogy that needs to be drawn. At the end of the 19th Century, the existing biological principles of that time offered Freud the opportunity to manipulate the patterns of psychiatric events and "neurological" disorders to establish a medically-based psychological model. Similarly, the study of cybernetics in the 40s offered the world of psychotherapy in the 50s the theory and nomenclature to manipulate the patterns of family behavioral and communicational sequences to establish a new model deemed scientific. It took into account behavioral norms, idiosyncratic patterns, feedback, and deviations. Psychotherapists now had a scientific means, or at least an operative metaphor, based on a hard science with which to monitor behaviors, to understand the problem pattern, and to resolve problems more quickly.

The cybernetic model, as exemplified in radar or in sonar, represents a *process*. Specifically, it is a way of *monitoring responses* by means of a steady beam of electronic stimuli. On the radar screen, the bleep represents a series of ongoing responses, a reflection of an electronic beam "hitting" the target. In an analogous manner, if a therapist poses a series of initial key questions, acting as a steady beam of relevant queries posed to a familial problem, the responses from the family members represent the feedback. The feedback, in turn, serves as a means of reporting the patterns and the recursiveness of the *family patterns* peculiar to that family. Subsequent questioning, either in the same therapy session or in subsequent sessions, will then reveal any *deviations from established patterns*, just as radar indicates a general pattern and deviations or changes.

Cybernetics, as in the case of radar, also has another major function besides reporting data. In addition to its capability to receive and process information, radar can also transfer that processed information and ultimately generate a brand-new capability into the scenario. It can, in fact, accurately direct radar-guided missiles into the target itself. Radar, which overtly monitors the position of a target and its deviations, can also inform radar-related equipment of those data. If radar is simultaneously connected to compatible apparatus which, in turn, controls weaponry, the radar could offer accurate guidance to a missile in pursuit of that target.

Similar to radar, in a therapeutic interview the therapist's monitoring of the recursiveness of family patterns and its deviations can in turn offer guidance, not only in creating a foundation for better quality questions, but also in being able to introduce a new component into the "target" family. That new component is *reframing*. This entails, first, processing sufficient information from the family to warrant moving out of an eliciting stance. From the information gathered, a *new perspective*, called a reframe, may be fashioned. After processing sufficient data, the therapist directs a reframe which re-introduces *specifics* of that information recast into a new perspective into the family system. Like a radar-guided missile honing in on the target, reframing embodies the "delivery" of this *new perspective* to the "target" family. In this sense, the reframe employs the use of the cybernetic feedback model.

The cybernetic tools offered new therapeutic options deliberately aimed at influencing and effecting positive outcomes, and extricating clients from their dilemmas. Reframing constituted one of the two major devices used by the MRI group in dealing with clinical problems of change. Naturally, there were no guarantees with the strategy of reframing. Basically, it represented a studied attempt at influencing change faster and more effectively. Reframing, as employed in therapy, involves first reshaping the client data elicited from the therapeutic conversation into a new perspective. Secondly, the therapist delivers the newly devised perspective hoping that the client might view his cosmos from that new position. In short, after eliciting sufficient client information, the MRI reframing efforts might be best described as attempting to effect a change by altering the conceptual and/or emotional context, that, preferably, will be reflected at a systemic level. In systems parlance, a change at the systems level is called a *second-order change*.

A reframe may be disarmingly simple and brief, merely a short statement or a question suggesting a new perspective. Offering a new perspective based on client data is its only major required condition. It might effect a perspective that the client has never before experienced, or simply a perspective that the client has forgotten or neglected. For instance, a client who has come for therapy because of depression may mention offhandedly, as if unimportant, that he has been painting landscapes for years and, in fact, has even sold some artwork not long ago. After a sustained series of relevant questions in the process of integrating the accumulated client information, a therapist might choose to respond in a positive and emphatic way with a simple reframe such as "So, you're an artist."

Reframes are unmistakably deliberate, persuasive attempts. A reframe is in many ways like its philosophical precursor, the *enthymeme*, which in Aristotelian thought was a rhetorical syllogism, a method of argument, usually consisting of *probable premises*, to be used for the purposes of *persuasion* instead of mere instruction. The reframe must be based on reasonable *probability* in that there exists a "fit" between the therapist's newly proposed perspective and the information thus far revealed by the client. The reframe is also reminiscent of the French word *essais*, which means an *attempt* to influence, such as in the phrase to write an essay. It signifies an attempt at persuading the reader to alter his or her perspective regarding a certain topic.

There are no guarantees that a reframe will have that desired effect. Reframes are attempts to influence based on substantiated information emanating from the client and/or the client family. A reframe's proposed perspective must be founded on information that is congruent with the clients' ongoing narratives. Depending on the context of the interaction of the therapist and client, a seemingly innocuous reframe may in fact rouse many positive feelings and thoughts in the client. Hopefully, it will have an effect in the immediate session and beyond as it is meant to make the client re-evaluate his "position."

A reframe must relate to the problem and have something new to offer as far as the problem defining the system is concerned. Gratuitous remarks do not constitute a reframe. A reframe should represent an attempt at effecting the system. Naturally, the client's reaction to the reframe is crucially important and should be examined by the therapist in the form of follow-up questions. The client may agree or disagree with the new perspective offered. If the client disagrees, the reframe's development is dropped. If the new perspective seems to contain relevance for the client, then the therapist explores its implications and amplifies the client's position in this matter. Likewise, just as the reframe could effect behavior in the session itself, it could also influence the client outside of the session after the therapeutic hour is ended.

The strategy of eliciting and reframing client information for the MRI group became, then, a more palpable way of exploring and analyzing behavior in the here-and-now, hoping, therefore, to effect a more efficient and more effective change in the client. Psychotherapeutic change in this model necessarily involves effecting major components of the system or effecting the "rules" that govern the system as defined by the problem. The MRI here-and-now approach, the reframe, having its distantly historical roots in the classic enthymeme, contains an *embedded interventive aspect.* "So, you're an artist," becomes interventive in nature *if* the client accepts that reframe. In sum, the reframe, as developed by the MRI group, represents an approach based on Bateson's theories and on Erickson's experiences and practices. Indeed, for its time, it represented a distinctly different and highly innovative strategy after about sixty years of psychoanalysis.

The second major area identifiable with the MRI group involves the use of *paradoxical interventions* or *prescribing the symptom.* They are also very new on the psychotherapeutic scene. Again, like reframing, they are linked both with Bateson and his introduction of cybernetics into family therapy and with Erickson and his psychotherapeutic experiences and practices. They emphatically represent a huge benchmark in the history of psychotherapy. They were and have since remained useful techniques to date.

In the dominant form of therapy at that time, psychoanalysis, the solution to a client's problem was found by establishing *insight*, i.e., getting the client to understand and bridge past trauma and present pathological behaviors. However, the MRI argued that this typically linear, non-systemic approach in the quest for psychoanalytic "insight" was short-lived and ineffectual. Paul Watzlawick argued in his *Language of Change* that psychoanalytic insight was unproductive primarily because its overall process becomes emaciated in the realm of "secondary thinking." Watzlawick viewed insight as too cerebral and too abstract to achieve any effective duration. While insight may effect a mental leap between the patterns of an old pathology and a newly related one, insight has a built-in limitation. This limitation helps to explain why the experience of "insight" may seem to make so much sense to the client during the therapeutic hour, yet is sapped of impact and relevance in only a matter of hours or days. Similarly, for many behaviorist-oriented therapy schools the "solution" usually involves, to a significant degree, a do-the-opposite-of-what-you're-doing approach. For instance, a client, who presents shyness as a problem, might be induced by the therapist to become outgoing, a depressed person to do "happy" things, and an agoraphobic person to become socially interactive. Watzlawick and associates demonstrated that these approaches, which emphasized "doing the opposite," were characterized as merely first-order changes, and therefore by their nature ineffectual and useless with little possibility of being long-lasting.

First-order change clearly had no place in the MRI's problem-focused strategic approach which sought a second-order change in their clients. The use of simple oppositional tasks in a programmed incremental fashion usually discovered that the long-range trajectory involved a tendency to return to the old unwanted behavior. The reversion to the old status has been proverbially described by the MRI as "more of the same." Watzlawick would also say that the "more of the same" condition recurs when the oppositional tasks eventually deteriorate in strength and again "the attempted solution becomes the problem" once more.

Rather than focus on solutions in the traditional sense involving psychoanalytic insight or the behavioristic performance of oppositional tasks or acquiring oppositional attitudes, it made more sense for the MRI researchers to focus cybernetically on the problem, the recursiveness of behavioral patterns, understanding their underlying semantic strata and discerning how elements of the system created and continued to perpetuate the problem in the form of recursive behaviors (Watzlawick, Weakland, & Fisch, 1974). This became the focus and orientation of their therapeutic thrust and the basis for designing interventions. Specifically, the immediate strategies involved restraining the client from reverting to old, apparently ineffectual, and failed solutions. It also involved understanding the special nature of the interplay between the behavioral and cognitive contexts, understanding the current behavior that continued to maintain the problem. Once these three things were accomplished, a specific and achievable goal could be established. Then the therapist team could create the last strategy, an intervention. The intervention served to manipulate the system and work within its parameters to effect change at a systemic level by changing the system's structure, its functions, or its "rules." This method clearly avoided the pitfalls inherent in "insight" and oppositional tasks. This is called a paradoxical intervention, also known as prescribing the symptom.

In essence, the MRI's strategic therapy, as a school of thought and practice, does study part of the past, but only to ascertain behavioral patterns. It seeks neither to prove anything of an intrapsychic nature, nor to fulfill the understanding of a prescribed pattern of psychoanalytic theory. It studies past recursive behaviors sufficiently enough to obtain information about "failed solutions" so that a comprehensively designed plan, the intervention, may be appropriately devised.

The practitioners of this method deemed their problem-focused approach more effective than psychoanalysis' "insight-based" therapy.

The MRI Brief Therapy Project • 81

Watzlawick argued convincingly that psychoanalysis primarily effects the left-hemispheric activities of the brain. He suggested that ample research had shown that left hemispheric activity focuses on rational and intellectual functions. This fact strongly implied that the methods of psychoanalysis, which essentially dealt with secondary processes, became unfortunately *systemically limited* as a therapeutic process and, therefore, less effective in effecting long range change (*The Language of Change*, pp. 40–126). Longer lasting change would be effected, Watzlawick argued, if and when therapy was based on a therapeutic process that influenced *right-hemispheric* activity. This side of the brain is less abstract and more analogic in nature. It is more open to change precisely because of its close links to primary process thinking (pp. 36–37). It remains closer to a systemic orientation, or, as Watzlawick would say, closer to viewing and appreciating reality in its totality or "world image."

The new "royal road" to conducting more effective therapy decidedly involves taking a detour around the "intellectualism" of left-brain activities and heading straight for the right-brain hemisphere. It implies heading directly for those areas deemed "mythical," the deep-seated operational beliefs, the analogical, the metaphoric, and the poetic. In the MRI model, the therapeutic focus was placed on dimensions that were more closely related to primary process thinking. In availing itself of the more useful avenues offered by the right hemisphere, problem-focused therapy avoided the pitfalls and limitations imposed by the left hemisphere's "rational" demands.

In their classic text, *Change: Principles of Problem Formation and Problem Resolution* (Watzlawick et al., 1974), the authors depict many scenarios that exemplify the approach of the MRI Brief Therapy Project's problem-focused model. One major tool involved the use of the *therapeutic double bind*. It is related to the double-bind hypothesis, and it represents therapeutically the outgrowth of the MRI's research on the double-bind studies. To appreciate fully this 1974 text, it is important to backtrack to 1967 when Watzlawick and associates published a book entitled *The Pragmatics of Human Communication*, which was, in turn, a natural follow-up to the article "Towards a Theory of Schizophrenia." It was the classic that Bateson and his associates had written describing the conditions of the double-bind hypothesis.

Viewed as a natural sequel to that article, the 1967 MRI text offered specific ways to handle clinical problems that involved double-bind situations, i.e., those situations whose traditional solutions only seemed to further deteriorate the problem situation. The 1967 text described its approaches as "paradoxical techniques," *prescribing the symptom*. While based on Bateson's cybernetic theories, prescribing the symptom was dissimilar to reframing. Prescribing the symptom acted differently in that the intervention involved *selectively* amplifying the symptom in the family system to effect change.

For example, a beleaguered wife goes for therapy. She is at her wit's end with her husband's habitual after-work drinking away from home. She has discovered that her preaching and genuine expression of concern for his health and their marriage, which usually created more marital conflict, have absolutely served to no avail. In fact, it reached the point where, when they argued, they knew each other's lines as if reciting a script. Her apparent "solutions" of preaching and expressing her concerns to him had failed repeatedly, and unfortunately she now finds herself at an impasse where her attempted solutions have become the problem.

In the course of the therapeutic sessions, through effective eliciting questions, she is encouraged to *pinpoint the exact nature of the behavioral transactions* whose solutions have failed. Ultimately, she describes them in great detail, both past and present patterns of "failed attempts." She describes specifically the behavioral and communicational transactions with her husband. She also depicts her *position,* i.e., her beliefs and how they influenced her behavior, especially in the area of communications.

When these two major steps are fully concluded, the client must then describe a very specific achievable goal. It must be specific enough so that when it is achieved, it could be easily identified, and the client would be convinced of the intervention's effectiveness. For instance, the wife might describe the specific goal as her husband regularly coming home right after work without drinking. The strategic therapists then devise an intervention plan that, first, would incorporate the safety of the wife. Secondly, they include a strategy that would scuttle the idea of a client, in this case the wife, reverting to traditionally "failed" behaviors or old solutions. Thirdly, the plan would also include the client's commitment to the intervention, adhering to the newly acquired position, the desired conceptual and behavioral changes needed to *change the system defining the problem.*

In this instance, the participants in the system are the husband and wife at a marital impasse. Were the system larger, the therapist could devise a plan that would also account for the care, concerns, and relative safety of the children or other significant participants such as in-laws. The strategic therapists would take into account the behavioral patterns, the particulars, and idiosyncrasies, case by case, so that the behavioral and conceptual changes would have a direct effect on the system (i.e., a second-order level) that defined the problem. Obviously, in this kind of therapeutic modality there are no easy formulations because each client and each client family presents different relationships which in turn reflect different systems.

An integral part of prescribing the symptom, the intervention, in this situation might involve the wife *"joining the resistance"* of the husband. This means "agreeing with him," telling him expressly that she "understands that a little drinking and socializing is almost necessary after a hard week's work," almost "as if" giving him tacit approval to pursue his drinking habit.

Prescribing the symptom also involves the use of adjunct behaviors that are part of the effort in effecting change at a second-order level. In this situation, these behaviors would include her desisting from preaching to her husband about not drinking and her refraining from sharing her concerns for his health and their marriage. Prescribing the symptom also includes behaviors regarding her own activities, doing something for herself that would potentially serve to counteract or counterbalance her husband's time devoted to his drinking habit which is the targeted, unwanted behavior. Specifically, this might involve an activity whereby the wife *does something different* for herself. Perhaps, she might have dinner ready for him, yet not be "available" to dine with him, attending to other reasonably sanctioned activities that do not include her husband. Or, even after having dined together, the wife might become involved in a regular group activity or enrolled in a program that would necessitate her being out of the house while he is left alone at home. The intervention just described includes changes that conceivably could effect the "system," the relationship that defines them as a couple and defines the problem area.

The initial changes that the wife attempts as part of the paradoxical intervention are *not* to be interpreted as "solutions" in and of themselves. An interpretation of that kind would constitute a shortfall in understanding the complexity of the therapeutic model. Those changes, instead, constitute only intermediate steps which are ultimately designed to effect the system. Joining her husband's resistance, not arguing anymore about the obvious, and doing something for herself are all geared to making an impact at a systemic level. Specifically prescribed behaviors constitute a strategy, a planned cluster of behaviors designed to effect change and involve the cybernetic use of feedback mechanisms in the problem system. It comprises a deliberate set of new behavioral sequences aimed at manipulating the set of established patterns, the unwanted behavior, by paradoxically "encouraging" an increase in their activity and creating a positive feedback effect.

Prescribed behaviors contradict so-called common-sense approaches. Conventional wisdom, by contrast, advocates the client remain steadfast to her old attempts and keep reiterating her "feelings" and her "being honest" in the hope that her husband would realize the meaning behind her efforts to openly communicate. In no way would a common sense attitude condone her telling him that she understands his need to stay after work and have a few drinks. In essence, prescribing the symptom precisely represents the use of introducing behaviors that will have the effect of creating *more* positive feedback in the system. By definition, positive feedback occurs when something encourages the repeat of a pattern of behavior. In this case, the positive feedback acts to encourage the drinking habit, which is the symptom. To those unfamiliar with this model, prescribing the symptom will naturally raise a few eyebrows and raise the question: why encourage a pattern that is not wanted? The answer to this question entails the necessary addition of other components to the paradoxical intervention.

The intervention is incomplete as it needs other interventive corollaries. Again, this involves the wife who will have to make changes in *her* behavior. For instance, she will not be at home on the evenings when her husband returns from his ritual drinking. Prescribing the symptom avails itself of the *quid pro quo* submerged "logic" in marital relationships. In this case it involves an equation of sorts that implies a special kind of reasoning, "Now that I'm telling you that it's okay for you to drink, it should also be okay for me to do something different for myself, which might include the very real possibility that I may not be here for you when you return home after drinking." This rather decisive "exchange" behaves in fact like a *new rule*, a new exchange agreement in their expressed or unexpressed marital *quid quo pro*.

This intervention is called paradoxical because it bears a double nature, a *therapeutic* double bind. The husband is caught unexpectedly in a strange new logic: having permission to drink but not finding his wife home after his drinking. He is now compelled to start making some decisions since one of the unwritten rules of their marital relationship has changed. It is this kind of "logic" that, while offering no guarantees, often leads to effecting a change in the marital relationship. The paradoxical intervention where a change in the "rules" of the relationship becomes fully realized constitutes a second-order change.

The following example also illustrates prescribing the symptom in a different kind of situation. A therapeutic interview reveals that the parents' nagging their only teenage son and that their son's verbal protests against them have escalated in recent weeks. They are all at their wit's end as the in-house fighting has resolved nothing. In cybernetic terms, the undesirable condition of familial fighting is the problem situation, and it has actually increased in the last several weeks. Thus, there now exists a relatively high positive feedback regarding the problem behavior. After a thorough interview that takes into account specific behavioral and communicational sequences peculiar to this family unit, the therapist asks the three-member family to describe a specific, mutually desired goal. It may well be a goal that is simply characterized by their ability to sit down together to discuss a specific issue and to find a specific compromise.

The therapist team, then, based on this specific familial situation and based on their experience with similarly related familial situations, creates an intervention in which the team prescribes the symptom, i.e., paradoxically, *escalating that unwanted behavior even more*. The therapist will instruct them in such a way that they are overtly encouraged *not to change* in their "positions" and to increase the unwanted behavior of arguing. The prescription will obviously involve all three family members having to argue more. The intervention also requires that they can only argue at designated intervals and on specifically assigned days.

This procedure has as its overt purpose to make the family continue to argue and *exaggerate their symptomatic behavior* all the more. Yet, a closer view of this prescribed situation shows that prescribing the symptom does represent a *paradox*. It means that they have to argue even if they don't feel like arguing at those assigned times. This strange design will put the family unit in a double-bind situation which may prove to be therapeutic. That is the reason it is called a *therapeutic double bind*.

While on the one hand they are instructed to perform more of the same unwanted behavior, supposedly reinforcing the very behavior they wanted to change, they are on the other hand compelled not to make any favorable changes in their situation. This constitutes the double-bind situation, and the MRI model views this as a *therapeutic*. It is viewed therapeutically in the hope that the paradoxical situation (i.e., the escalation of the symptom so "mechanically" prescribed) allows the clients to experience and deduce for themselves essentially two major ideas that will hopefully help them resolve their own dilemma.

First, the inflated situation will metaphorically point out to them that their interactive patterns, both the parental nagging and the adolescent's opposition, *now* no longer serve the family needs which might earlier have been based on developmental family rules. The "forced" periodic arguing rings hollow showing its emptiness. Secondly, the periodic imposition of arguing at prescribed times puts them in a paradoxically revealing situation which is actually empowering. They realize that they do have the power and capacity to attempt positive alternatives. In a sense, prescribing the symptom compels them to see their arguing as contrived and pointless. It compels the clients to choose to change the "rules." If the family accomplishes this change on their own, it constitutes a second-order change.

In *Change: Principles of Problem Formation and Problem Resolution*, Watzlawick and associates devoted many pages offering specific examples that illustrate their model's technique of prescribing the symptom (1974, pp. 116–157). While the essential idea is deceptively simple, the therapeutic scenarios often differ to a considerable degree and, correspondingly, so do the interventions. Many factors are at work in the creation of the intervention. Client personalities vary as do ethnic, gender, socioeconomic, political, religious, and economic considerations. Additionally, there are the contextual particulars that vary from situation to situation. The authors' very first illustration is a scenario entitled: "Less of the same."

The problem. It deals with a young couple seeking therapy because "the wife feels she can no longer put up with her husband's excessive dependence on and submission to his parents." In fact, he is doing well financially and professionally, but he cannot say "no" to his parents who have perpetually showered him and his wife with gifts, have inundated them with advice, and have meddled persistently in their affairs to the point of selecting furniture for them and arranging its layout at the couple's home.

The attempted solutions. As a couple, they have attempted to diminish the problem by fighting over the payment of restaurant checks when dining out with them. The young couple also attempted to return gifts only to receive replacements that were even more expensive than the originals. In brief, they now feel helpless since their attempts to break away from the parents have ended in failure. They are at an impasse and can find no way out.

The goal. Initially, they discussed what they generally wanted to achieve as a couple; namely, the right to live as adults, "make their own decisions" and not be treated "like children." However, the team of therapists deemed their description too general a goal. A more specific and achievable goal was needed. Additionally, that goal would have to be described in an accurate and recognizable context that could serve as "tangible proof" of success when it occurred. Finally, the thirty year-old husband opined that the goal would be achieved if his father would say something to the effect that: "You are now grown up, the two of you have to take care of yourselves and must not expect that mother and I are going to pamper you indefinitely."

The intervention: The therapists designed an intervention that prescribed the symptom, the young couple being treated like children. It would be an intervention that would necessarily fit into the "only *language* the parents could understand, namely the overriding importance of being good parents." In other words, an intervention which attempts to effect the "system," defined by the young couple and the parents must, by design, "fit" with the components of the system. The strategy must account for the fact that the parents in this particular case think themselves as good parents by virtue of doing things to their son in the name of loving parental generosity.

Before the parents' next quarterly visit to the couple's home, the couple is informed to be prepared to do the following. First, beginning within a

The MRI Brief Therapy Project • 89

few days before their parents' arrival, the house is to be deliberately neglected. Dishes should mount over the sink area, the laundry should be left to accumulate to an all-time high, the cars should be left dirty and lacking fuel, the groceries and kitchen supplies should run low, and the garden left unkempt. Moreover, unlike in prior times when they would go out as a foursome and argue over who would pay the bills, the young couple was now asked *not* to argue and let the parents pay for groceries, restaurant tabs, entertainment, and the like. Moreover, in each instance the couple was to "wait calmly" until the parents paid for everything. In addition, for the all things the parents did, the young couple was to thank them but only in a most perfunctory manner (pp.118-119).

When the newlyweds returned to therapy several weeks later, they admitted that they were able to execute only some of these suggested tasks. Nonetheless, they reported that things did change. His parents cut their visit short. More importantly, before leaving, the father in an aside to the son said that "he (the son) and his wife were very much pampered, that they had gotten much too accustomed to being waited upon and supported by the parents, and that it was now high time to behave in a more adult fashion and to become less dependent on them." This rather explicit statement seemed to match very closely the specific goal that the son had uttered during the discussion of goals. Here again, as in prior examples, the "rules" of the system had changed sufficiently enough to effect a second-order change reflected in the way the parents would treat the newlywed couple (pp. 118-119).

Similarly, the remainder of the examples of stories that Watzlawick and associates relate repeats the same paradoxical approach of prescribing the symptom. Naturally, the therapeutic challenge to the therapist lies, first, in understanding the exact nature of the behavioral patterns; second, in delineating the specific nature of the intervention that would meet the fulfillment of a specific goal. The intervention must also take into account safety factors and the idiosyncratic qualities of the problem's context. For example, in the case of the meddling parents' controlling attitude, it was important that the therapist had taken into consideration their character and their "position." It contained a certain amount of generosity and care which *they*, the parents, obviously had assumed as being part of good parenting.

The MRI group drew much of its vigor to devise their model from Bateson's study of cybernetics and from his communications work. However, as Watzlawick and associates revealed, the practical successes of the MRI model in therapeutic practice ultimately and necessarily led them to explain more and more the theory behind their specific methods. At this point Watzlawick and associates felt the need to "conceptualize" the uniqueness of their approach, systematizing the "premises" to illustrate their "conceptual framework" since so many others, impressed by the MRI model, wanted to understand the model at its rudimentary, theoretical level (Watzlawick et al., 1974, p. xv).

Interestingly, Watzlawick also revealed that in their early history, in the prelude to its Project's creation, the MRI group had been simultaneously "frustrated by the uncertainty" of their methods and yet were "intrigued by the unexpected and unexplainable success" even when they employed interventions that seemed to be "gimmicky" (p. xiv). In fact, how their brief problem-focused therapy model functioned became the topic of their 1974 book entitled *Change: Principles of Problem Formation and Problem Resolution*. The book critically dealt with the important themes of *persistence and change*, which corresponded exactly to the subtitle of the book.

In short, in their 1974 book Watzlawick, Weakland, and Fisch dedicated themselves to not only discussing change and illustrating their strategies which they had already done "through lectures, demonstrations, and training courses" (p. xv), but also to discussing the *theories relevant to their success*. As a start, Watzlawick and associates thought it important to distinguish between the existence of *first-order changes* and *second-order changes* in systems theory. The essential difference between the two orders of change represents the decisive characteristic for understanding the difference between temporary change and long-lasting change. This challenge, in turn, led them back to Whitehead and Russell whose mathematical work in 1910 on the Theory of Logical Types had proven crucial for 1940s' cybernetics, and ultimately, for family therapy (Watzlawick et al., 1974, p. 6). They also availed themselves of another mathematician's work, a Frenchman, Evariste Galois, who in the early 1800s had been responsible for introducing the term *group* into Western thought because of his work in Group Theory (p. 3).

The necessity of explaining their model from a very theoretical perspective also led them to Ashby, a cyberneticist, who had completed work more recently in the area of first-order and second-order changes (1952, 1956). The MRI group's unique elaboration, differentiation and integration of these phenomena, first-order and second-order changes, group theory and logical types, comprised much of the substance of their classic 172-page text. From Whitehead and from Russell, Watzlawick and associates illuminated second-order change, and from Galois they illustrated first-order change.

From Galois' "Theory of Groups" work in mathematical logic, Watzlawick and associates reiterated, strictly from an analogical point of view (p. 2), the characteristics of a *group* and their postulates, which were "concerned with relationships between *elements* and *wholes*," their characteristic qualities and properties (p. 3). In short, they described the attributes that constitute a "group." According to group theory, then, a group is "composed of *members* which are all alike in *one* common characteristic" (p. 3).

Group theory, however, is not limited to numbers as in mathematical relationships. A group can also consist of "objects, concepts, events, or whatever else one wants to draw together in such a group" (p. 3). Since members of a group are bound by only a *minimum of one characteristic*, it means that there literally exist innumerable combinations to any given group. Thus, each member of a group is permitted to be different, except for one minimum characteristic that remains common and constant for all members, even in the most disparate combinations. For instance, fire trucks and red apples may be part of a group that may define itself as containing those things bearing the color red. So, with the exception of the commonality of redness which incorporates fire trucks and red apples into a group, they really have little else in common.

Group members inherently contain a high probability of varied, and often bizarre, combinations. Ironically, employing the same strict logic, one may see that group relationships also contain a certain *invariance* in that within *any group* "a combination of any group members is again itself a member of the group" (p. 4). In other words, members of a given group, whose commonality for instance is redness, may also contain within themselves varying kinds of subgroups that consist of smaller but different kinds of combinations. Despite the fact that vast numbers of combinations or subgroups may exist, depending on the size of the initial group, they still remain tied to the initial group because of the commonality of redness. This characteristic is called invariance.

The importance of these observations lies in the fact that they have important therapeutic implications, especially when one is considering familial behaviors and family patterns. The MRI thinkers accepted the work of mathematicians such as Keyser (1922, p. 203) and cyberneticists like Ashby (1954, 1956) as foundational in the identification of the *theory of groups* as a model to explain *first-order change*. Namely, the combinations of *changes within the group's members* make "it impossible for any member or combination of members to place themselves *outside* the system."

Out of a myriad of possibilities, let us take one specific group defined as *cars*, which obviously have different *combinations*, varieties of size, shape, color, and horsepower. Now, if a car were to perform a different task, a recognizably clear combination such as pulling another vehicle stuck in the mud, it still remains a car. It is neither a tractor, nor a tow-truck, nor a wrecker. It cannot change its key quality which has defined its essential nature, being part of that group called cars, not trucks, not vans, not wreckers.

Hence, by identifying Galois' description of group theory and that of subsequent theorists, group theory and its inner workings and configurations became viewed as a framework exclusively dominated by first-order change. "Group Theory gives us a framework for thinking about the kind of change that can occur within a system that itself stays invariant" (p. 10). In other words, Galois' initial study of groups served as the foundation to illustrate those varieties of theoretical changes, all of which are reducible to *first-order changes*. In effect, Watzlawick and associates linked the *invariance* factor found in group theory to the *invariance* factors in psychotherapy with *clients whose repeated efforts to change proved fruitless*.

By definition, first-order changes represent those changes *within* a given system that *do not change the structure or basic organization or the rules of the system itself*. As in the previous example, a car may be temporarily used for towing which is a combination, but it still remains a car, not a tow-truck. Hence, a car can have combinations, but the car is invariant. The ideas inherent in group theory are particularly useful when applied to therapeutic contexts because they account for understanding first-order changes, changes that really do not effect the system in question. A family/group, presently characterized by conflict, may have its members attempting behaviors with one another, designated as combinations that repeatedly change little or nothing because no real change to the group or family system has taken place.

The ensuing examples, however, are somewhat different. Unlike the previous example which showed no change, the following do show some positive change. However, despite the fact that they effect some positive change, they still retain their identity at the level of first-order changes because they *do not effect the system in question*. According to Galois, most first-order changes take the form best described as "do-the-opposite reaction" to something. Those changes usually act to maintain a certain *status quo* condition, trying to maintain a "balance" that is *internal* to the system but not the system itself.

The following example presents situations involving a typical "common sense" decision-making first-order change that effects the given situation in a positive manner within the system yet *not* the system. Again, first-order changes usually suggest an idea involving the performance of a *maneuver* that stands in opposition to some other condition *within* the system in question whose resolution returns to a *status quo* condition. To illustrate this point in another context, consider the *weather system*. An early morning TV weather forecast speaks of incoming cold weather and unusually strong winds throughout the nation in the afternoon. It might suggest to one TV viewer in the North to wear heavier clothes that day. To another viewer out West, it might suggest canceling his ski trip that day. Or, to another viewer living down South, it might suggest shortening his deep-sea fishing trip expedition and returning home by noon.

In these examples, it becomes important to figure out what is the system or the "group" and what is the "member," the participating entity called member that is implied in each case, and to identify what really changed. An examination shows that in each case what might be described as the *system*/group is *not* effected by the individual member's actions. Those maneuvers by the individual member remain, in fact, just *internal changes* with respect to the system. In the first case, wearing heavier clothes, the member concept, does not have any effect on the weather system. In the second case, the member concept, canceling a trip also has no effect on the weather system. Similarly, in the third case, shortening the duration of a fishing trip has absolutely no effect on the weather.

In short, the actions and behaviors taken by the individuals are considered *member* concepts vis-a-vis the system that is the weather. The individuals' behaviors are identified as first-order changes precisely because the system, as defined by the weather, remained unaffected. The changes that did take place were *internal* to the system. They might be described as the members' preventive actions that effect the members themselves in some way, but do not change the system itself.

In this kind of first-order change, both Bateson and Jackson developed some interesting applications to understanding family behavior and therapy, the idea of psychological or behavioral *homeostasis*, the concept of dynamic equilibrium. The whole notion of homeostasis was based on Walter Cannon's 1932 studies in physiology (Goldenberg & Goldenberg, 1991, p. 38). It was essentially a biological idea that described homeostasis as the body's natural tendency to retain equilibrium, a "balance" of its functions, such as metabolism and blood pressure.

Bateson and Jackson utilized the homeostasis idea, restating it in psychological, familial terms, suggesting that it essentially represents a linear cause-and-effect relationship. It's a first-order change that might be characteristically viewed as simply a reactive maneuver to maintain psychological maintenance of *balance or equilibrium within a given system*. For instance, with the introduction of a newborn baby into family system, family members will adjust to compensate for the newborn's presence. Or, when the last of a household's young adults goes off to college, the parents will similarly do things to maintain a balance in the absence of that person and for the new conditions created by the absence of that person at home. These kinds of positive first-order changes illustrate how first-order changes may, in fact, be very useful in certain everyday situations for the maintenance of equilibrium.

There is a flip side or counterpart to the aforementioned positive first-order changes. It consists of those ineffective, pointless, counterproductive efforts that attempt to create change but neither effect a change in the equilibrium internal to the system nor change the system itself. In other words, this is where neither the member/concept nor the group/system changes. One may clearly see this phenomenon in everyday situations: for instance, when a depressed person is told "to cheer up and be grateful to be alive," when a shy person is told "to try to be outgoing," when a grieving person is told that "in a few months, surely things will get better," or when an overweight person is simply told "to eat less."

The thinking in these examples, patently first-order thinking, while seeming so ostensibly true from a common-sense perspective, becomes in a therapeutic context superficial, very irrelevant and potentially harmful in the long run. The responses to these given conditions represent faulty thinking because they are erroneously suggesting that *simply doing or feeling the opposite* of the problematic condition will somehow present the solution to the depression, shyness, mourning, or weight loss. According to the MRI, experience in psychotherapy has shown that this simplistic thinking, which is typically a "common-sense," doing-the-opposite kind of activity in a therapeutic context, will usually produce "more of the same" *unwanted behaviors*. It induces no enduring *change* despite temporary spurts of remission of the problem.

The MRI theorists spent many pages ascribing to these failures the explanations of the various forms of unprofitable changes at the first-order level. They argued that while many first-order changes employed in many everyday situations may work well for the moment as in temporary combinations like the car acting like a tow-truck, they usually produce no positive long-lasting results for problems presented in therapeutic situations. They reasoned that this is so because first-order changes do *not create change* at a systemic/group level, but only move components around internal to the system at the member level. It does not effectively change the structure, the organization or the rules of the system. The MRI researchers had dubbed this ineffectual, first-order scenario of failed attempts as insidious and characteristically deluding "games without end" (Watzlawick et al., 1967, pp. 232–236).

As depicted theoretically by Galois and by subsequent thinkers, Group Theory represents an understanding of first-order change: the occurrence of *change within a given system* whereby *the system* still remains *invariant, unchanged.* If this is so, then where do we look for a theory that explains second-order change whereby the system does change? As mentioned earlier, following in the steps of Bateson and other cyberneticists, Watzlawick and associates necessarily returned to Whitehead and Russell and to their work dating back to 1910–13. Among other things, their philosophical discussions included a Theory of Logical Types. Basically, logical types represent a series of mental categories that reflect a vertical progression from the most *specific abstractions* to the most general, all-encompassing abstractions.

This philosophical scenario of logical types involves the use of not only two key words, *class* and *member*, but also a vertically-oriented framework. Driven vertically from a less abstract to an increasingly more abstract level, the logical types become ever broader and more inclusive. Let us begin by starting with a *member*. A member may be defined as a person, a specific entity, object, or event. As a member moves vertically to a higher level of abstraction (i.e., into another *class*), the latter has the capacity to incorporate that member automatically. The higher the member travels upwards the more it becomes subsumed by broader abstractions (i.e., a broader class). To illustrate our point, let us select persons as members of a class (abstraction), and let us choose to begin with an obvious starting point of the class, the *family*. If we follow the theory of logical types and we move vertically from the least to the most abstract, it follows that *family* as a class in turn belongs to a larger class called *neighborhood*. If we continue this sequence upwards, what ensues are classes that keep getting larger and more abstract, the *community*, the *city*, the *state*, then the *country*. Clearly, all these categories are abstractions and in ascending order, each one becomes more abstract, broader, and more inclusive than the preceding one.

Any abstraction, however, has a *double role*. At any given point, an abstraction represents itself as an abstraction by the Law of Identity: anything is equal to itself. Simultaneously, it is also a member of the logical abstractions above it. This vertically-driven compartmentalization of a member standing as part of a class, which is in turn subsumed by a higher abstraction, represents the nature of logical types, a continuous vertical process in which the higher abstraction subsumes the prior one. To make this example more concrete, a person in any given family may be, all at once, not only a member of a family, but also subsumed automatically as part of a neighborhood, a city, a state, and a country.

Watzlawick and associates underline the fact that the Theory of Logical Types does *not* focus on what goes on *between the members* of any given class (i.e., its "group"), which brings us back to the limitations of first-order changes. Instead, the Theory of Logical Types "gives us a frame for considering the relationship *between member and class*, and the peculiar metamorphosis which is in the nature of *shifts from one logical level to the next higher*" (p. 10). This, then, becomes the crucial distinction. There are *two types of changes*. First-order change deals with what goes on *within a given class*, the "group" and its combinations. As in the case a car that acts temporarily as a tow-truck, it is a "combination" that has no effect on the class. The group (cars) still remains unchanged. This scenario essentially represents group theory, and it represents one type of change, positive or negative, which only effects the combinations of its members.

The second type of change involves what goes on between a member and its class and the movement from one level of class to another. This vertical mobility is facilitated by the fact that any "member" at a lower level of the vertical framework is represented consistently in each higher level. It is in this theoretical framework that second-order change becomes feasible.

Like first-order change, second-order change also has two sides to it. Let us recall when we originally discussed first-order changes. We realized that first-order changes had their useful, positive side. This aspect is usually illustrated in those practical, common sense, everyday decisions based on elementary notions whereby something or someone performs an action to counteract a possible problem (oppositional behavior). For instance, a weather forecast in the morning predicting rain for the afternoon will often allow one to take an umbrella. This change, taking an umbrella, does not effect the weather system. Obviously, the presence of the umbrella will have no effect on whether it will actually rain or not. Taking an umbrella merely reflects an "internal" change (combination) within the system whereby an individual member may do something different (a combination), but that action has no effect or influence on the weather *system*.

First-order change, we recall, also has its down side. The negative aspect is usually illustrated when it involves clinical problems, in or out of a therapy session. For instance, despite the use of a seemingly common sense, practical approach in trying to cheer up a bereaved person, a typical, yet ineffectual remark might be "Try to feel better. In a few months it'll be ancient history." The speaker is obviously attempting to comfort an individual. The system (class), in this instance, might be defined as bereavement and the bereaved person as the member. Even if for a moment the bereaved person is momentarily consoled, that attempted remedy will still not effect the bereavement (system) in any significant way. *As long as the bereaved person maintains membership* in the group of the bereavement *system*, that member will not experience a second-order change, only temporary relief or other combinations in the realm of first-order changes.

Second-order changes also have their positive and negative aspects. Ensuing are two examples illustrating the negative side. Each contains an easily identifiable error in reasoning, an error in logic. They involve a faulty generalization going from a specific "member" situation to its "class" generalization. For instance, a woman might say, "I just broke up with my boyfriend. *All men* are lousy!" Or, a man might say, "I know a good-for-nothing neighbor down the street who receives public assistance. *All public assistance recipients* are lazy." The error in reasoning in both cases illustrates the transparently clear example of confusing logical types between a "member" and its "class."

In the first example, a "member" of a class, *a particular man*, who has been assumed "lousy" by the speaker is identified with the whole "class" of men, *all men*. The member clearly gets confused with the class. Similarly, in the second example, a "member," a recipient of government subsidies who is perceived as lazy, is identified with the "class" to which he or she belongs, *all* recipients of government subsidies. While one particular individual (member) may be in fact "lazy," or may be "lousy," it does not necessarily follow that the whole class is lazy, i.e., *all* recipients of government subsidies are lazy, or, that *all* men are lousy.

In fact, many racial, ethnic, or demeaning remarks involve this kind of faulty reasoning whereby the example of an individual of a specific background is used to denigrate all others that may share any particular feature or quality with the individual. Similarly, political propaganda, political speeches, and many advertisements overflow with these logical paradoxes (illogical statements) using the language of logical types where a "member" is confused with a "class." This appears often in more subtle ways. For example, a campaigning politician might say, "Any person that votes for me will reap all the rewards of my administration." Or a salesperson might say, "If you buy this car, you'll feel the way all wealthy people feel when they drive." These statements are simply not true because of the fallacy in the logic of confusing member and class.

Complications in communication arise in this hierarchically construed scenario of logical types as "the result of ignoring the paramount distinction between member and class and the fact that a class cannot be a member of itself (Watzlawick et al., 1974, p. 7). While any class by definition includes all its members, the class per se is not a member of its own class. A class contains all its members, but a class cannot be one of its members. Hence, in a class under consideration, one cannot "jump" from member to class and assume what is true for one member is necessarily true of the class. For instance, all novelists (member) are human beings (class), but one cannot say that all human beings are novelists. Obviously, in trying to prove or illustrate any special relationship between member and class scenarios, it may require utilizing other means of reasoning and other information. For instance, one could say that all novelists are human beings, but all human beings do not have the same opportunity to become novelists. The study of logical types, dating back to classical Greek philosophy, has designated these errors in reasoning as *logical paradoxes*.

The MRI Brief Therapy Project • 101

In returning to our original thought, let us consider logical types, the relationships between a member and its class, and how unique shifts that often take place *between one abstraction and another* may constitute a positive movement in the nature of second-order change. Watzlawick underlines the view that since "second-order change is always in the nature of a *discontinuity* or a *logical jump*, we may expect the manifestations of second-order change to appear as illogical and paradoxical" (*Change*, p. 12) as a shift takes place between abstractions.

Take an example previously used in this text to illustrate reframing. When a client was detailing his script to the therapist, by outlining his depression, he also revealed, almost off-handedly, that he had painted landscapes and had even sold some of them recently. Naturally, the therapist could favorably react to the client's statement, "So, you're an artist." This statement represents a *shift in context* or category, a completely new *class* which we might designate as *creativity* or non-depression. In a shift of perspective, the therapist subsumes the client as creativity's *member* by virtue of the client's avowal of his artistic talents.

In other words, let us suppose that a therapist concludes that a client's depression is most likely situational. Additionally, she has also ruled out organicity and any immediate need for medication. She sees a male client who says he is depressed and who has tried a host of things to lessen his depression in the last few months, but to no avail. In the world of logical types, the client's present condition might be best described as "positioned" as a *member* of a *class* designated as *depression*. Apparently, all of the client's attempts, defined as combinations in that class, to decrease his depression have proven to be fruitless, and the therapist might reasonably assume that those attempts were, unfortunately, only first-order changes. However, after the therapist asks an appropriate number of relevant questions and the client's answers strongly substantiate the notion of the client as artist, she may attempt to employ a new strategy to help effect change in the client. She might compliment the client by saying, "So, you're an artist." The therapist has in effect, almost magically, *switched context* from

102 • *Breakthroughs in Six Brief Psychotherapies*

the client's membership in a class called *depression* to membership in another category, *creativity*. This represents an attempted second-order change called a reframe.

This bold attempt of the therapist represents an apparently "illogical" yet inventive leap. Since both client and therapist were ostensibly discussing depression, the leap has, in effect, created a switch in membership in one logical category (depression) to another (creativity). Indeed, it represents a *jump* to an area that is entirely different from the immediacy of the vertical continuum of abstractions. The therapist's statement has defied the so-called "logic" of the immediate conversation, and the therapist has availed herself of an appropriate class (creativity) in the kaleidoscope of logical categories. Based on the client's own information in which he relates his artistic talents, the therapist assumes that theoretically the *client also must be a member of another abstract category called creativity*. The switch in effect represents the process of redefining the client from the vantage point of a totally new perspective, the client *as artist, not just as depressed person*. The therapeutic leap is, no doubt, always based on concrete information divulged by the client. Through this strategy, reframing, the therapist avails herself of the manipulation of logical types in an effort to draw the client out of his dilemma of failed attempts at overcoming his depressed condition.

Similarly, when a therapist employs the paradoxical intervention of *prescribing the symptom*, the same attempted shift to a new logical category takes place. In the case of parents who are constantly locking horns with their teenage son, their dilemma consisted of not being able to reach any conclusion to their predicament despite threats, ultimatums, and discussions. However, when prescribing the symptom, an intervention which involves both parents and son having to argue periodically for 10 minutes every hour on the hour for specified periods of time on Saturday and Sunday for the next two consecutive weekends, might also have the same "illogical effect" on the threesome. They might make the mental leap in realizing that they must alter their old ways of "solving their problem" and try a different manner that redefines the way they look at their problem, their roles, and their situation. In short, they may alter or *change their rules of behavior*, a second-order change.

Since most clients come to therapy unable to effect a second-order change in their lives, it is usually assumed that they have reached an impasse, having struggled in vain with first-order change. To describe the variety of these impasses, Watzlawick and associates have elaborated three headings that contain the related kinds of initial problems. When these problems are compounded in severity because of the persistence of failed first-order attempts, they become a newer and greater problem (1974). The three headings that describe the failed first-order attempts are *avoidance* and *two basic forms of pseudosolutions*, taking action when it should not take place and taking action based on a wrong logical level.

As the word itself implies, *avoidance* involves the outright minimizing or denial of an apparently existing, undesirable situation. For instance, "Dad isn't really an alcoholic; he just has a few drinks too many, too often, that's all." Or, "Mom isn't really doing drugs; anyway, not the way she used to." Or, "My husband sometimes beats me, but he really can't help it. He was battered as a kid by his own father." The verbalization of this kind of thinking, which in essence denies or tends to undercut the presence of those realities, has the ultimate effect of compounding or exacerbating the initial problem.

The first of the two pseudosolutions involves *taking action when it should not have taken place*. This generalized statement obviously needs qualification. The unique identifying quality of this pseudosolution involves its usually being based on *utopian* or *quixotic* or *grandiose* premises. It involves a distortion of reality in which an impractical solution, most likely doomed to failure, blindly holds sway over the patently clear presence of the availability of more practical alternatives. For instance, "Who says I shouldn't drive at two in the morning? I've only had six drinks. I've always driven myself home." Or, "Smoking cigars is okay. My grandfather smoked them and used to drink a shot of bourbon every day until he died at eighty-two. Isn't that proof enough?" Or, "Casual sex isn't

104 • *Breakthroughs in Six Brief Psychotherapies*

a problem for me. I check out whom I sleep with. I haven't caught AIDS yet, have I?"

The third form of mishandling problems, the second of the two pseudosolutions, involves *taking action based on the wrong logical level that characteristically contains an internal contradiction.* This pseudosolution is characteristically more difficult to decipher since it doesn't deal with obvious impracticalities in the face of reasoning, but with subtle contradictions. This faulty reasoning or miscommunication may be clearly visible to observers, but, unfortunately, not at all obvious to the persons immersed in the communication of the relationship in question. Those contradictory expressions are identifiable by the uniqueness of an attempted "solution" that involves a "logic" that tends to create a double-bind or a "logical" lose/lose situation. As Watzlawick and associates put it, it creates "the peculiar impasse which arises when messages structured precisely like the classic paradoxes in formal logic are exchanged. A good example of such a message is 'Be spontaneous,'-i.e., the demand for behavior which by its very nature can only be spontaneous, but cannot be spontaneous as a result of having been requested" (1974, p. 64).

Another example characteristic of this third form could easily involve an overbearing mother who might say demandingly of her child, "Love me anyway! I'm your mother." Or, "Clean up your plate! The kids in India are starving." Or, similarly, it might be a self-indulgent, belligerent father who might say, "I may be wrong in pushing you around, but I'm still your father." In actuality, these kinds of contradictions abound in everyday conversation, and, coincidentally, are expressed as themes in many jokes and pranks. One such example is a sign posted in a work place that reads,

There are two rules in this establishment.
Rule #1: The boss is always right.
Rule #2: If there's a problem with that, refer to Rule #1."

In summation, the three common ways by which clients' faulty attempts at solutions become exacerbated typically deal with pursuing behaviors whose processes may be uniquely identified by the sustained use of *denial, utopian/quixotic thinking,* and *semantic* or *formal contradictions in logic.* They are typically first-order attempts and therefore offer no real hope of dealing effectively with the problem. In order to effect long-lasting change, the MRI version of brief therapy employs both *reframing* and *paradoxical interventions* to create change. Both approaches, either a sustained series of reframes which act to dissolve the problem, or a paradoxical intervention, are designed to effect second-order change in the client-problem system.

Reframing remains primarily a cognitively-based approach. It represents a broad term involving a therapist's reworking or reshaping client data into a new and useful perspective. It involves manipulating the client's "position," yet, it is always based on sufficient client data which potentially will offer a "back-door" out of a psychological impasse. It is established on the notion that a new perspective at a systemic level may invite new responses and new behaviors in handling the problem.

Prescribing the symptom, the paradoxical intervention, is both behaviorally and cognitively based. Paradoxical interventions are driven by boldly designed strategies, all aimed at the possibility of effecting second-order change. In designing an exact strategy, therapists must have at their fingertips a broad range of skills and experiences because prescribing the symptom usually involves creating a unique match of the intervention with the client's specific problem situation and its characteristics. These considerations involve client safety factors, the client's "position" (his or her cognitive perspective), the precise knowledge of the client's history of failed attempts at resolving the problem, and a general knowledge of the client's repertoire of possible behaviors. At the heart of their function and rationale, paradoxical interventions ultimately involve purposely placing the client in a situation known as the "therapeutic double bind." This might be best described as placing the client in a deliberate dilemma of having to choose between difficult alternatives. This purposeful dilemma often leads the client to select an alternative and act upon it, thus effecting a real change in the system, a second-order change.

In sum, given strategic therapy as practiced by all the aforementioned MRI group members, including Haley and problem-focused model practitioners, given the model's abundantly rich literature, its track record (Segal, 1982), and given its broad influence (Bodin, 1981), many critics have designated the problem-focused MRI model as a major breakthrough and one of the most significant achievements in what has been generally called brief therapy in the last four decades. The determined nature of its non-pathological interviewing techniques, its energizing reframing approach, its "therapeutic double bind" interventions, its communications-oriented and systemically-founded and cybernetic approaches have drastically shortened the number of visits to therapy which would have otherwise involved, for many patients, years in psychoanalytic inquiry and psychological excavation. The MRI group's strategic interventions, ensconced in a systemic framework, proactively designed, excluded psychoanalysis' existence and its protracted regimens (Lambert & Bergin, 1994; Wells, 1993).

The accomplishments of the Mental Research Institute, its Brief Therapy Project, its nationwide seminars, its many individual and coauthored publications, and its problem-focused therapy model indeed effected a major breakthrough in modern psychotherapy. Viewed synergistically, the MRI group developed and integrated many innovative ideas and perspectives. It has been a major catalyst in affecting the course of the brief therapy movement, its growth, its development of subsequent models, and it has irrefutably constituted a paradigmatic change in psychotherapy in the last forty years.

Chapter 3

The Milan School's Circular Interviewing

In psychotherapy, the concept of circularity came into existence when Bateson introduced it as part of his theories on cybernetics and its related application to family therapy in the 1950s and 1960s. Circularity also became involved with systemic thinking in dealing with problems, and it was precisely in those two decades that family therapy began creating its foundations from a rich variety of influences. These influences have already been discussed at length both in Chapters 1 & 2, and their culmination, as far as early brief therapy is concerned, was realized in the MRI's problem-focused model.

In the history of psychotherapy, the 50s and 60s decades presented a major shift in thinking. It was a radical change of direction, away from inferential psychoanalytic inquiry which was usually based on interviewing one client. Instead, the newly evolving family therapies found different therapeutic avenues in the study of observable phenomena in the "behavioral consequences of interpersonal relationships" (Goldenberg & Goldenberg, 1991, pp. 62–63). The switch involved a new emphasis on familial and social considerations. During those two decades the methods and theories surrounding circularity came into being and enjoyed great distinction in an abundance of literature and research. Proof of that abundance remains, not only in Bateson's more recent texts (1972, 1979), but also in the fruitful and practical writings of many notable family therapists (Fleuridas et al., 1986, p. 113).

Circularity as a working concept in systems thinking and circularity as in circular questioning have grown in prominence. Circular questioning,

110 • *Breakthroughs in Six Brief Psychotherapies*

as a widely used technique, is found not only in the various brief therapies of systemic thinkers, but also in the short-term therapies such as psychodynamic and cognitive-behavioral. Circular questioning has become an integral part of the general *corpus* of today's psychotherapeutic literature (Cooper, 1995, p. 65).

Cooper's text, *A Primer of Brief Psychotherapy*, represents a highly condensed version of the psychotherapeutic approaches under the generic heading of brief psychotherapies. The text exhibits the clear acknowledgment of the influence of the research and practices of family therapy, in general, and the importance of strategic and communications theories. In particular, the Milan School (Italy), a strategic school of thought in psychotherapy, is credited for the development of circular questioning.

Of course, the Milan School's development of circular questioning should not eclipse the fact that it also developed one of the most noteworthy achievements of its time, the *systemic family therapy model*, which obviously contains circular questioning (Goldenberg & Goldenberg, 1991, p. 200). The Milan School began with the initiatives of Mara Selvini-Palazzoli, M.D. In the late 1960s, she organized a team of psychiatrists whose efforts focused on treating severely disturbed children within a family therapeutic setting. Also, claiming to be the first group to practice family and couples therapy in Italy, they initially employed the traditional psychoanalytic model of the time. But their subsequent experience showed that both family and couples psychotherapies did not fare as well as they had imagined. The psychoanalytic model proved to be time consuming and not very practical in family settings.

Disappointed by the negative results she had encountered in the treatment of anorectic children, Selvini-Palazzoli, a psychiatrist trained in child psychoanalysis, became ever more attracted to the theories of the Mental Research Institute. Many other therapists of this fledgling Milan group also experienced a positive influence from the MRI's work. The writings of Bateson, Haley (1963) and Watzlawick, Beavin, and Jackson (1967) and, generally speaking, the influence of all those writers who presented

The book contains a description of their work with families, particularly their work with anorectic and schizophrenic children. Based on Haley's influence of symptom-related strategic therapy and on other strategic therapists of the MRI group, and on much of their own heuristic experiences (Tomm, 1984a, p. 122), the Milan group developed their own theories and techniques. Working with the symptomology, their underlying principles espoused the fundamental notion that no major change could take place within the family system unless a complementary change

the amalgam of communication/interactional and strategic approaches (Bodin, 1981) became important to the Milan School.

The Milan group learned that both in strategic theory and practice, the symptoms, as presented by the family in the therapeutic setting, were derived from the study of the family's interpersonal behaviors. The behaviors overtly served the purpose of "maintenance" (homeostasis) in the system as defined by the network of familial relationships. This represented a complex and ongoing dynamism in the interactive nature within the family system and, also, between the family system and those systems which the family contacted (Haley, 1963).

Apparently the influence, particularly of Haley's work and that of the MRI's literature, was so great that it effected a change in the composition of the original Milan therapeutic cluster. Four key members of that group split off to form the Institute for Family Study in Milan in 1972 (Goldenberg & Goldenberg, p. 200). This four-member group consisted of Mara Selvini-Palazzoli, Giuliana Prata, Luigi Boscolo and Gianfranco Cecchin. In the literature, it is this original foursome that has since been referred to as the Milan School or the Milan group. In the development toward a model of their own, the Milan group adopted the communications, cybernetics (interactional), and strategic perspectives. At a point in time, Watzlawick became a consultant during the Milan group's early years. In a remarkably short duration, less than a decade, the Milan School published an impressively written book entitled *Paradox and Counterparadox* (Selvini-Palazzoli et al., 1978).

The book contains a description of their work with families, particularly their work with anorectic and schizophrenic children. Based on Haley's influence of symptom-related strategic therapy and on other strategic therapists of the MRI group, and on much of their own heuristic experiences (Tomm, 1984a, p. 122), the Milan group developed their own theories and techniques. Working with the symptomology, their underlying principles espoused the fundamental notion that no major change could take place within the family system unless a complementary change took place in the system as a whole. They believed that change would have to emerge, not as a unilateral development, but as a multi-lateral, systemic phenomenon. They employed circularity in the interviewing process together with the use of a team approach in a systemic framework. This combination became a key feature of their distinctively emerging systemic model.

In 1980, after their basic therapeutic model was well established both in practice and in their literature, the group of four splits into two pairs, one pair was Selvini-Palazzoli and Prata while Boscolo and Cecchin comprised the other. Each pair focused on different aspects of their original model, already established in the literature two years earlier. Again, whenever a reference is made to the Milan model, it usually refers to the original model prior to the foursome's separation into two groups.

The Milan group's centerpiece, its breakthrough known as the *circular interview*, employs the *circular questioning* technique (Selvini-Palazzoli et al., 1978, 1980). The apparent reasons for developing the circular interview involved its effectiveness in gathering family data, discerning behavioral patterns, and acknowledging the consequences of those behaviors. It also utilized that information for developing the therapeutic dialogue and expanding the perceptive possibilities of the family members' mindset. Its purpose involved eliciting meaning from clients' personal explanations and the meaning (semantic ramifications) that they attributed to their relationships and to the noticeable differences of those relationships that occurred over the course of time. The therapist used a working hypothesis to guide the thematic quality of the questions while the circular questioning process focused a systemic exploration for *differences* in family behaviors and relationships.

As the clients became more disposed to integrating newly found meaning to their behaviors, both during and after the sessions, their cosmos hopefully expanded while integrating and incorporating these new views and perspectives. For a long-lasting therapeutic change to be effected, the Milan group theorized like the MRI group, that change would have to take place at a systemic level, a second-order change. In order to be effective at that level, family members would have to recognize both the overt and covert existence of *family rules* whose transgression was often at the core of familial problems. Whenever these codes were broken or stretched to the limit by familial transactions called "family games," it was not uncommon for problems to arise. Circular interviewing became the major vehicle for obtaining and utilizing that kind of data in the therapy session.

The *circular interview* represents the general infrastructure of the Milan group's modality, and *circular questioning* remains its major operational component. Functioning hand-in-hand with a working hypothesis, the efforts of circular questioning became involved symbiotically in redefining and in fine-tuning the therapeutic team's working hypothesis and also the nature of the intervention that would be prescribed at the end of the session.

Perhaps one of the main reasons for circular questioning's innovative usefulness and philosophical wisdom deals with letting family members experience their own individual and collective transformation. In the beginning of treatment family members usually tend to hold on to delimiting and simplistic notions of cause-and-effect in viewing their cosmos. Properly employed circular questioning effects a definite therapeutic transition whereby family members' initially jaded perceptions move toward a new *position* of viewing intrafamilial causality more and more as *multi-causal* and a *socially reciprocal* phenomenon. Hence, the once reductionistic perceptions of family members become transformed into a useful expansiveness of mind.

The Milan group believes that family change may be initiated either by change in behavior or by change in meaning. Since change in behavior is usually "not directly accessible" in the therapeutic session, effecting a change in meaning is the more practical route. Often, this may be realized immediately through *reframing* (Becvar & Becvar, p. 247). Effective circular questioning, which by design persists in finding descriptions, or, as Bateson would say, finding a *double description* of behaviors and their

114 • *Breakthroughs in Six Brief Psychotherapies*

attributed meanings, expands the dialogue for newer multi-causal explanations and ever broadening perspectives.

According to Tomm (1984a), Bateson's influence, from *Steps to an Ecology of Mind*, on the Milan group is clear. The latter apparently saw, for one thing, the overriding importance of differentiating between behavior and thought. In particular, they pursued the tact of searching for the *differences in behaviors* and the *differences in meaning* attributed to those behaviors. It was discovered that the very process of circular questioning where the therapist found a way of "introducing new connections or new distinctions between thought and action" was *interventive* and often immediately useful to the client family. The circular interview is the Milan group's innovation. It clearly demonstrates that it is therapeutic whenever the therapist employs relevant circular questioning that *expands* the client's capacity to see new meaning in familial interactions which usually have the effect of freeing up simplistically conceived, rigidified explanations. In military terms, it is analogous to recognizing and eventually demolishing fixed fortifications that the mind has imposed upon itself in its defense, its homeostasis.

Whether it is the use of *positive connotation* (the reframing of the client's good intentions) where specific prescriptions such as *rituals are offered*, or it is the use of another technique that proves to be effective, the goal of the circular interview involves raising the awareness level of the family members and encouraging the expansion of the client's "meaning" world. Family therapists had already invented a word to describe this positive phenomenon depicting the client's ever expanding view of causality. Despite its unfortunately negative-sounding name, *negentropy*, it has a very positive meaning. Negentropy describes a therapeutic phenomenon that includes promoting a tendency where family members lower their defenses and their hostilities through new input and different interpretations of interrelated family data and social transactions. Over a period of time, this has an overall effect of allowing the emergence of a new interpretational cosmos (Selvini-Palazzoli et al., 1980).

The circular interview, in essence, explores the *recurring contextual patterns* that describe the family's behavioral dynamics (Penn, 1982).

MacKinnon (1983) describes the Milan School's approach as sharply in tune with Bateson's pioneering circular epistemology (1972) in which Bateson emphasized his by-now-famous definition of *information* as "*a difference that makes a difference.*" Systemic inquiry naturally involves the sustained search for *differences*, particularly those at behavioral and perceptual levels. In becoming aware of those differences, family members, hopefully, could avail themselves of the opportunity to both disclose and dislodge linkages that apparently have kept the family in deadlocked, embedded positions. Newly acquired awareness of the family system's workings serves, instead, as a major component to liberate the clients from their old self-imposed interpretative scenarios and to motivate them for positive change.

The circular interview, in essence, explores the *recurring contextual patterns* that describe the family's behavioral dynamics (Penn, 1982). The process of circular questioning might be best described as exploring the "overlay" of evolving, recursive loops or interactional sequences of behavior in the system (Papp, 1983). Behaviors, beliefs, and feelings do not transpire independently, but occur interrelatedly. Thus, raising the awareness of the affective, behavioral, and cognitive linkages between family members, their familial transactions, became so crucial in the therapeutic process of circular questioning that it was often not uncommon to report that in the therapy session "spontaneous change" would take place (Penn, 1982).

Tomm (1984a, p. 122) has described the Milan approach as "long brief therapy". While the therapeutic plan usually calls for ten sessions, much like the MRI's brief therapy model, the clients are scheduled at one-month intervals, making it just about a one-year process. At first, the large spacing of intervals between sessions was established purely as a practical means of accommodating those families having to travel long distances to the Center in Milan (Goldenberg & Goldenberg, p. 202). With time and experience, the therapists discovered that the one-month spacing, given the nature of their interventions, focused on changing the system rather than any one

116 • *Breakthroughs in Six Brief Psychotherapies*

given individual. This proved to have better results than similar therapy that was tried at shorter intervals. Thus, the Milan School established a firmly enforced time constraint of approximately one meeting per month. They argued *a posteriori* that, given the nature of the circular questions and the time-sensitive development of the interventions, monthly meetings whose cumulative effects involved close to a year seemed to work best (Selvini-Palazzoli, 1980).

Milan group therapists would usually interpret any family member's insistence on changing appointments as a strong indicator of the accelerated occurrence of family change. Since the family members' dynamic integration of change within the family system, especially outside the therapy session, was part of the treatment model, the Milan School would adamantly refuse the rescheduling of appointments, especially those of clients who requested the shortening of meeting intervals.

A typical session consists of five parts and the method requires a team approach following specific guidelines. First, the team members have a presession consultation, which may last as much as twenty minutes, during which they discuss the available family information. They hypothesize the more significant family relationships that are possibly involved in being more responsible for the problem.

Secondly, the interview session with the family then takes place ranging from fifty to ninety minutes. One therapist usually conducts the session while the rest of the team observes behind a one-way mirror. The portion of the team that observes behind the one-way mirror has been dubbed the "Greek chorus." It is reminiscent of ancient Greek drama in which the chorus' function often involved adding relevant information to the dramatic development, or commenting on the unfolding of the drama story line. In fact, today, depending on the style of the team therapy approach, the observation part of the team or the consulting group behind the one-way mirror will often phone in a statement as a form of observation. They may also pose a relevant question during the session's progress for clarification purposes, or as a challenge to the family's "position."

The Milan School's Circular Interviewing • 117

Thirdly, there is an intrasession break during which the therapist leaves the session room and meets with all the team members privately to discuss the family session. This may range from fifteen to forty minutes (Tomm, 1984a). From the experiential data accumulated in the therapeutic session, the team discusses what appears to be occurring in the family's observable manifestations and the family members' presentations of their explanations and meanings for what they perceive is occurring. It is during this intersession phase that the team may revise its original hypothesis and formulate an appropriate intervention.

Fourthly, the therapist returns to the family session with the intervention. While the rest of the team observes this final interaction portion of the session, the therapist relates the "findings" of the team and assigns the task to the family members. Even to a member unable to attend, the task is assigned, and it is usually presented to the absent member by means of a letter. The task is generally a paradoxical prescription. It takes the form of a "ritual," i.e., a specific family-centered activity that is repeated during the one-month interval between therapy sessions. A ritual could be simply having a family "conference" or the family having dinner together as a unit at regular intervals.

Part of the paradoxical nature of this assignment involves directing the family *not to change*, to keep things as they are between therapeutic sessions. This maneuver, obviously, represents a deliberate tactic constituting, in effect, a "therapeutic double-bind" message. The purpose involves undoing the family's own double-bind dynamics that have been maintaining their "family" problem. Clearly, the Milan School's paradoxical tactic, the use of a therapeutic double-bind message, is employed to match and correct the family's own double-bind problem.

The Milan group based much of its intervention tactics on Bateson's "double-bind" theories. Bateson essentially presented the idea that the confusion and frustration caused by the contradictory messages that family members send to each other is significantly involved in creating family problems. Taken to the extreme, these contradictory messages, repeated and sustained over a period of time, may even be involved in the development of psychotic behavior. Emotionally and perceptually, this repeated behavior creates a "double bind" in a personality. The double bind then becomes a trap in which the individual gets caught in a proverbial "lose/lose" situation in the familial relationship. If the family's own double-bind communications behavior represents the "paradox" sustaining the family homeostasis which is apparently "balanced" yet dysfunctional, then the "therapeutic double bind" message, the therapist's directive to maintain the assigned ritual consistently, yet *not change*, serves to counterbalance the family system and represents the *counterparadox* (Selvini-Palazzoli, 1978).

Much care is taken to avoid a direct intervention which would involve the therapist putting an *individual member* of the family in a position to change the family "rules" of operation. In putting the onus on only one shoulder, there is also an inherent risk that it might invite an unwanted reaction. The other family members' dissension, reprisal, or defensiveness may further embed the problem. Similarly, assigning a different task or intervention to each person in the family would also defeat the means of obtaining change through interactive ways. This would be the same kind of impasse a client might often encounter, for instance, if he or she were implementing a behavior modification task or assignment whose problem really involved a group situation.

The "therapeutic double bind," instead, thrusts the whole family into a repeated interaction (the ritual) with the added directive "not to change" for that monthly interval. This directive has systemically more validity and effectiveness. The family assignment to collectively perform a ritual and directing its members paradoxically "not to change," represents, together, an innovative and effective systemic approach to paradoxical therapeutic change (Selvini-Palazzoli, 1978).

As the fifth and final part of the therapeutic interview, the postsession meeting consists of the entire team not only discussing the family's immediate response to the presentation of the intervention, but also starting to

The Milan School's Circular Interviewing • 119

plan for the next session (Boscolo et al., 1987). Invariably, whenever the therapeutic team meets to discuss the family meeting on any given day, they routinely hypothesize, incorporating newly presented information elicited both from one another and from the family session, to ascertain which factors might be responsible for sustaining the family problem.

Hypothesizing, circularity (circular questioning), neutrality, positive connotation, linguistic sensitivity and family rituals remain among the principal areas considered in the way the Milan group presented its circular interviewing model, dubbed systemic family therapy. The Milan group, essentially based on the ideas of systems and communication theory, examined the clients' cosmos as patterns and information (Becvar & Becvar, 1993). Therefore, learning the behavioral and recursive nature of family feedback becomes crucial in establishing the possible nature of the problem in the patterns of social interaction, not from any intrapsychic perspective.

For the Milan group, *hypothesizing* embodies a fundamental technique in its systemic approach. This involves the therapy team preparing, in a presession setting, a working formulation to be tested in the therapy session about what may be responsible for the family's apparent ongoing problem. This kind of preparatory thinking has often been referred to as *mapping*, a kind of shorthand for deciphering the family's interactive patterns. In some ways it is similar to computer flow-charting. Obviously, the working hypothesis is subject to change as new information is acquired from the next session's content.

For the Milan group, hypothesizing has an immediate twofold purpose. It is a deliberate attempt to preclude the efforts of the "client" family members from surreptitiously dictating their own, possibly faulty, definition of the problem which would have the consequence of incorrectly affecting the orientation of the therapy sessions and resolution. Secondly, hypothesizing serves as a guide to the kinds of questions that need to be raised during the session. The hypothesis is always integrated into the concept of circularity, i.e., family relationships and interactions rather than "symptoms residing within a person" (Becvar & Becvar, p. 248).

The team preparation is based on preliminary presession information supplied by the family which is provisionally interpreted by the therapist team. During the session, if the therapeutic questioning does not confirm the validity of the provisional path chosen by the team's hypothesis, then a necessary reformulation of the hypothesis takes place. To insure their agreement or to air their disagreement with one another's interpretations during the postsession discussions, the team members often cast their observations in the form of metaphoric imagery to help demonstrate vividly the purpose that the symptom serves in the family system and how the family system organizes itself around the symptom (Becvar & Becvar, p. 248).

Since the systemic concept of *circularity* is constantly employed in this modality, the questions are contextually and relationally founded. They take their lead from the initial hypothesizing. For instance, from the beginning of the therapeutic session which defines the nature of the presenting problem, circularity is employed. When asking what prompted the family to seek therapy or what was the nature of the problem, the therapist's questions clearly invite the response of each family member for individual reactions, interpretations, and ascribed meanings.

After family members offer their explanations of family phenomena regarding the problem, they are asked to further pursue the issues presented through elaborating upon the *differences* by relating who in the family would *agree or disagree* with the explanations. Inviting several members to express their views on the same question about a specific relationship serves to further the acquisition of additional information, new meaning and significant differences that ultimately expand familial awareness and diminish the embeddedness of their problems in nonthreatening ways (Selvini-Palazzoli, Boscolo, Cecchin, & Prata, 1980).

Cross-checking other family members' behavioral observations and personal perspectives, in short, their points of agreement and disagreement, is essential to the circular questioning method as it encourages the amplification of family members' differences in their affect, their perceptions and their behaviors. Circular questioning, as conceived and practiced by the Milan group, serves to stimulate an ongoing in-session dialectic to clarify confusion and introduce fresh information to the family members based on those proffered differences. In this regard, the relationship between the hypothesis and the ongoing circular questioning remains crucial. The hypothesis serves as a guide for maintaining the unity and integrity of the circular questioning (Tomm, 1984b).

Circularity, as conceived by the Milan group, goes a step further into a special kind of circular question called *triadic questioning* (Tomm, 1984b). As the name implies, this involves addressing a *third* person present in a questioning sequence about the *relationship* between two other members and their respective observations. Under the unitary guidance of the thematic issue dictated by the hypothesis, the questions represent significant queries about relationships and behaviors. The sustained use of triadic questioning within the circular-questioning format achieves an added dimension. It helps to make family members further aware of exercising their own circular questioning about the dynamics of the family. This influence will ultimately help dissolve the old family homeostasis, which has been perpetuated and rigidified by "solutions" that characterized only first-order changes (Watzlawick et al., 1974, p. 17). The overall effect of circular questions, together with the intervention, involves the whole notion of the family's constant interaction in the agreement and disagreement of the other members' perceptions. This in-session interchange serves as a model and as an example whose influence will encourage negentropy both at the individual level and family group level after the therapy session concludes and during the monthly interval between sessions.

In the early formation of family therapy terminology, the word "coalition" was introduced into its working vocabulary. Of course, coalition has political and military overtones. It describes the joining of two or more forces in opposition to a perceived common adversary. In therapy, the term, coalition, still maintains that same adversarial connotation, obviously, on a smaller scale. So, for example, a daughter could be in a coalition with her mother against a perceived common "adversary" in the family. This kind of alliance is usually covert in nature, and it could be of a temporary duration or part of a long-term scenario. Since coalitions imply conflict, the therapist usually assumes the existence of difficulties resulting from familial interpersonal rigidities, trauma, and power struggles.

This working concept of coalition brings us to the issue of therapist *neutrality*. The Milan School developed the idea that the therapist's position should include a determined attempt to avoid participation in any family coalitions. In a sense, it is a paradox that the therapist be "allied" with all members of the family. At least, in a general sense, this is achieved by virtue of his or her therapeutic presence and involvement with all participants and by not showing any kind of inclination with one member over another.

Obviously, then, the meaning of the Milan School's concept of therapeutic neutrality involves the notion that the therapist actively avoid the emotional entrapments often set up by some family members hoping to gain access to the therapist's support in perpetuating their behaviors. By the same token, neutrality does not imply indifference, lack of empathy, or quiet "objectivity" in regard to the members of a family and their troubles. Neutrality represents, in actuality, walking within a very fine line of systemic thinking and avoiding the human penchant to side with the immediacy of a family member's who might be especially adept at playing "family games."

While maintaining a posture of concern for all the family interactions in the therapy session, the therapeutic focus should remain on how the dynamics of that particular family work. The Milan School firmly believes that the family structure, as it presently maintains itself, could not be any other way because of its collective reasons. The therapist does not participate in agreeing or disagreeing with family members' evaluative responses whether right or wrong judgements. Rather, as Tomm suggests, the therapist takes the lead in creating circular questions regarding relevant areas of interest around any statements that may offer more useful information (1984b).

For instance, a family member may report that Dad is away from home too much and he often comes home inebriated. The negative implication is implicit. However, this may serve the therapist as a basis for creating many more circular questions regarding behavior and meaning in regard to this relationship. To accept at face value that statement without circular questioning in regard to its meanings would be tantamount to missing a good therapeutic opportunity. Similarly, making that a moral issue or a springboard for a moralizing critique would also mean losing a good therapeutic opportunity.

As Penn points out (1982, p. 271), circular questioning attempts to emphasize the co-definition or simultaneous meanings of any given family relationship. It is, in fact, encouraging the bilateral development of individual family members. In therapy, a family in crisis usually presents individuals who typically seek "unilateral control" over others. Circularity, and in particular circular questioning as a tool, represents a most natural way to "punctuate" the co-evolution of individuals out of the embeddedness of past relationships.

Therefore, the key therapeutic issue is not so much how the therapist may immediately effect a change in the family, but how the neutrality of the therapist, as reflected in the quality of relevant circular questions and of the corresponding family members' responses, stimulates the family's powers to regenerate itself by creating its own solutions. Unlike many models where the therapist provides solutions, systemic family therapy compels the family to come up with its own solution (Boscolo, Cecchin, Hoffman & Penn, 1987). This view is heightened by the fact that the Milan School firmly believes that only the family as a unit can change. The process of circular questioning, interventions, and other techniques represent only the means of assisting the family in regenerating itself, in re-inventing itself.

The Milan School strongly believes that the family may choose to find its own solution; or, as Selvini-Palazzoli stated, the family may also choose, unfortunately, *not* to create a solution for itself (Simon, 1987). The necessity of therapist neutrality helps to insure that the change process remains uncontaminated by a therapist's coalition with any particular family member or by a therapist offering a solution to the family as a whole.

Therapeutic neutrality is necessarily applicable to other situations outside of the therapy session. For instance, if a member of a family phones the therapist between sessions, the therapist must be consistent with exercising neutrality. Barring an explicit emergency, such as a potential homicide or suicide situation, the therapist advises the caller to defer the apparently pressing issue for the next session. Again, the therapist does not participate in any kind of special treatment, coalition, or favoritism. This is especially significant when one considers the relatively large gap of time between sessions. During the intersession intervals the onus of working out difficulties and creating positive change lies with the family members and within the family setting.

Another important concept of the Milan group involves *positive connotation*. The therapist obviously plays a key role in his or her relationship with all the family members in therapy. To maximize the effectiveness, the Milan group advocates that the therapist function in a "positive" manner, i.e., positively connoting all the family information, avoiding judgmental, moralizing or accusatory stands. This *positive* stance lessens the probability of shame, guilt and anxiety interfering in the therapeutic process. Helm Stierlin, in his foreword to the Milan group's book, *Paradox and Counterparadox* (1978), incisively posits positive connotation as one of the quintessential elements of the Milan model.

At a philosophic level, the Milan School considers that family members are being essentially motivated by a desire for family cohesion. Therapists might, therefore, assume that beneath or behind symptomatic behavior there exists a *positive motivation* for actions that unfortunately do not eventuate into positive behavior. For this reason the Milan School believes

The Milan School's Circular Interviewing • 125

in *reframing*, not the symptom itself, but the *intention* behind the behavioral symptom.

Positive connotation, then, does not seek to rectify a "wrong" behavior as much as to open the possibilities for change in the wrongness, at least at the motivational level. It prefers to focus on the existence of an *assumed positive intent* that may have been squelched along the way by unknown factors.

For instance, a ten-year old child's continually poor behavior with her classmates which causes her full-time-working, head-of-household mother to be a frequent visitor at the principal's office, might be positively connoted as reflecting the child's deep desire to experience seeing her mother more often, alone. The child, the youngest of four sisters, may have wanted or intended to be more connected to all her family members and, especially, to her mother. In reality, though, she may have felt that as the youngest child in an all-female household she had fallen through the proverbial "cracks" of a busy household of "older females," each one concerned with her own schedule.

When the therapist establishes a positive intent through reframing, e.g., a family member wanting to be connected to the others, that *ipso facto* becomes a positive and validating comment on an individual's unfulfilled, yet positive, intent in the familial relationship. In the reframing process, the symptomatic behavior undergoes a change of focus from blame and wrongness to an underlying unfulfilled desire seeking a positive effect in the family relationship. Positive connotation acts in many ways like a template that forges out of a fluid mass of thoughts an unsuspecting foundation, something redeemable upon which more constructive elements may be built. Here again, like circular questioning, positive connotation assists in broadening the perspective of possibilities in the process for greater interactional understanding.

Positive connotation, when applied universally to all family members through the circular interview, in effect, creates more vigor in the possibility of the family creating change. It shapes and creates a paradox, placing the family in a challenging "dilemma" demanding some kind of change. It creates an interesting, tantalizing scenario whereby if there is such an abundance of good will and positive intentions on behalf of its family members collectively, how is it that the family unit has had to resort to symptomology?

Positive connotation of the family members' intentions avails them the possibility that hereafter they may view each other differently, in a more favorable light, perhaps inducing greater family cooperation and understanding. As Tomm points out, the in-session use of positive connotation with each family member when combined later with the assignment of the paradoxical intervention further enhances the impact of the "therapeutic double bind" counterparadox, thus helping to promote change (1984b).

Along with the formulation of circular questioning and positive connotation, the Milan School's philosophy professes the overwhelming and incisive importance of *linguistic sensitivity* and its expression in therapeutically-informed *languaging*. Working together as a unit, the amalgam represents one of the major tools in the model. Since expanding the clients' cosmos is by definition inherent in negentropy, the Milan School considers both the overt and covert perpetuation of stereotypes, negative labeling or wording, trigger words, or reductionism of wording as definite forms of interference and interruption in the therapeutic process.

One of the useful ways to insure greater negentropy involves the therapist's selection of words and wording. Its implementation becomes a vehicle that both subtly and deliberately compels the clients, in a non-threatening and tactful way, to be become more aware of the limitations of their simplistic cause-and-effect, non-productive generalizations about family relationships. At the same time, it assists the clients' efforts at making more accurate and sensitive descriptions of family members' interactions. This has the consequence of clients elucidating, not only their own affect, their belief systems and their social transactions, but also those of others during the therapy session and especially during the one-month interval between sessions.

The therapist employs the tools of linguistic sensitivity especially when he or she rephrases ambiguous blanket statements or dubious generalizations into circular questions for the clients to answer and clarify. The opportunity to employ this tactic becomes particularly apparent whenever a client grossly generalizes or labels another family member's symptomology, problem, or unwanted behavior. First, the therapist replaces the "generalizing" verb from the original client statement with more appropriate verbs such as "to seem" or "to show" (Selvini-Palazzoli et al., 1978). Secondly, the therapist poses a series of circular questions that invite the client to revisit his or her statement and focus on the description of the behavioral transactions or issue.

For instance, as in the classic case of one family member characterizing the problem of another, one member might say, "Dad *is* always depressed." In this kind of situation, the therapist might reshape the idea of the original sentence into a series of questions whose answers would at once elaborate the behavioral specifics and dismantle the generalization, thus adding fresh information about what that family member more accurately means by "depression" in a behavioral context. Additionally, these circular questions would surely serve to debunk a client's biases or gross misconceptions about what constitutes "depression." The questions would also clarify what other factors might be operating in this relationship. This is where the therapist suggests calling into question the effects of a client's idiosyncratic meanings, the possible oversimplification of the client's phenomenological field, the possible polarization of emotions and the like. No doubt, this line of therapeutic questioning has the general effect of stretching the boundaries of the client's understanding.

In the actual questioning process, the therapist would, first of all, avoid using the verb "to be" and any of its variations in the immediate context of the questions. Since the verb "to be" and its variations by their very nature seem to imply the notion of a blanket equality, they can act linguistically like a linear equation, suggesting semantically that the father's existence must necessarily *equal* depression, obviously, with a

128 • *Breakthroughs in Six Brief Psychotherapies*

certain sense of permanence. This implied "equation" that the client verbalizes could be counterproductive to therapy. Therefore, the therapist would substitute words such as *shows* or *seems* for the word "is" in a series of related questions. The therapist might ask, "*When* does Dad *show* his depression?" "*How* does Dad *show* his depression?" "How *does* his recent depression *seem* to be different from that in the past?" "*Where* does Dad usually *seem* to experience depression?" "*Around which people* does he *not seem* depressed?" "*Who* gets treated differently from the rest when Dad *shows* his depression." "*Who would immediately benefit* if, all of a sudden, Dad's depression *seemed* to disappear?" "*Who would be hurt* the most if his depression continues to be *shown* this way?"

These questions represent a sample of many more elementary questions that could expand the description and the definition of what one family member perceives as depression in another. A time-frame differential, the difference between past, present, and future scenarios, could also be systematically applied so that revealing *comparisons* might be elicited and amplified between those scenarios. For instance, "How did Dad show his depression *six months ago?*" "How does Dad show his depression *this week?*" "How might Dad show his depression *in the future?*" Here the deliberate interplay of past, present, and future-oriented questions benignly compels the family member to differentiate the quality of behavioral sequences across the dimension of time.

This methodology that seeks "a difference that makes a difference," clearly reminiscent of Bateson's dictum, may be carried still further. The client may be queried as to reasons that account for any qualitative or quantitative variances offered in the descriptions. Stretching still further the systematic quest for differences in interactional sequences, the therapist might also ask the client who in the family, or the relevant system in question, would *agree or disagree* with his or her interpretational differences and why. In essence, if one were to metaphorically display the points of interception and the connectedness of the questioning as the reflective "interactional field" of the client's perception, it would materialize looking much like a spider's web. That is why asking relevant and meaningful questions make the client aware of the interconnectedness between affect, behavior, and meaning in a systemic way. This denotes that movement in one area of the web may impact other areas and to varying degrees.

More recently, however, brain researchers have become fond of employing holograms as a metaphoric example to demonstrate this interconnectedness between parts of the brain. A hologram, especially a spherical one, containing a crisscross of vertical, horizontal, and diagonal axes creates a pervasive grid that more clearly illustrates the interrelatedness of causality. Like any projected or envisioned axes in a hologram, relevant circular questions have a compelling affect on the client. They affect client cognition so that in the process of answering these questions the client more easily actualizes the linkages between the aspects of affect, behavior, and cognition of past and present experiences. Thus, old and erroneous perceptions begin to dissolve while newer perceptions encompass more liberating scenarios.

The Milan group obviously supports the utility of *not* accepting the implied permanence or perpetuity of a symptomatic condition as expressed by any therapy participants. The Milan group prefers to change the focus to one that encourages the expansion of the descriptive interactive contexts around the symptoms or unwanted behavior. This tactic is deemed more useful and realistic in obtaining the kinds of information that will promote negentropy and ultimately create the foundations for change. This tactic, of course, may be employed not only with symptomology, but also with any kind of negative labeling, a phenomenon that is fairly common in troubled families.

For instance, if a family member views another member as a bigot, the questioning pattern would essentially mimic the same basic kinds of wording as in the previous example dealing with the symptomatic conditions of depression. For example: "*When* does he *show* his bigotry?" "*How* does he *show* his bigotry?" "*Where* does he *show* his bigotry?" "*Around which people* does he not *seem* to display his bigotry?" "*Who gets hurt* the most when he *shows* his bigotry?" "*At which preferred occasions* does he *seem* to display his bigotry the most?"

Linguistic sensitivity, appropriate languaging, and circular questioning in combination with each other become powerful tools in the therapeutic process. As a combined strategy they allow the family members to elucidate their world. The family is supported and encouraged by the circular questions into expanding and more meaningful interpretative dimensions. Since clients are indeed the "experts" in knowing and describing their world best, they must necessarily verbalize their perceptions, their explanations, and their affect. This process broadens their understanding of the patterns of their behavior that have influenced both the weaknesses and strengths in their lives.

With the focus placed on clients answering circular questions, this frees the therapist to concentrate on the affective, behavioral, and perceptual transactions described by the family members. The clients' newly verbalized descriptions, in turn, offer the basis for new information from which the therapist continues to pose more circular questions. However, the process of circular questioning is obviously not an end in itself. In answering the circular questions, the clients are usually in the process of widening the parameters of their understanding, gaining awareness of the complexity of social interactions and seeing the limitations of simple cause-and-effect pat answers.

Since there is no psychoanalytic point to prove or Freudian patterns to embrace, the therapist may spend time creating more of the useful and powerful kinds of questions that will consistently keep expanding the ways the family members see their collective cosmos. Circular questions, as a whole, are behaviorally focused and transactionally described. They lend themselves easily to descriptive elaborations that, while certainly inclusive of past experience, are more focused on the recurrence of behavioral interactions in general. As a methodology, the circular interview has great maneuverability. In many ways, it is less inclined to get stuck in the embeddedness of long unproductive segments that center on the past.

The Milan School's Circular Interviewing • 131

Circular questioning, instead, is focused on uncovering the connections and the linkages that operationally maintain the *unwanted* redundant interactional familial patterns. The answers evoked by circular questions make it possible for clients to experience sensing and perceiving the redundancy of their unwanted patterns from a multicausal perspective without the necessity of the therapist's "interpretation" or "insight." In turn this process can become empowering to the clients as they become aware of a newly emerging and enlarged perception of *their* interpretative reality. This growth process is deemed inherently superior to many other kinds of therapeutic scenarios where the therapist, by virtue of the modality's scope and design, is compelled to explain the "interpretation," or worse, to discuss the "insight" with the clients.

The integration of *family rituals* is also an essential element of the Milan group's systemic model. Religious and personal holidays that punctuate life transitions are deemed essential to family cohesion. Therapists will often design tasks or paradoxical prescriptions around these special days. Interventions may also be rituals of a very general nature, such as going out or eating together as a family, or gathering for a family conference at specific times. Proposed generally *as experiments* to the family, the tasks that the therapist suggests usually involve full family participation. The net effect of these rituals challenges the present "family rules" and the embeddedness of their family behaviors. The task is described in much detail to the family members, and the therapist underlines it with the proviso that it is merely a *suggested exercise* which may prove to be useful. The ultimate purpose of family rituals is to provide clarity to family structure and relationships and to effect change (Tomm, 1984b).

The Milan group may also espouse the use of other family "rituals" without any reference to specific holidays or personal or religious rituals. The former is reminiscent of Jay Haley's interventions and those of the MRI group. For instance, these rituals often deal with issues of parental approaches and family discipline. The therapist will often prescribe an "odd day-even day" ritual in which each parent alternates being responsible for the daily family decisions. Unlike many of Haley's prescriptions which often incited defiance in the clients, the Milan group's prescriptions are aimed at offering the family members the opportunity to discover "new" information about themselves, and thus offer the family a foundation for change (MacKinnon, 1983).

More recently, another technique has been advanced. It is called the *invariant prescription*. Developed from research begun with Giuliana Prata (Goldenberg & Goldenberg, p. 208), Selvini-Palazzoli formulated a variation on the process of employing family intervention with severely troubled families in the case of families with anorectic or schizophrenic children (1886). The invariant prescription was originally meant to be used when, after the first session, it was clear that the family was deeply immersed in what was described as "psychotic family games." The invariant prescription is a strategy that has been deemed controversial. At a later date, she proposed it "be applied to all families with schizophrenic or anorectic children" (Goldenberg & Goldenberg, pp. 208–209).

The invariant prescription represents a highly focused and decisive attempt at breaking down family coalitions and highly dysfunctional "family games." It achieves this by strengthening the parental alliance in a specific way. It bears a distinctively structuralist flavor in dictating the establishment of stronger boundaries between the parents and the sibling subsystem. For example, it might involve parents doing things by themselves like going to the movies, but the activity is never specified or revealed to family members. "The parental alliance, reinforced by joint action and by secretiveness" acts both to cement the parental alliance in the eyes of the family members and to disrupt the negative influence of "psychotic family games" and their divisive ways. The invariant prescription, as the name implies, remains constant throughout the entire length of therapy.

The Milan group's systemic model as presented in 1978 in their fundamental text, *Paradox and Counterparadox,* and in their seminars and subsequent writings, found a receptive audience in Karl Tomm of the

University of Calgary in Canada and in the members at the Ackerman Institute for Family Therapy in New York (Goldenberg & Goldenberg, p. 201). This latter group included Peggy Papp (*The Process of Change*, 1983), Peggy Penn, Joel Bergman (*Fishing for Barracuda*, 1985), and particularly, Lynn Hoffman (*Foundations of Family Therapy*, 1981). The Milan group whose initial steps and development were directly influenced by the MRI group was now, in turn, in a position to influence psychotherapy in the United States. Deemed as one of the most systemic and effective models to have evolved out of the 1970s, it continues today as one of the most useful modalities in brief psychotherapy.

However, its usefulness goes beyond its effectiveness as a family or as a group modality. Despite its originally intended use in therapeutic family settings, many of the interviewing techniques associated with circular interviewing are applied to individual clients where a team approach is not used at all. Tomm (1987a,b), basing his thoughts on circular interviewing, developed his own model called *interventive interviewing*. The model involves the use of circular questions that are categorized into four stages: *linear, circular, strategic,* and *reflexive.* The first two stages are characterized as *orienting questions*; the second two stages are characterized as *influencing questions.* In the first two stages the questions are structured so that by the time the client arrives at answering strategic and reflexive questions, he finds himself ably positioned to influence himself to change behavior or to think differently. Tomm cautions the therapist, especially in the first two stages, to exercise both therapeutic neutrality, by never implying a judgmental role, and proper languaging.

The first stage is characterized by eliciting information at a semantic or meaning level. The linear questions are meant to be cause-and-effect in nature. The questions involve contextual concerns over "who, what, when, where, how, how much." They also require the client to make some amplification in regard to "why, in what way, how come." The essence of this stage involves ascertaining the closest approximation to understanding the *nature and meaning of the problem* within the client's system. For instance, in the case of depression as the presenting problem, the client might be asked, "What do you think about when you're depressed?" "What were you doing immediately before feeling depressed?" "What do you do to diminish the feelings of depression?" "When does it occur most often?" "Where does it usually happen?" "Why do you think it happens?" "In what way does the last time seem different from prior episodes of depression?"

The second stage is characterized by circular questions. Like the first stage, it is an effort to gather information. However, unlike the first stage which is semantically oriented and focused on the client meaning-system, circular questioning, as the name implies, seeks to draw information that necessarily involves *recursive interpersonal linkages*. It therefore needs to ascertain behavioral sequences between people and whatever differences occur in a behavioral context. For instance, again in the case of depression, the client might be asked, "When you are depressed, who notices it first?" "Who notices it last?" "Who doesn't notice it at all, but you wish would notice?" "How do those individuals who notice your depression treat you differently?" "What is the most difficult part of other people noticing you depressed?" "Who becomes the most difficult person to deal with when that person notices you depressed?" "Who is the most understanding person when you get depressed?" "Who do you avoid showing your depression to?" Circular questions whose answers imply differences may also be rephrased and asked as differences over time, indicating past, present, and future possibilities.

The third stage is characterized by strategic questions, and it has one important element in common with the first stage. Both stages deal with the client's system at the meaning level. The therapist's questions in the third stage depend more on stage one information about the client's own meanings than on stage two recursive information. Thus, the intent of the third stage is meant to trigger change in a client's interpretation of his world, or, at the very least, challenge the client to begin to think about new interpretations. The intent is to "correct" or influence the client to think more constructively and less simplistically. Indeed, the questions may even become somewhat confrontational in nature. In this challenging mode, the therapist might ask the following: "If you thought your wife to be a loving person instead of a person who is distant from you, especially when she plays with the kids after dinner, how would you react to that?" "If you believed in total commitment to your spouse and to the household, how would that change the way you think about spending money that you don't have to spend?" "If you believed that continuing to take mind-altering drugs meant that your kids would probably not have you as a father a few years down the road, how would you see yourself?"

The fourth stage is characterized by reflexive questions. This stage depends heavily on information from stage two as both stages focus on circularity or recursive interpersonal linkages. This last stage, like stage three, is meant to influence the client to find new solutions regarding its effects on others. In contrast to stage three, stage four is quite behavioral as it is meant to deal with interactional sequences. For instance, the therapist might ask the following which is always based on prior "circular" information: "What do you think your husband would do if you insisted on having sexual relations at least once a day for the next two weeks?" "If your husband sees you continuing to drift closer and closer to your mother, what do you think he might do a year down the road?" "If you were to argue, what do you think your husband would do if you didn't cry and didn't get visibly bitter at him?" "If you decided to go on strike around the house, what do you think his reaction might be?"

Stages three and four, in a sense, are somewhat like "reframes with a challenge twist." Like reframes, they offer no guarantee they will produce their desired effects. The process may be slow to act in the client's reframing process, and it may require returning to more elementary questions as in stages one and two. The intent of the last two stages involves influencing the client to think in terms of greater self-understanding.

Similarly, in one-on-one therapy Terry (1989) also illustrates the application of circular questioning with special emphasis on the use of three kinds of questions: *monadic, dyadic, and triadic*. In the early part of a therapeutic interview, problem-definition questions might be handled in this fashion. The therapist might simply begin with a series of monadic questions: "What brings you here today?" "How long have you had that problem?" "Has there been any change recently in that situation?" When the series of monadic questions seems completed, the therapist then might ask the client a series of questions typically categorized as *dyadic*, necessarily about another person: "Who else thinks there is a problem?" "What would he or she say is the problem?" "Who was the first, second, third...last, to notice the problem?"

In the course of interviewing, *triadic* questioning ensues. In effect, they involve asking the client what a second person, obviously not present in the interview, might say about a third person's (also not present in the session) view of the problem. For instance: "If your father were alive today, what would he say is your brother's view of your situation?" In essence, this method provides a broad interactive, contextualizing, systemic perspective despite the fact that there is only one client present. Naturally, to complete this series of questions and make them circular, the therapist would focus on more questions that deal with the *differences* and the *meanings* behind those differences, and how they all were effected by time.

Similarly, Sheinberg and Penn (1991) have more recently developed the notion of circular questioning in a specific area called "gender questions." This is aimed at individual clients or couples. It is an attempt at encouraging them to explore gender-informed norms and ideals. Essentially, it assists clients in examining the current or prevailing norms in regard to what it means to be masculine or feminine in specific behavioral contexts. Once an agreed upon "norm" is established as a basis or benchmark for therapeutic inquiry, circular questions, usually in the form of future or hypothetical contexts, are presented.

These questions designed by Sheinburg and Penn specifically examine the relational consequences of that context *if* that "norm" gets modified or manipulated. In addition to the use of a circular-questioning framework, it also employs questions, which recall much of Olga Silverstein's work, specifically her "dilemmatic" and "what if" kinds of questions. For instance, at the monadic level, the therapist might ask the male client: "What do you think might happen if your wife initiates sexual relations for the next two months?" On a dyadic level, the male client might be asked, "What do think your wife might say if she were to carry that out?" This might even be carried to a triad level as, for example, if the male were asked: "What would one of your friends say that you're thinking if your wife carried it out?" This type of gender-driven questioning is just one more specific application of circular questioning's protean character.

The Milan group's influence has traveled far and wide, effecting counseling textbooks not only for those dealing with "family therapy," but also counseling textbooks of a more general nature (Brammer, Abrego, & Shostrom, 1993, pp. 159–160). The Milan group's basic principles of circularity are reflected in the quality use of its circular questioning techniques. The therapist's use of working hypotheses, positive connotation to a reframe the symptom, therapist "neutrality" and linguistic sensitivity offer untold avenues of therapeutic opportunities. Since the Milan School's original model was founded on systemic thinking, it accommodates not only varying numbers of clients in therapeutic session, but also a wide continuum of therapeutic relationships. In the therapy session, the number of participants may range from an intergenerational cluster, a nuclear family, a single head-of-household family, a heterosexual or homosexual couple, or one client. Obviously, then, when there is only one client in the session, he or she becomes the conduit for gathering information about the "system" of significant figures in which he or she belongs. Circular questioning realized through the individual client offers access to the client's system (Terry, 1989).

A most useful and detailed instructional outline of the basic circular interview model and its applicability to many varied relationships or combinations of clients was developed and written in 1986 by Fleuridas, Nelson & Rosenthal. It is found in the *Journal of Marital and Family Therapy* (*12*, 113–127). Their outline and commentary represent a highly useful tool in assisting therapists who wish to familiarize themselves with the art of formulating effective circular questions.

This article may prove to be helpful in illustrating the extreme maneuverability and resourcefulness of circular questions as the angle of observation adds more dimension or depth. Since by their very nature circular questions are designed to access information efficiently and comprehensively, they go well beyond the contextual constraints imposed by linear questions. Linear reasoning, which involves two points and the movement between them has its limitations. For instance, before the invention of radar, two points were insufficient to chart a course in navigation. A navigator needed three points to navigate a course accurately. This is called triangulation. Similarly, circular questioning possesses its own dialectic and is ultimately based on three necessary elements. Two contextualized positions containing psychological phenomena, whether feelings, behaviors, or thoughts, separated by a time interval, need a *third* element, which is characterized by the notable *differences* between the two phenomena.

Linear contextual questions, by themselves, are obviously important because they deal with the specifics of time, place, and situation. So, when a client says, "I am depressed," a series of linear contextualizing questions posed by the therapist will invite the client to more concretely render the feelings or notions of the client's initial generalization regarding depression. However, the strength of linear contextual questions is intensified when they exhibit contextualized *differences over time*. Thus, the time dimension is crucial in that the contextualization of two specific situations is ultimately compared.

Circular questioning, as the name implies, is *not* one question, but the manner and quality of questions that raises linear contextual questions to more penetrating and more relevant heights. Metaphorically, full circular questioning is like raising a linear equation to an exponential equation or like moving from a simple first-order mathematical operation to a logarithmic expression. In circular questioning there is a similar exponential or logarithmic effect in and around the contextualization at the systemic level, and this phenomenon occurs when *differences in time*, which are relatable to affect, behaviors, and cognition, are compared and amplified. To that end it may be helpful to analogically visualize the characteristics of circular questions in the tridimensional shape of a hologram. As the observer witnesses the hologram from many different angles, each vantage point offers new information. Yet, as each view adds something new and different, the accumulation of the data offers the viewer an enlarged global effect that is something more than the mere sum of its data. Because a hologram is tridimensional, each new view contains a "systemic" flavor. It might more easily be considered as exponential in nature which suggests the fundamental existence of a more comprehensive view previously unavailable to the observer.

The Milan School has offered the world of psychotherapy a tried and tested operational model. It is effective and relatively short in duration in terms of actual contact hours with the client family. It has also proven to be very adaptable to modifications. A team of therapists may use circular interviewing with families as it was originally designed, or a therapist may use the model's basic ideas and techniques in working with individual clients. From an aesthetic and philosophical point of view, the model is systemic and elegant in overall design. While the Milan group's systemic family therapy model is structured and focused around circular questioning, it is hardly a closed system of thought. It is a highly adaptable model that allows for modifications and utility. The unique design of circular questioning, the centerpiece of the model, represents a major breakthrough in the history of modern psychotherapy.

Chapter 4

Steve de Shazer's
Solution-Focused Therapy

In the following pages, when referring to the ensuing brief therapy models, it will be important to recognize the differences between these headings "problem" and "solution," and, by the same token, the words "focused" and "oriented." It will mean making a concentrated effort to recognize a new set of semantics beyond the ordinary definitions and meanings found in the dictionary. It will also be important to bear in mind the meanings of the words resolution and dissolution. Their meanings and implications will be particularly important to understanding, for instance, the shift from problem-oriented therapies, such as the MRI and Milan models, to "solution" therapies. Solution therapies find two basic forms of expression: solution-focused and solution-oriented.

Yet before discussing at length the solution-focused therapy model, the topic of this chapter, one needs to briefly return to the origin and growth of the Mental Research Institute founded in 1959. Its founding members and its subsequent formation, referred to as the MRI group, is our more immediate point of departure. Collectively, their influence has been far reaching, effecting many schools of psychotherapeutic thought in the last four decades, both in the United States and abroad. The MRI has become synonymous with a variety of therapeutic perspectives, designations and labels, such as systemic, interactional, strategic, communications, and cybernetics. The MRI model can be viewed as a matrix of modern systemic psychotherapy. While designated by many different names and labels, its penetrating influences run far and deep.

144 • *Breakthroughs in Six Brief Psychotherapies*

The MRI's psychotherapeutic labels include "problem-focused," "problem-oriented," "problem-resolution," or "problem-dissolution" therapies. Obviously, in these hyphenated word clusters, the common word *problem* accurately represents the key idea as it identifies and informs much of the MRI's therapeutic perspectives and approaches. Globally, if the MRI had a "mission statement" through these labels, it would likely imply that these related terms express a therapeutic process whose goal and fulfillment would take place by *resolving* or by *dissolving* the *problem*.

In essence, the MRI's goal prescribes or indicates that the completion of the therapeutic process would *not* necessarily imply the search for a *solution* as we ordinarily use that word. In our everyday conversation when the word "problem" is mentioned, it immediately suggests its associated counterpart, the word *solution*. One term almost automatically seems to suggest the other. However, the MRI group had something very different in mind in the evolution and development of their model. It had proposed, instead, the notion of seeking a *resolution to* or *dissolution of* the problem by tackling the problem itself. This is accomplished by *dissecting* and *dismantling* the constituent elements of the problem.

It is essentially an analytical process, but its analysis is not at all associated with Freudian psychoanalysis. Instead, the MRI's analysis achieves its ends by *dismantling elements of the problem*. This specific way of dealing with the problem designates the essence of its style and perspective. Generally speaking, this form of therapy has also been called strategic therapy as it is symptomatically based. In order to resolve a problem, one needs to understand the symptoms and their functions. There is, however, an important caveat at this point. The word "symptom" obviously has a medical or pathological flavor to it. However, the MRI model is not interested in any psychological excavation whereby the symptoms lead to understanding the "mental disease" as a psychiatrist might typically approach a troubled mind. To the MRI group, a symptom essentially means an *unwanted behavior whose repetitive presence constitutes the problem.*

Much of the MRI's foundation hailed from the work of Milton Erickson, an M.D. trained in psychiatry and traditional psychoanalysis. He had a long history of experimentation that chronicled an interesting array of non-traditional approaches in psychotherapy. He was interested in dealing with the "symptom" as a way of resolving the problem, but *not* through Freudian analysis and etiologies. They would have obviously suggested oedipal conflicts, developmental fixations, childhood trauma, and a host of childhood problem experiences.

The MRI has also been called strategic therapy. As a general term, strategic indicated that interventions and related strategies had to be used. It acquired that label due to Haley's introduction and usage of the label at the MRI and then, later, in his writings after leaving the MRI. This term became further disseminated when the MRI as a whole was labeled in the same way. The MRI's theoretical foundations, however, also hailed from a multi-faceted framework which involved communications systems and cybernetics for which Gregory Bateson and his associates represented key and pivotal figures.

In fact, it was from the MRI's influence that the Milan group drew much of its inspiration in the 1970s. The Milan group's resulting model, circular interviewing, bears a strong kinship to the MRI's strategic practices and theories. The Milan model also brought to fruition a systemically envisioned strategic methodology that heavily incorporated Bateson's interactional sequences (cybernetics). The Milan model of circular questioning focused on eliciting client *differences* of affect, behaviors, and cognition. The articulation of these differences was referenced through the dimension of time and the substantiation of meaning (semantics) that the clients attributed to their problem. This was all done within a systemic framework.

Many critical commentators of family therapy seem to agree that the Milan model, while still maintaining a strong kinship within the order of the MRI's "problem" perspective, went on to become, methodologically speaking, the most consistent with Bateson's circular epistemology

(Goldenberg & Goldenberg, 1991). In essence, the Milan model offered the psychotherapy community a very effective modality for treating family problems. The Milan model also offered a model which was the most systemic of its time, incorporating many prior theories and practices that dealt with conducting psychotherapy as essentially working with a *problem* in a process that involved a dismantling effect.

In this light, then, it becomes relatively easy to appreciate the Milan group's emphasis on dealing within this *problem* format. For them the symptomatic situation, defined as inextricably holding back the family, becomes the *locus* around which therapy must take place. The circular interview, the core of the Milan group's model, provides a unique and comprehensive approach which both unifies and systemically enriches the approaches that deal with "dissolving" the various developmental components of the *problem*. Thus, through the course of the therapeutic process the clients stretch their perceptual boundaries, see the interrelations and the patterns of their behaviors in a systemic perspective, and the problem is said to begin "dissolving."

The emphasis on the word "problem" becomes all the more evident in that the practitioners of the Milan model emphatically do *not* purport to offer a "solution" to a problem in a traditional sense. Indeed, like the MRI model, the Milan group's model presents an approach that deals with problem "resolution" and "dissolution." As the Milan group's initial leader and organizer, Selvini-Palazzoli has pointed out, *a fortiori*, that the Milan model might be described as a problem resolution process in which the family, as a unit, must decide for itself to bring about its own resolution in the course of its therapy (Simon, 1987). Clearly, the Milan School's model, the culmination of a strategic, family-systems based, cybernetically inspired therapy, realizes the idea that the therapist neither offers, nor finds, nor presents a "solution" for the clients.

To the contrary, the course of therapy involves the therapist pursuing appropriate strategies to create the conditions for eliciting useful information. The therapist also asks a series of contextualized questions and circular questions that will bring to the surface recursive family patterns at the behavioral, affective, and cognitive (belief systems) levels. In particular, the model employs systematically and systemically circular questions, and, from time to time, reframing (positive connotation) family behaviors to emphasize family members' positive intentions. Ultimately, circular questioning, the very core of its model, creates the conditions for the family members to perceive the interrelatedness of the components of their interactive and reciprocally influenced cosmos through their recursive patterns.

In summation, this kind of therapy examines interactive patterns and offers an opportunity for family members to decide to make significant changes based on their growing and ongoing awareness of themselves as a unit. Through the course of time, usually ten months to a year, family members increasingly accede to their own understanding based on the interrelatedness of their existence. Working with "assignments" or rituals during the intervals between therapy sessions, the family will often make the therapeutic leap into its own family "resolution" of their problem. It is not so much finding a "solution" to the problem as it is finding a "dissolution" or "resolution" of the problem in the sense of a melting away or a dissipation of the problem.

Interestingly, when the "resolution" to the therapeutic problem is realized, the therapist will, accordingly, attribute that "success" phenomenon as being realized by the family through its own efforts by having expanded its understanding of itself over a period of time. In the interim, the therapist has neither proposed nor suggested any kind of "solution" at any time in the course of therapy. It is for these reasons that the Milan model, after being identified primarily as a strategic and systems model, is also a problem-focused or problem-oriented model and definitely *not* a "solution" model.

This, then, represents our new starting point. Despite the variety of names and labels, the "problem-focused," "problem-oriented," "problem-resolution," or "problem-dissolution" therapy approaches unintentionally generated another scenario. They unwittingly invited some psychotherapeutic practitioners and thinkers to undergo an almost obligatory reaction to this "problem" style perspective. With the passing of time, it seemed that their very strengths that had been exerted through the "problem" perspective in a systemic context, as exemplified by strategic therapy, the MRI group, Jay Haley and the Milan group, created a backlash. The *problem* approach and its nearly two-decade-plus record elicited dissatisfied reactions among some practitioners.

This reactive movement often consisted of individuals who were family therapists, practicing or experimenting with strategic therapy, who were also seeking a different way to effect change through brief forms of therapy. Yet, as reflected in most movements in history, the dialectic process (change) is rarely as simply as it appears on the surface. Its trajectory contains many components, some carried forward from the past and some which are left behind. And so, the reaction to the established MRI and Milan models was complicated, and the change necessarily involved many components, some of which were utilized by the newer models, and some of which were left behind.

Generally speaking, the "strategic style," by its definition, concentrated its efforts and steered its strategies in and around the *problem*. Practitioners of strategic therapy had decided, both individually and collectively, that they would specifically deal with the problem through resolution or dissolution. That was the quintessential premise of their approach. It comes as no surprise that this factor would eventually become the major philosophical issue at hand. It became an issue over this fundamental premise dealing with the *problem*, its *emphasis* and *direction*. Given the advent of newer methods and models on the horizon that superseded the prior problem-oriented one, where would one now find the *locus* of the "problem?" Would it vanish as a consideration? Would it still maintain the position of "front and center?" Or would it be relegated to a different location in the therapeutic process?

When practitioners sought to create alternative "brief therapy" approaches to those practiced by the MRI and Milan groups, both the emphasis and the direction for dealing with the "problem" as systems of "dismantling" the problem components became the necessary questions at hand. However, it is very important to underline the fact that the ensuing shift that defined itself on a trajectory as moving from "problems" to "solutions," in no way means or implies that everything that was related to the "problem" approaches was left behind or summarily abandoned. To the contrary, a close study shows that many components of the "problem" approaches were merely re-utilized in different capacities to the ends of a different philosophical persuasion.

The new response manifested itself in a significant shift in perspective. The previously placed emphasis on the so-called "problem" shifted to a focus on "solutions" to the problem. This shift involved a change in direction, which reflected a new way of thinking that necessarily called into play employing therapy as a means of finding "solutions." This "solutions" movement ultimately produced two new, relatively distinct, schools of thought. Both are generally traceable in development to the family/systems thinking of the 50s, the Mental Research Institute, and the Milan model. It is important to emphasize that with these changes there also persisted a relatable continuity to the 50s' paradigm shift, effecting a switch from the medical model to cybernetically-informed therapy.

One school appeared on the scene in the late 1970s and early 1980s. It called itself, at first, eco-systemic therapy, and then later dubbed itself "solution-focused" therapy. The other school, which followed somewhat later, called itself "solution-oriented." These two groups, of course, have most aptly ascribed to themselves in their very titles the carefully, well-chosen term *solution*. Their commonly held, one-word self-descriptor embodied the basic underlying notion that would distinguish them from prior brief therapies that had labeled themselves using the word *problem*. Thus, there clearly emerged "solutions" schools of thought that counter-balanced the previous "problem" approaches.

150 • *Breakthroughs in Six Brief Psychotherapies*

Yet, given the major influence of the MRI's wide range of innovations and its rich diversity, both in practice and in theory, and given the Milan School's highly developed model with its many detachable and adaptable components, the "solutions" groups availed themselves of prior successfully operating components. The "solutions" groups did not evolve without the influence of the two antecedent problem-oriented schools. In reality, many of the "solutions" developers and advocates were themselves family therapists or strategic therapists who were, generally speaking, *ipso facto* systemic in orientation and who had embraced, to varying degrees, strategic, communications, and cybernetics perspectives.

It is no surprise then that the developers of the "solutions" models, as is evident from their writings, were immensely familiar with the Milan group's systemic model, Virginia Satir's work in communications, Haley's strategic perspectives, Milton Erickson's innovative legacies, Bateson's cybernetics, the MRI's own brief therapy model, and the writings of the MRI group's very visible practitioners and theoreticians. In fact, Steve de Shazer, who initiated "solutions" thinking, had been a strategic "problem-oriented" therapist in the 1970s. Based on clinical case studies, in 1975 de Shazer published an article in *Family Process* where he reported and commented on the effectiveness of his practice of "problem-oriented" therapy. De Shazer's influences are evident in his abundant writings about Milton Erickson's methods (de Shazer, 1979) and Haley's work (1967, 1973). De Shazer's early books also reflect the influence of Bateson (1979), and others at the Mental Research Institute, in particular, the work of Watzlawick, Weakland, and Fisch entitled *Change: Principles of Problem Formation and Problem Resolution* (1974), the Milan group's influence, and in particular, their use of circular questioning techniques (Selvini-Palazzoli et al., 1978).

Even a perfunctory view of "solutions" therapists' writings shows how many aspects of "solutions" therapy are immediately relatable and akin to the vast richness of specific components of antecedent models. The solutions schools became, in a sense, both subscribers to and modifiers of antecedent modalities. However, the solutions schools, despite overlaps in the usage of similar components with the "problem" schools of thought, did in effect go on to create new modalities. What became the crucial factor involved the significant changes in theory and the subsequent emergence of "solutions theory." It was the orientation and the reasoning, in short the new philosophy, which uniquely informed and described the solutions modalities that were important. Obviously, effecting change in a brief manner had been, and still was, the object of their therapeutic efforts. However, it was the new solutions philosophy that determined how change might be handled differently and, perhaps more effectively, despite overlaps and carry-over elements from prior models. From a theoretical perspective, the solutions models clearly presented distinctly unique models when compared to their antecedent "problem" modalities.

Today, Steve de Shazer still represents the most important proponent of "solution-focused" therapy, both from a theoretical and a practical perspective. Having written several books (1982, 1985, 1988, 1991, 1994) and many articles, he was principally responsible, along with his associates, for establishing the Brief Family Therapy Center (BFTC) in Milwaukee, Wisconsin in 1978. Publishing his first book (1982), a foundational text entitled *Patterns of Brief Family Therapy*, he proposed a host of "solutions" approaches, couched as they were in what he described as an "ecosystemic epistemology" perspective.

De Shazer particularly emphasized the effects of *reframing* (de Shazer, 1982, pp. 24–26), clearly an idea relatable to the MRI group (Watzlawick et al., 1974). However, de Shazer employed the MRI's use of *reframing* in a different manner, emphasizing more its applications in a broader perspective. Going beyond reframing's immediately recognizable usefulness as a firsthand technique, he employed it as a means of helping the client achieve a greater "world view" or perspective so that solutions seemed more feasible. He emphasized reframing's effectiveness in achieving a wider range of solutions through change in perception, affect, and behavior (1982, p. 25). De Shazer reiterated the same global notion in his later work, *Putting Difference to Work* (1991, pp. 54–55).

Indeed, de Shazer did agree with the MRI group and with other strategic thinkers that the clients' attempted solutions and their repeated failures constituted a problem, or, "the problem" (de Shazer, 1985). However, unlike the MRI group's brief therapy model which had placed the focus on the "problem" and on "problem resolution," de Shazer preferred to *focus* philosophically on the family members' more immediate capacities within themselves to generate creative *solutions* to their problems. While in many ways this may echo the same basic notion as in the prior MRI model, it is in fact different. Indeed, the *locus* of change is still situated within the family system and its individuals, but the orientation in time has made a radical shift. In MRI theory, change is effected *in the here and now* through interventions, through prescribing the symptom. Instead, in de Shazer's approach, change is effected through a "future" context. Taking the lead from Milton Erickson's 1950s pseudo-orientation in time, de Shazer created a model that utilized a *future* context whereby therapist and client could co-construct hypothetical and future solutions as the primary step in change. This led de Shazer to the creation of the "miracle-question" model, discussed at length later.

Generally speaking, solution-focused therapy might be summarily described as a philosophically broad "exception-based" approach within a systemic perspective whereby the therapist works in collaboration with the client(s) in centering immediately on solution-building strategies and change through the medium of future and hypothetical contexts. The new *focus* posited in the search for solutions relegates the "problem" approach, which analytically "dismantles" the problem aspects to a secondary position in the process. The problem is neither denied nor dismissed; rather, it is treated more like a benchmark, a touchstone for comparisons or better, a baseline from which positive change is measured and monitored with regularity throughout the interview process. Hence, de Shazer cleverly introduced the *scaling technique*, a highly expeditious monitoring procedure and empowerment tool, which will be discussed later.

In de Shazer's model, time is viewed as having three basic periods: past, present, and future. The model's broad reframe in the search for solutions assumes a different angle of attack with each different time period. Hence, problem and solution are manipulated very differently. While the problem is reframed as something that obviously existed in the past (and is referred to from time to time during the interview), and while the problem is patently de-emphasized in the present (used only for obtaining data verification and comparisons), the solution-building process is focused upon a future or hypothetical context, which is the heart of the model. Hence, the therapist maintains a stance whereby the problem and the details of the complaint become subsumed within the greater framework of "change" expectations couched in the "solutions" talk. The "solutions" approach denotes a definite second-order style, emphasis on changing the system, where the dialogical posture, the collaboration between therapist and client, emphasizes and encourages change through "solutions" talk on a future or hypothetical context.

De Shazer's solution-focused model does share a similar concrete relationship with the MRI problem-focused model. The MRI group, as practitioners of a second-order model, and de Shazer have rejected both the structuralist elements of traditional family therapy and the psychoanalytic elements of psychodynamic therapy. Yet, despite the similarity in attempting to achieve second-order change, de Shazer experiences a major discomfort with the MRI's strategy which retains a "boundary between therapist and client and the subject-object split of traditional therapy" (1991, p. 56). He therefore appraises the MRI approach as being a *transitional* model between the era of "structuralism and post-structuralism" despite its second-order qualities.

As de Shazer reiterates, he and his associates effected a new and radical shift in 1978 at the Brief Family Therapy Center (BFTC) in Milwaukee. Rather than accepting the unit of analysis as consisting of "client-plus-problem," he insisted that the new unit be "the client-plus-problem-plus-therapist-plus-team as the *system-under-consideration*" (1991, p. 57). Thus,

154 • *Breakthroughs in Six Brief Psychotherapies*

he emphasized the BFTC's broadened concept of collaboration with the client, and this inherently suggested the lessening of the "distances" between the client and therapeutic team. In effect, he viewed the BFTC as bringing the "systems" of systemic therapy to newer and more liberating heights. He later identified and labeled this kind of accomplishment as the "death of resistance" (de Shazer, 1984).

The focus on solutions brought many implications. For instance, specifically in the area of termination, reaching the client's goal or solution was deemed, by far, more important than the problems presented and discussed in the sessions. Inevitably, this led de Shazer to a redefinition of the unit of analysis: "client-plus-therapist-plus-goal (or solution)-plus-team" (1991, p. 57). In other words, for de Shazer, as his thinking emerged, each session potentially represented a concluding session in the sense that the client's solution could be reached at any time during the process, irrespective of established deadlines. Theoretically, the therapist cannot really set any limits on the number of sessions, since even a single session may prove sufficiently conclusive for a solution to be found. De Shazer had originally kept to a five-to-ten session format. Thus, by limiting the number of sessions as Erickson and the MRI group had done, he had hoped to naturally enhance the expectation of change. However, his very latest thinking does go one step further.

At the Brief Family Therapy Center, de Shazer and Insoo Kim Berg co-developed the Solution-Focused Therapy model, which has often been referred to as the Milwaukee model. There are two versions of this evolving model. They range from its earlier, somewhat more structured model, consisting of a six-step session interview to its later model, which represents a similar yet more fluid version, typically beginning with a "miracle-question" sequence after an introductory interval of joining.

From *Patterns of Brief Family Therapy* (pp. 31–46), the interview in the earlier model is divided into six distinct steps: *pre-session planning*, the *prelude*, the *data collection*, the *consulting break* (intervention designing), the *message giving* (intervention), and the *study efforts* (postsession assessment). De Shazer qualified this brand of family therapy as "ecosystemic." The word stem "eco," which in classical Greek designated the term for "house" or "household," has come to mean the relationships between living organisms and their environment. In the tradition of systems and family thinkers, it was aptly chosen and reiterated by de Shazer to emphasize the interactional relationships between not only family members themselves, but also all the other systems around the family which affect its members.

A team usually conducts the therapy, which lasts about one hour. One therapist actively participates with the family members while the other team members observe the session from behind a one-way mirror with the availability of intercom systems where the team acts as a "Greek chorus." Without the clients, the therapeutic team first discusses the available data in the *pre-session planning* portion of the therapeutic program. They also do some temporary or open-ended strategizing, which is meant to serve as a guide and *not* as a format.

The *prelude*, which may take up to 10 minutes after meeting the client family, is a kind of extended "joining" or "socializing" period with the emphasis placed on rapport-building with the client family. The therapist attempts to avoid any deliberate discussion of the family members' complaints that might have been instrumental in their being there. Rather, the therapist deals with learning specifics about the family, especially its specific resources and its members' positive qualities which usually would not have appeared on their intake forms. In the Ericksonian tradition, these resources and positive personality qualities could be used in the session as useful tools in a utilization strategy.

Data collection comprises the major portion of the interview. During this interval of time, the family is invited to consider and verbalize how therapy might be most useful. Then, proceeding into the specifics of the complaint(s), family members are encouraged to answer circular questions, particularly, triadic questions. The latter involves a family member discussing the nature of the complaint by making no necessary observations about

156 • *Breakthroughs in Six Brief Psychotherapies*

himself or herself, but discussing two or more other family members and how they are involved with the complaint and its description.

In the spirit of the Milan group's circular questioning, the solution-focused therapist capitalizes upon the triadic aspect of this questioning technique to obtain valuable family information, its communicational and behavioral patterns, and their meanings. However, while similar to the MRI group's approach and to the Milan School's approach, this information gathered is not used for systemically "dismantling" the specifics of the problem; rather, the information collected is utilized systemically as a foundation on which to initiate and create "solutions" building. Again, by employing circular questioning, particularly triadic and dyadic questioning, the therapist assists the family in creating realistic goals. In particular, these questions will focus on how any given member of the family "will know" *when* change has taken place, or, *when* a given member will know that another family member "thinks" that change has been taking place.

Circular questions, grounded in future, hypothetical, or in presuppositional contexts, serve to metaphorically measure the differences from past unwanted behaviors to the client's desired change. So, while goal setting is ostensibly going on, solutions building is already taking place in the family interaction. Circular questions employed in the data collection process will usually involve all family members. Each person will be a respondent to the therapist's questions or will be the "subject" of another family member's answers. The data collection portion of the session concludes by the therapist announcing that she will take a break to consult with the rest of the team which had been observing the proceedings. During the *consulting break* the team members make observations and assessments for the purpose of designing an intervention to be delivered by the therapist.

Upon her return to the therapy session, the therapist delivers the *intervention* message, usually consisting of two parts, the *compliment* and the *task*. As the former name implies, the compliment is targeted at bringing forth a positive statement to the family members to which they all may relate. It is founded on actual data that have been presented by the family during that session. The compliment also serves an important function as a bridging statement for future action in helping to animate the family. It thus creates a stronger likelihood of greater family participation in the suggested task that follows.

The *task* may vary, but it usually involves all the family members. The assignment typically involves an observational task such as those described by Molnar and de Shazer (1987) or simply the task of doing "something different" (de Shazer, 1985). The observational task may be to track certain behavioral sequences of certain individuals' behaviors or specific key family interactions. Additionally, the therapist recommends that particular attention be paid to observing the *consequences* of those behaviors.

The task of reporting observations that involve the tracking of behaviors is not new to therapy. However, the tracking behavior and, in particular, the noted consequences, when presented by the clients to the therapist at the next session, become the foundation and new context for more "solutions" building, obviously based on the clients' experiences and observations. Similarly, suggesting that clients try *something different* behaviorally between sessions may also prove to be useful. The clients' efforts to do something different during that interval become the focus of the next session's agenda.

After the delivery of the intervention, additional time is offered to the family members for their reactions to the interventive message, both to the compliment portion addressed to the family members and to the task portion where clarifications might be needed. When this phase is completed to the family's satisfaction, the therapist quickly concludes the session.

The *postsession assessment*, naturally, takes place after the family's departure. The team discusses its assessment of the day's therapy session: the dynamics, the patterns of interaction between family members, and the possible behavioral meanings. The team also discusses the possible family dynamics occurring in the interval before the family's next session. The number of therapy sessions is usually limited to between five and ten, reminiscent of the tradition of the MRI and the Milan groups.

The Brief Family Therapy Center of Milwaukee has also developed a more recent version of the basic model just outlined. The new version has been produced for instructional purposes in a series of videotapes (Berg, 1994, 1995a, 1995b; Berg & Reuss, 1997) which easily lend themselves to in-depth study, both by individuals and by groups in training. The videotapes employ the didactic use of subtitles that identify the various techniques during the course of the therapy session. The format also employs periodic "suspensions" in the client interview during which the videotape's narrator and Insoo Kim Berg, the therapist, discuss, in a question-and-answer format, the significance of the methods being employed. These videotapes present clear and highly effective examples of solution-focused therapy.

In 1997, after much success of her video presentations, Insoo Kim Berg, joined by Norman H. Reuss, produced a sequel to the solution-focused series of videotapes. The videotape, entitled *Solutions Step By Step*, presents the video version of their coauthored book bearing the same name. As in the prior tapes, the therapist makes comments upon the interviews in a didactic format using a conversational, easy-to-follow style on the solutions-techniques used, couched in its theme of moving "step by step."

The spirit of de Shazer's second version of the solution-focused format does indeed capture much of the essence of the original "ecosystemic" version. It is similar in that it is focused on the future, and it is interested in achieving, more and more, the details of a solution. The therapist continues assuming a non-judgmental attitude, a position of "not knowing" and creates a rapport with the client which might be best described as very "cooperative" and collaborative. However, unlike the earlier version, the latter version does not assume a range of five to ten therapy sessions as the general rule. There is, instead, no predetermined number of sessions at all. In fact, De Shazer individually views the entire first session and subsequent sessions as potentially the last session *if* the apparent problem becomes quickly dissolved, or, *if* a solution to the problem becomes quickly accessible.

The first session typically consists of three components. They are designated as the *interview,* requiring most of the hour, the *intrasession break,* lasting five to ten minutes and which may or may not include questions from the observation team, and the *delivery of the message* by the therapist, lasting only a few minutes. If this is a team-approach session, then the team devises the message; otherwise, the therapist, alone, would utilize the break time to formulate a message consisting of a compliment and a task.

At this juncture, it is important to point out that the first session is unique and different from the subsequent sessions which employ a format whose acronym has been designated as *E.A.R.S.* Discussed later in the chapter, the format's acronym signifies elicit, amplify, reinforce and start over. However, the initial session format and the format for all subsequent sessions are highly structured and integrated so that any session becomes a natural progression and extension of the preceding one.

A significant difference between the initial and subsequent sessions involves the discussion of both the problem and the main goal desired by the client. In the beginning of the first session, the therapist and client reach an understanding of the problem that the client wishes to address first. This facet of the model is important because, as the name of the model (solution-focused) implies, the object of solution-focused therapy remains that of finding specific solutions, *not* elaboration of the problem in a "dismantling" resolution or "dissolution" format as in the MRI Model, and *not* elaboration of any psychoanalytic inquires.

Once the problem is identified and generally described, the therapy session involves finding solutions. Again, it seeks neither an excavation of the problem's origins, nor an extensive description of the problem. It is a philosophy that de-emphasizes the problem's etiology and its historical timeline details. With the problem placed in a secondary perspective, it then functions more like a benchmark or a touchstone from which the change generated by therapy is gauged. Change is usually described as a series of "small changes" in a process that is gradual and paced toward a solution. This characteristic tact is philosophically significant as it is one of the trademarks identifying the uniqueness of this modality. It is based on the Ericksonian belief that small changes can lead into a progression of changes in the "system." The system is not fixed as one might prematurely assume it to be. The client's system, instead, will be viewed as evolving and in constant flux; and it will include the therapist's interaction and whatever new meanings the client adapts into his beliefs and overall perspectives.

Once this preliminary portion of the session is achieved and the client identifies the main change he would like to see effected in the coming weeks, the therapist immediately embarks upon the major portion of the session called the *interview*. It consists of a series of questions which may be categorized as four main kinds: *the miracle question, relationship questions, exception-finding questions*, and *scaling questions* (Berg, 1994).

In brief, the *miracle question*, couched in a hypothetical context, has as its main objective allowing the client "space" and freedom to be able to think unencumbered by the problem, *as if* the problem has suddenly disappeared. Once this hypothetical stance is accepted by the client, the mindset created allows the client to talk about the positive differences present in this new mental landscape free of the problem. In the course of the interview, the miracle question's effect also functions as a negotiating tool where therapist and client discuss small achievable goals.

Relationship questions, as the name implies, assist in contextualizing the client's social environment and in creating an accurate assessment of the available social resources for future solutions. *Exception-finding questions* function in the search and enhancement of past and present accomplishments, thereby rendering a possible foundation of available resources for future solutions. Lastly, *scaling questions* serve two purposes. As an assessment tool, they assist in evaluating the comparison of past situations to present or future situations through the use of numeric values using a scale, usually one to ten. Together with presuppositional questions, scaling questions also function as motivational instruments by bridging past and present, or future, once an exception-finding sequence has been established.

This newer version of solution-focused therapy highlights the employment of the miracle-question sequence as a major strategy. After the "joining" takes place as a preliminary step, the therapist enters into a relatively brief discussion about what the client specifically seeks in therapy. From the beginning, the solution, and *not* the problem, takes precedence. The *interview* usually begins with the posing of the "miracle-question" sequence. The miracle question takes its lead from Milton Erickson's 1950s' "crystal ball" question and its concomitant effects through the positive use of "time distortion." The miracle question, as posed by the therapist to the client, represents a momentary "miraculous" leap into a future, or hypothetical context where the client's problems are deemed as completely removed. Naturally, the therapist's presentation of this "miracle" sequence specifically consists of a very brief narrative description that is well paced and smoothly delivered. The therapist describes a supposed miracle that occurred while the client was asleep. At the client's awakening, the miracle would manifest itself as a place in time where the client's problems suddenly ceased to exist.

The therapist's presentation of this supposed "ideal" state is done in such an affirmative and aesthetic manner that it bears a vivid immediacy and a definite credibility. Despite its obvious hypothetical qualities, the miracle question, when presented accordingly, does not possess the abstractness of a cold project or the all too transparent contrivance of a stratagem. The therapist simply presents this miraculous event to the client as an immediate and operational in-session consideration which will be examined and developed together by client and therapist. The miracle-question sequence, another trademark of this modality, offers the client the possibility to consider and "speculate" as to *what* the conditions could be like when his problems no longer exist.

162 • *Breakthroughs in Six Brief Psychotherapies*

Once this preliminary phase of the interview is subsumed by the client, as witnessed by his cooperation in answering the introductory questions regarding *what is different* in this new, problem-free dimension, more questions ensue that involve the development of "solutions building." Once the client has agreed to consider and embrace this temporary, ideal "condition" as a reality, the therapist then proceeds to pose a series of questions that concern and elaborate the context of this co-created, albeit hypothetical, "problem-free" time zone.

The therapeutic questions are geared to evoking client sensibilities to critically perceive *what is different* in this time zone without the shackles of his problems. Paradoxically, in the very act of describing "what is different," the client is already signaling the beginnings of possible solutions. The elegance of this stance is its obvious immediacy toward solutions. In varying degrees of spontaneity, the client's responses to the therapist's questions continue along the lines of solutions-talk within the client's "semantic" framework and behavioral and affective infrastructures, *not* those of the therapist.

Building upon the effects of the miracle question and its ensuing sequence, the therapist poses many questions from three major categories: *relationship questions, exception-finding questions* and *scaling questions*. These questions are interrelated and artfully blended to remain focused and geared towards finding and creating solutions. These three basic categories of questions are generally presented in order, and they necessarily follow the miracle-question sequence. Relationships questions usually come first since they serve to expand the base of the context of the possible social resources divulged in the miracle-question sequence. Once a social context has been established, *exception-finding questions* naturally seem to follow. In turn, the "exceptions" (i.e., instances when the client's past *positive* behaviors confuted his script of negative behaviors) serve as a foundation of resources of past success. *Scaling questions* naturally seem to follow whenever conversational sequences reveal opportunities for measurability to take place. For instance, if a client reveals that his confidence

Steve de Shazer's Solution-Focused Therapy • 163

level went up to a 6 a week ago when he cut down on his use of illicit drugs, the therapist might ask: "What would it take to move the confidence level to a 7?" This kind of scaling question is just one of hundreds that serve to motivate and empower clients. In fact, once the miracle-question sequence is initiated, scaling questions possess extraordinary flexibility and maneuverability in finding solutions.

Essentially, the quality of questions posed includes some that are linear in nature, but the preponderance of questions is circular. They are focused on behavioral sequences and on semantic qualities whose descriptions are filtered through a "lens" that sees "what is different," how it is perceived differently, and what new meaning may be ascribed to those perceived differences. De Shazer's meaningful allusion to Bateson's "a difference that makes a difference" is especially clear in this context. It constitutes the principal idea of de Shazer's modality.

Additionally, the questions involve asking the client not only what *he* considers as different (*monadic dimension*), but also what he thinks others would notice as different (*dyadic dimension*) in this miracle "dimension" of time without problems. Juxtaposed around the originating miracle question, the ensuing contextual and circular questions essentially carry forth the dialogue between therapist and client. These questions not only influence the quality and quantity of desired changes which are apparently recounted quite freely by the client in this "miracle" interval, but also serve as "interventive" questions. This is witnessed in the phenomenon of suggestibility posed by imbedded commands. This *interventive phenomenon* truly represents the paradox of the miracle question in that the client is, at once, able to put aside the embeddedness of his old script while "trying on for size" new scenarios in a problem-free interval. The miracle question, which poses the question "*what is different* now that the problem is gone," in its proper therapeutic development, becomes among the most clever and useful therapeutic interventions ever devised.

The miracle question creates the opportunity for therapeutic change, and more importantly, it is the client himself who is effectively determining what changes need to occur and how they might be handled. In this process the client creates his own itinerary and his answers seem to come naturally. This situation undoubtedly confirms an old and interesting paradox: clients have known all along many of the answers to their problems. It is one of this model's major corollaries that the client represents the only real "expert" on *his* own problems, not the therapist. Accordingly, it is the client who already "knows," to a considerable degree, the solution to his problems.

After establishing the "miracle" interval, *relationship questions* generally constitute the major ongoing segments of the process. These questions deal with the client's newly discovered affective, cognitive, and behavioral sequences in the miracle interval. They particularly involve interactive sequences that are reflected in questions such as: "How will other people describe the differences they notice in you?" or "What would they say to you about this change?" These questions, circular in nature, serve to stretch and expand the positive expectation levels of the client. In addition to the client's avowal of his "changes" in this "miracle" interval, he also has the opportunity to "speculate" on those changes as possibly seen through the eyes of others in response to the therapist's use of dyadic or triadic questions.

Once the client posits these changes by answering the miracle question (i.e., what is different in this trouble-free zone), another significant component in the enactment of this model ensues, *exception-finding questions*. This includes selective therapeutic digressions into the client's past in the search for related client "successes," however small they might have been. Small successes from the past, simply overlooked or benignly neglected by the client because they somehow seemed insignificant, are amplified for new meaning. The elaboration of these small, yet significantly positive elements, represents the "exceptions" that specifically belie and contradict the negative contents of the client's old script. Exceptions questions play a key role in evoking the hidden and untapped resources that the client brings to therapy. This is reminiscent of Milton's utilization strategy which de Shazer has incorporated into his model.

The therapist's subsequent use of *amplifying* a past success (an exception) which may have seemed small is then skillfully *bridged* and connected with the "miracle" and its trouble-free time zone. The past is thus connected to this hypothetical condition, the miracle. The total effect of this *bridging* allows the client not only to alter his view of the old script, once ostensibly stymied and filled with negatives, but also to recreate a newly expanded script from his past into the future. These positive connections serve to motivate the client to speak the language of change and to effect change in his life during the coming weeks.

Amplification, a rhetorical tool dating back to the Greeks and their many treatises on rhetoric (Watzlawick, 1978), and notably utilized in Milton's strategies, finds new aesthetic life and significant meaning in de Shazer's model. It becomes an instrument by which the therapist shapes the quality of the questions that allow the client to explore and bring forth the once forgotten, or dismissed, positive elements of the old self. The amplification of past successes, together with the use of circular questions, presents a potent combination for inspiring change. Again, it is the client who suggests the ingredients to solutions that he, in a sense, "already knew." Additionally, the client's acknowledgment of the positive "differences" experienced in this new trouble-free dimension, together with answers to relationship questions, allows the implementation of scaling questions. Exceptions offer the specific contexts in which the scaling questions can "measure" (i.e., relative ratio measurements) and again help inspire the possibilities for change. The scaling questions are ostensibly cued, not only to eliciting information about the content of past successes, but also to "speculating" about what else might be achieved in the coming days and weeks after the current session is completed.

Scaling questions can become powerful instruments because they may be employed not only for the purpose of scaling the severity of a problem, but also for *scaling motivation* and *confidence*. They also may be used in combination with relationship questions, thereby allowing the process of scaling to be employed in a dyadic fashion. For instance, assuming a scale of one to ten, where one represents poor behavior and ten optimal behavior, a therapist might ask: "If you feel that you're at six today in your confidence for finding new ways to stop smoking, what number will *your wife think* you are capable of achieving by next week?" Scaling questions, when used effectively in the interview, often create an almost magical therapeutic effect where motivation and confidence are encouraged. This effect derives its energy through a subtle associative process where "exceptions" sequences are *bridged* between the client's past "successes" (exceptions) and the miracle "trouble-free" time zone. It builds strength by *suggesting* that past success is replicable in a future scenario.

The bridging effect necessarily builds on past successes, however small. However, locating and ascertaining past successes may often be difficult because the range of successes may often be narrow and their frequency low. As therapeutic experience has shown, especially in the case of chronicity in long-term polysubstance abuse clients, exception finding is indeed difficult precisely because of the low frequency of positive exceptions. Thus, great therapeutic skill and patience necessarily go hand-in-hand with the therapist's in-depth ability to elicit exceptions, however small, and to process them "one step at a time" (Berg, 1994).

Towards the end of the initial therapeutic session, the *intersession break* occurs. Immediately prior to the break, if the interview is employing a team watching behind a one-way mirror, this then may become an opportunity for the therapists, via telephone, to ask the client or client family to elucidate an area of concern. When that is completed, the therapist leaves the client or client family for several minutes to consult with the team to prepare the *intervention message*. If there is no team format employed, then the therapist will use the break to prepare the message alone.

Upon the therapist's return from the break, the interventive message is delivered. It usually consists of three elements. First, it includes a *compliment* or a series of compliments. They are based on the client's accomplishments, however minimal or small, and on the client's apparent desire for change, which were rendered palpable by his prior descriptions when responding to the miracle question. Berg reiterates that it is very important to amplify the client's *desire to change* because that's where the "energy is" (1994) especially when exceptions are few and limited.

The client's desire for change then necessarily becomes an integral part of the utilization strategy. This portion of the session becomes particularly critical with clients whose problems may bear the additional problem of chronicity such as with polysubstance abuse or alcoholism. Generally, they report few "past successes." Thus, along with the amplification of small, often barely recognizable and retrievable successes, amplifying the client's desire for change must be especially emphasized.

Secondly, there follows an articulate *bridging statement* realistically founded on the compliments just expressed and the importance of the forthcoming "homework assignment." Finally, the third element, the "homework assignment" is announced. The therapist usually suggests that the client *track his behavioral sequences* specifically in regard to the observation of consequences, especially if it might involve an "exception," something positive. This also includes tracking not only his behaviors but also his thoughts and feelings, and how he reacts to them. The homework results, when reported at the next session, usually become the major focus of the session.

In many respects, the solution-focused model is highly structured. Therefore, the second session and all subsequent sessions follow a different format whose acronym, *E.A.R.S.*, represents *elicit, amplify, reinforce,* and *start over*. E.A.R.S., generally speaking, embodies the notion of intensive thematic development. It means working therapeutically in a coherent unifying manner with the changes that have taken place since the last meeting. This even includes the notion of a possible client relapse, which is common in cases of chronicity. Thus, the results of last session's homework assignment serve as the content for the forthcoming session's discussion and development.

Elicit basically deals with questions that, in effect, draw information from the client, especially in relation to his successes and progress towards a goal. *Amplify* deals with the elaboration of the positive changes reported by the client. *Reinforcement* highlights and reiterates the positive changes that have taken place in order to effect a sense of empowerment in the client. The therapist asking the kinds of questions that reveal "what made the difference" that allowed positive change to take place, however small the change, achieves this.

In effect, the process of reinforcement involves, at once, focusing not only on the client's successes, but also on his ability to produce more change from his available resources, both internal and external. Reinforcement focuses on the constant possibility of change and its realization. When one thematic aspect is sufficiently reinforced, it is time to *start over* and develop another aspect of change. This is typically introduced by the therapist asking: "So, what *else* is better?"

The three primary components of this model, elicit, amplify and reinforcement, all serve to thematically focus on finding solutions, even if there are only small, positive increments of change at the outset. The process of E.A.R.S. operates synergistically. Once the therapist initiates an eliciting sequence in a session, the two other primary components, amplification and reinforcement, become the respective repertoires from which the therapist accesses a multiplicity of questions such as relationship questions, scaling questions involving client progress, confidence, presuppositional questions, and negotiating questions. Questions may blend and crisscross with each other, but they all have the purpose of processing client achievements. Once a "small success" has been developed thematically, the therapist must *start over* and develop another area, and the *eliciting stance* begins anew. Like the first interview, the second and all subsequent interviews repeat the use of the intrasession break with its components: compliments, bridging statement, and homework task.

Philosophically, de Shazer (1985) operates on the assumption that the client is the "expert" on himself and on his problem. In fact, the client "already knows" the general, and often, the specific solutions to his problem. If this is so, a question might be aptly posed at this point. Realistically then, what is the purpose of the therapist *if* the client "already knows" all of this? The therapist's function is to *create the conditions* for getting the client to become more fully aware of what he already knows and to get him started in constructing solutions based on the knowledge that he already possesses. The therapist is more correctly viewed as the "expert" only in so far as he or she assists clients in getting started in the solutions process (Berg, 1994).

Solution-focused therapists obviously begin the process by asking the client the right kinds of questions that promote self-awareness and empowerment, and generate more motivation to effect the initiation of change that creates solutions. De Shazer's model, in a sense, behaves like an exemplary reification of Adler's notion of therapy as "encouragement." Yet, it is definitely *not* a perceived encouragement through an advice-giving maneuver or a simplistic problem-solving modificational ploy. Rather, it is an aesthetically-informed process of empowerment through "solutions" thinking, typically beginning with the miracle question and its "trouble-free" condition that temporarily unshackles the client from his problems. There is also a certain "Rogerian" quality that fully respects the client, his pain and suffering. It is a process whose "exception-finding" format systemically bridges the successes of the past and present together with the future to form solutions.

De Shazer's approaches present some paradoxical ideas. A client's solution, for instance, need *not* be perfectly matched to the specific problem in order to be effective. In explaining this paradox, de Shazer presents the interesting metaphor of "skeleton keys" and its related "locks" for understanding this modality (*Keys to Solution in Brief Therapy*, 1985). The "skeleton keys" and the "locks" are metaphorically dialogic. Both metaphors are needed to fully understand the underlying meaning of the solution-focused therapeutic approach.

170 • *Breakthroughs in Six Brief Psychotherapies*

Metaphorically, the *complaints* that clients bring to therapy are likened to *locks* on doors. A family, or an individual, seeking therapy have probably invested much time in trying to decipher why the "locks" on the doors are stuck, or why the doors won't open. These symbolically represent the clients' old rigidified scripts. It is assumed, then, that the clients, in presenting themselves for therapy, are obviously lacking the *key* to the locks. De Shazer suggests a metaphoric analogy of therapy to the use of "skeleton keys" for opening the locks. By definition, skeleton keys are not intended to fit perfectly into any particular lock. Their sole purpose is very specific and unique. It merely involves being able and sufficiently capable of opening locks *even if* doing so "imperfectly." Skeleton keys represent a means to an end, and they represent means that need not be *perfectly* matched to achieve a solution. They need be only capable of "opening the door."

This analogy helps to explain the essence of de Shazer's model and specifically why solutions need *not* be perfectly matched to the problems to be effective therapeutically. The implication of this metaphoric description of skeleton keys also serves to explain why the therapist need not be overly concerned with the whole issue of *why* the "lock" is stuck and *why* the "door" won't open. In this manner, de Shazer purposely avoids having to deal with etiological issues which often turn into stalemates or impasses generated by traditional psychoanalysis or, to some extent, by the analysis of problem-oriented scripts. De Shazer's point is well taken. It is therefore more important to find a "skeleton key" that opens the way than to persist in the uncertain and protracted search for the perfect "key" and thereby run the risk of its not being found.

The corollary to this paradox contains an equally important notion: finding a solution does not require that the therapist know and understand the history of the problem, all of its contributing factors, all of its details, or what keeps maintaining the problem. De Shazer's model makes wise use of an experiential principle borrowed from the very beginnings of strategic therapy itself. Haley (1973) espoused the view that knowing the "history" of a client, at least in the "excavational" sense of the word, was time consuming and offered no guarantees. De Shazer's "solutions" perspective, like that of many strategic problem-oriented therapists, made a 180-degree turn away from one of the principal ideas of the original psychoanalytic model, historical excavation.

De Shazer's model presents another perspective that is crucial for understanding the workings of the model. It goes back to the theory proposed decades ago by Erickson who espoused the radical idea that, despite resistance, change is inevitable. In a sense this slew, once and for all, the omnipotence of the psychoanalytic dragon of "resistance." The "solution" models follow Erickson's lead and regard resistance as part of a utilization strategy, purposely using client resistance for positive ends. Freud had generally viewed resistance, by his own definition, as a phenomenon counterproductive to therapy.

More than familiar with Freud's negative and, at times, ambivalent concept of resistance, Erickson viewed resistance instead as something quite different and far more useful and functional for therapy. In many ways, resistance might be likened to an unassuming trail in the woods. It is obviously not a road, but it does serve as a path, an indicator, a useful guide. De Shazer and the MRI strategic thinkers followed in Erickson's footsteps and found utility in the phenomenon of resistance. Watzlawick devoted many pages in his book, *The Language of Change* (1978), to discuss "utilizing the patient's resistance," citing some Ericksonian examples. De Shazer, then, very much like his contemporary strategic problem-oriented therapists and like Erickson himself, had chosen to bypass the Freudian view of resistance and to embrace resistance as immediately useful.

De Shazer also viewed resistance from another interesting perspective, although it is one that therapists do not like to acknowledge. He believed that clients who willingly come to therapy for change basically resist because they view the interventions and the therapists-centered interpretations as not "fitting" the general view or perspective of "where they [the clients] are at" at that moment in life. A therapist's poor handling of a willing client will usually be reflected in the wrong kinds of questions being

172 • *Breakthroughs in Six Brief Psychotherapies*

asked throughout the therapy. There is a mismatch between what the client is immediately experiencing in the therapy session and what the therapist is imposing upon the client. In short, "resistance" might be a client's situational reaction to poor therapeutic methods. This kind of resistance will persist as long as the therapist is out of sync with the client. A therapist is, therefore, advised to keep to a firm position of "not knowing," as advocated by many contemporary therapeutic schools, particularly the originating Houston-Galveston School. A therapist assumes nothing and should start from scratch with every new client, despite fully completed intake forms and the client's avowal of prior therapy.

De Shazer believes that ultimately most clients are essentially cooperative and do want to change. This is one of his major assumptions. It therefore becomes the business of the therapist to make the client's desire to change become a reality by providing the right therapeutic conditions for change. In a nutshell, those conditions are asking the right kinds of questions in a collaborative relationship. De Shazer shares wholeheartedly the Ericksonian perspective, which in turn reflects an old Buddhist idea that assumes change as inevitable. As a corollary, de Shazer also espouses the Ericksonian view that therapy, done correctly, allows one to have the expectation of *when* change will happen, not *if* change might happen.

As practiced by the MRI group and by the Milan group, the Brief Family Therapy Center in Milwaukee employs a variety of team formats and one-way mirrors. Team formats afford the precious pooling of ideas during consultation breaks for the eventual forging of an intervention. When the therapist returns to the session with the intervention message, it usually consists of a well-thought-out compliment and a homework assignment. Both are geared to creating the groundwork to form solutions.

Homework assignments may simply consist of *observational tasks* as in the time-honored behavioral tradition of tracking one's behaviors and their consequences. In the solutions approach, however, it goes on to include tracking changes in one's affect and cognition, and their respective consequences. Since de Shazer's approach is based on "exception-based" sequences, the homework assignments essentially focus on the client taking note of positive outcomes in thought, action, and affect that contradict, confute, and challenge the client's traditionally held beliefs of past scenarios that had been problematic. The client is encouraged to track and then relate all changes, both big and small, that may seem relevant for therapeutic discussion.

As foundational to de Shazer's method, it remains crucial to deliberately debunk the potentially negative aspects of the client's verbal manipulation of reality and the semantics of the client's belief systems in accordance with the client's complaints. Often, the client has conditioned himself and manipulated these areas to such a degree that his "scripts" abound with embedded generalizations whose contextual elements have created a self-defeating reality for him.

Thus, whenever the client keeps track of overcoming problems in communication which confute his past history, especially in his abuse and misuse of words, the client is already on his way in the process of solution-formation. When the client brings to his next therapy session examples of success, no matter how small, they are amplified and reinforced. These examples then become the focus of discussion and basis for building solutions. Throughout the process, the emphasis is placed on reinforcing *change,* even *small* change. The amplification of "exceptions" behavior and its reinforcement become tools for empowering the client. Even when a client reports a "relapse" into unwanted behavior, that event is handled in a positive manner. A client's relapse into an "old," unwanted behavior gets reframed by the therapist as only a temporary event, a transition. By the same token, the client's attitude is connoted as positive because he was cognizant and aware of the relapse. The client's attitude is immediately posited as positive. As in the Milan model where positive connotation is important, in de Shazer's model, the client is similarly recognized and empowered for his *conscious awareness of that phenomenon* and for his positive intentions. In short, a relapse becomes reframed and viewed as one of the goals of maintenance activity.

De Shazer is particularly interested in word choices made by the client. The misuse of words, such as "trigger" words (i.e., words that tend to escalate confrontational behavior or relay miscommunication), miscommunication in general, and abusive communication frequency can cloud up and complicate social and personal relationships. Similarly, a client's tracking of behavioral sequences and their consequences should also include the client's conscious "non-use" of troublesome "trigger words" which would represent, then, positive "exceptions in a very special way." They, therefore, become very important behavioral sequences to be noted as changes at both the behavioral and cognitive level and need to be amplified and reinforced.

De Shazer, most likely, had been mindful of Virginia Satir's classic enumeration of the notorious ten "trigger words" that negatively influence our thoughts and speech (*Making Contact, 1976*). Trigger words, especially those like *always* and *never*, that are used all too frequently but rarely reflect reality, are examples of the many areas that are the subject of homework tasks or assignments. The question of language, wording, and semantics are crucial notions for de Shazer throughout the interview process. Often, as a necessary preface to the actual solution-talk or solution-formation, de Shazer will spend concentrated effort in helping the client focus on specific meanings in the process of redefining the problem.

Semantics, therefore, becomes another major area of emphasis in de Shazer's model. This is especially true in the early portion of the initial interview where an accurate description of the problem is essential. For instance, if a client says he is "depressed," de Shazer will ask the client what does the word *depression* mean in general. More specifically, he asks the client to explain depression in his own words. After the client's definition is expressed, de Shazer will ask the client to talk about what he does when that condition (depression) *is present*. On the other hand, he will also ask the client what he does when that condition is *not present*. In sharply contrasting these two behavioral conditions, de Shazer arrives at a new and unique definition, that of *non-depression*. By emphasizing the behaviors that are prevalent when depression is apparently *not* present, a new door is opened that allows other conversations to take place. To couch this in another way, de Shazer and the client arrive at a position where they can not only understand the client's view of depression, but also a definition of *non-depression* by having a description of what depression *is not* (1991, pp. 47–48).

Somewhat akin to the behaviorist tradition, de Shazer might also ask about antecedent behaviors and consequential conditions around a specific interval of a depression episode. However, the whole purpose of his approach remains within the realm of the creation of solution-talk and solution-building by the therapeutic process confuting the errors in languaging and in semantics. The reason why this semantic approach is important in "solutions" therapy involves the notion that clients often believe, or at least want others to believe, that as in the case of depression, they are *always* depressed. Clients commonly attempt to register complaints or problems as universalized conditions by their conscious or unconscious manipulation of language and wording.

Unlike many of the interventive types of models and the strictly behaviorist models, de Shazer's solution-focused model does not direct, teach, or instruct the client. It is a model whose general idea involves the therapist asking the right kinds of questions, using a conversational style in an exceptions-based strategy, where the use of the miracle question sets the foundation for the creation of a hypothetical time zone temporarily "free" of the client's problem. As the miracle question implies, this hypothetical condition creates an extraordinary solution-talk environment. It allows the client time to select which positive events did occur and what positive conditions did exist that constituted *exceptions* to his otherwise negative script, and how the former might be bridged positively to future behavior.

The solution-focused model is structured, yet open-ended. It is future-oriented and solution-focused, yet summons the past for the purpose of obtaining necessary data for solutions-building. The model is semantically sensitive. Languaging is critical, and directional shifts from problem-talk and negativity to solution-talk and positive connotation generally rule. It is also an exceptions-finding model. Focusing on exceptions and amplifying them is a major means for building on small changes, in turn becoming the basis for negotiating more change. This highly productive two-part model consists of a first-session format and another format that is relegated to all subsequent sessions. The first session is comprised of three components: the interview, the intrasession break, and the delivery of the message to the client(s). The format's interview portion contains the heart of the model called the miracle question. Four steps denote the second format whose acronym is E.A.R.S.: eliciting, amplification, reinforcement, and starting over again at eliciting. This highly effective approach is a cleverly devised and refined amalgam of many ideas adapted from prior thinkers and originated by de Shazer, all based on sound philosophical theory and enjoying a remarkable history in over twenty years of practice.

Chapter 5

Solution-Oriented Therapy

William O'Hanlon and Michele Weiner-Davis remain the two writers most often associated with the term solution-oriented therapy (O'Hanlon, 1987; O'Hanlon & Weiner-Davis, 1989; Weiner-Davis, 1992). In contradistinction to their solution-oriented therapy, which is characterized by a broad-based style of therapeutic solution alternatives, they spend several pages in their coauthored book, In Search of Solutions (1989, pp. 21–25), specifically referring to Steve de Shazer solution-focused therapy, which is characterized by a more structured solution model. They admire de Shazer whose relatively long history of accomplishments in publications and practice had clearly set the stage for the revolution in solutions thinking in the late 70s and the ensuing decades.

Since the use of the word *solution* may easily become a source of confusion, a few words at the outset will hopefully minimize that situation. The heading, *solution-focused* therapy, a title that de Shazer himself had aptly selected, dovetails accurately into his ideology. The hyphenated term, solution-focused, accurately reflected de Shazer's challenge to the antecedent MRI model which was labeled *problem-focused*. Specifically, his use of the word *solution* acted to confute some of the theory and practice of the MRI model whose interests, by contrast, had centered on the *problem*. Since both models do *focus* on their respective targets, in one case the problem and in the other, the solution, de Shazer's deliberate continuance of the word *focused* makes sense.

By contrast, O'Hanlon and Weiner-Davis, who incorporate and assume many of de Shazer's ideas and strategies into their broader based model, fittingly named their model solution-*oriented*, thus suggesting a wider range of therapeutic options along the lines of Milton Erickson whose work precedes de Shazer. Of course, both models constitute two reflections, one more specific and the other broader, that are ultimately united under the philosophical banner of solution-thinking.

Solution-thinking had naturally evolved as a mindset, starting as early as the late 1970s with emergence of theories based on the *constructivist position* which posited, for instance, the principle that access to understanding reality in absolute terms was virtually impossible. Werner Heisenberg (1901–1976), an atomic physicist, who drew upon Kantian epistemological notions together with his own scientific observations, came to the conclusion that even with sophisticated instruments the human ability to measure has its inherent limitations. He actually went a step further than Kant in exemplifying the limitations of human understanding by drawing upon an example from his study of subatomic particles. In articulating his "Uncertainty Principle" in his study of quantum mechanics, *The Physical Principles of the Quantum Theory* (1930), Heisenberg corroborated the Kantian notion that involved our phenomenological strengths as interpreters of data as well as our phenomenological limitations. Expressed in layman's terms, he suggested that "the more accurately we know the position of an electron, the less we know about its momentum" (Bullock and Woodings, 1983, p. 317).

Thus, at the quintessential level of subatomic particles, our knowledge still remains incomplete despite the use of sophisticated equipment. It seems that the workings of the universe are so complex and interrelated at such finite levels that as we, the observers, ascertain more knowledge of one aspect of a phenomenon, we seem to sacrifice a corresponding certainty in another aspect. Yet, understanding reality is possible and achievable even if *limitedly, not absolutely,* by understanding it through a causality that is viewed from multiple perspectives rather than through a unicausal perspective.

Perceiving the universe and its components from multiple perspectives is generally called constructivism, a philosophical position where the individual observer actively "constructs" reality idiosyncratically and where society "constructs" reality collectively. It inherently involves a systemic, interrelational notion of reality that includes both the dynamics of the external world and that of the inner world of the observer. Generally, the constructivist position not only describes the universe *as process*, but also as an *interactive* process, thus necessitating multiple perspectives in attempting to understand causality.

This simple yet explosive idea in science and philosophy generated new possibilities in psychotherapy. First, it implied that one could effectively avoid the rigidities imposed by most traditional models which "mechanically" tended to emphasize a linear or unicausal causality. Secondly, it focused on finding solutions by deconstructing the problem into its component areas and working on those interrelationships. Thirdly, and most importantly, since the meanings attributed both to behavioral sequences and to perceptual patterns are inextricably embedded in human language, it then meant that skillful and well-intentioned manipulation of language for therapeutic ends could become a vehicle for change and creating solutions (O'Hanlon & Weiner-Davis, 1989, pp. 60–73).

In their promulgation of the timeliness and resourcefulness of solution-thinking, O'Hanlon and Weiner-Davis summoned the name of John Naisbitt's 1982 bestseller, *Megatrends*, which detailed "some sweeping trends...in our society" (O'Hanlon & Weiner-Davis, 1989, p. 6). In a way analogous to the spirit of Naisbitt's popular thematic literary work, they proceeded to describe a megatrend that had been occurring concurrently in the field of psychotherapy. At the cutting edge of present-day therapies, they insisted that "the trend is away from explanations, problems and pathology, and towards solutions, competence, and capabilities" (p. 6).

As for positing the practical psychotherapeutic origins of these developments, they obviously had in mind Milton Erickson. They invoke his name in the opening pages of their text, citing him unequivocally as one of the foremost pioneers in psychotherapy especially, in search of generating solutions. For them, Erickson was an exceptionally gifted psychiatrist, a memorable classic who utilized both his psychoanalytic background and his professional training to consistently emphasize "people's competence rather than their deficits, their strengths rather than their weaknesses, their possibilities rather than their limitations" (p. 1). This sweeping statement represents the essence of all solution-thinking.

Erickson was a pragmatic practitioner who emphasized positive ways to deal with client problems, spending more time during a therapy session on the "how-ness" of what worked rather than the "why-ness" of what didn't work. The recognition of Erickson's greatness has become further appreciated even more in the last decade, and it seems to be growing with our entry into the new millennium. He was responsible for much of the early foundations of solution practices and approaches in the broadest sense of the word as far back as the 1940s and 1950s.

O'Hanlon and Weiner-Davis also called attention to Abraham Maslow's incisive critical warning, dating back to the 1960s. Maslow cautioned about the excessive emphasis that the worlds of psychology and psychiatry had placed on pathology and disorders, and conversely, to the meager amount of time and effort devoted to the "healthiest specimens of human beings to learn what we want to know about people" (O'Hanlon & Weiner-Davis, p. 7). Agreeing with Maslow, O'Hanlon and Weiner-Davis unquestionably profess their deep disappointment and utter discomfort with the traditional therapies which they have generically labeled "past-oriented" therapies.

In their argument against the methods of "past-oriented" therapies, they maintained the belief, based on their own repeated client observations and research, that "having a good explanation about the nature and origin of the problem does not necessarily produce the desired therapeutic outcome" (p. 10). The conceptual premise of "insight," attributable to the psychoanalytic model, was questioned and doubted. According to Freud, insight was supposed to assist the client in effecting a major mental leap, bridging the past with a similarly patterned present pathology. The client's recognition of this leap was supposed to liberate, freeing the client of the problem. Yet, its validity in regard to long-term effectiveness had remained suspect and unproven as early as the 1950s (Eysenck, 1952).

By way of indirect proof in their advancement of solution approaches in therapy, O'Hanlon and Weiner-Davis also cite *In Search of Excellence: Lessons from America's Best-Run Companies*. This 1982 bestseller's major themes dealt with the "effective management" of companies (Peters & Waterman). O'Hanlon and Weiner-Davis suggested that this bestseller could serve as a metaphor, an analogy for understanding the most recent direction which the newer methods of psychotherapy have taken with their emphasis on success, not on failure and pathology. Here again, O'Hanlon and Weiner-Davis pointed out that the thematic content of this bestselling business book reflected and emphasized the *how-ness* of success in business, not the *why-ness* of company failures. Similarly, they fully endorsed Maslow's ideology which advocated a positively oriented, humanistic and health-oriented approach in psychology and in psychotherapy. They reiterated that psychology and psychiatry had indeed devoted far too much time to pathology and not enough time to wellness studies. It is therefore not surprising that they also refer to Thomas Szasz, a longtime advocate of a movement to depathologize many areas of psychotherapy and psychiatry (Szasz, 1961).

Tracing the evolution of solutions therapy in very broad strokes, O'Hanlon and Weiner-Davis posited the 60s as the pivotal decade upon which subsequent decades would base their developments. They underscored the beginnings of a distinct trend that amounted to many therapies systematically turning their backs on searching the past "for the roots of the present symptoms" (p. 12). They admired, in particular, the innovators of that period who had explicitly posited the new *locus* of therapy in the "here and now" and not in the past. For instance, in addition to Milton Erickson, they referred to thinkers from Gestalt therapy such as Kempler (1965, 1966, 1967, 1968, 1969), from family and strategic therapies such as Virginia Satir, Ivan Nagy, Carl Whitaker, Jay Haley, Cloe Madanes, and Mara Selvini-Palazzoli. In different ways, these innovators had initiated a dismissiveness towards prior modalities and replaced them with models that emphasized the immediately pressing psychotherapeutic need to understand symptom-maintenance or problems *in the present* (pp. 12–14).

Alluding to Bateson's cybernetic principles, O'Hanlon and Weiner-Davis reiterated the phenomenon of symptom-maintenance in the present as the fundamental event that set the stage for newer, more positive developments. This essentially represented the initial portion of the solutions trajectory, but O'Hanlon and Weiner-Davis also viewed this as transitional in the sense that the next part of the solutions trajectory moved forward away from the study of symptom-maintenance or problems in the present to a *future-oriented* solutions approach.

Solutions-thinking, clearly a phenomenon developed in the late 70s and in the 80s, received many of its influences and much of its foundation from specific notions of several preceding thinkers who had characteristically emphasized the strengths and efforts of individual clients and client family members. O'Hanlon and Weiner-Davis argue that these positive notions surely had been present in the works of Milton Erickson and in those of thinkers previously mentioned (pp. 12–13).

The solutions therapists that eventually emerged in the 80s and 90s included de Shazer (1979, 1982, 1985, 1988, 1991, 1994), O'Hanlon, Weiner-Davis, Wilk (O'Hanlon & Wilk, 1987), Gingerich (Gingerich et al., 1988), and Lipchik (1986). Of course, they subsume de Shazer's work, which historically precedes the work of the others mentioned, because of their commonly shared emphasis on solutions and their commonly expressed discomfort with past-oriented therapies.

O'Hanlon and Weiner-Davis, of course, reiterate the importance of Milton Erickson, often referred to as the "father of brief therapy," the harbinger of solution thinking (Erickson, 1954; Erickson & Rossi, 1983; Erickson, Rossi & Rossi, 1976; Rosen, 1982). Erickson's influence was so vast that he not only influenced the MRI group and its pioneering "problem" model, but also the entire group of "solutions" schools. Citing Jay

Haley (1985, Vol.1, pp. 83–84), an ardent student and admirer of Erickson's strategies, O'Hanlon and Weiner-Davis alluded to Haley's illustration of Erickson's early innovative genius in the case of a particular client, a recently hired bank employee. Of special note is how the client's long list of on-the-job mistakes was skillfully *reframed* by Erickson's *reiteration of the procedure* by which the client had made his corrections. Erickson *never* reiterated the details of the client's process of making errors.

Erickson, a master of reframing, proposed his remarkable *utilization strategy* (Erickson & Rossi, 1983)). He advanced the notion to utilize whatever a client brought into the therapy session. To Erickson, this maneuver was a crucially important operative procedure. The utilization could involve a wide range of possibilities such as a client's reported life experiences, his overt behaviors, nonverbal behaviors, beliefs, resources, attitude, talents, and sense of humor. Erickson uniquely perceived things from a different perspective. What many therapists interpreted as "pathology" in a client Erickson saw as potential "skills" and "mental mechanisms" that conceivably could be employed to generate "healing as well as problems" (O'Hanlon & Weiner-Davis, p. 15).

O'Hanlon and Weiner-Davis also alluded to Erickson's other important strategy referred to as *pseudo-orientation in time* (Erickson, 1954). This therapeutic tactic is used to "distort" time in a positive sense to allow the therapist, with or without the use of hypnosis, to let the client's thoughts move back and forth in time in a fluid manner. This served to allow successful events often neglected, forgotten, or simply minimized by the client to emerge from the client's repertoire of experiences. The events could then be utilized in a supposed "future scenario" in the search of solutions.

Thus, while substantially bypassing the use of traditionally client-chronicled, excavated past scenarios, Erickson would nonetheless visit some relevant past episodes of a client's narrative. His sole purpose, however, would be to extract from them positive elements. Erickson "distorted" time in the sense that past successes could and would become transformed in the therapeutic process as *repeatable successes* in the future. In a way reminiscent of the Aristotelian notion of the ontological interplay between "actual" and "potential," Erickson seemed to magically evoke a resemblance of that interplay whereby past sequences of positive "actuality" could be viewed and transformed into a future "potentiality."

The vivid flavor of this movement from a positive actuality to a transformational potentiality may be noted throughout Haley's studies of Erickson's work. For instance, in the discussion of diagnostic classifications, Erickson was quoted: "The problem isn't trying to adapt therapy to that particular classification, but: What *potentialities* does the patient disclose to you of their capacity to do this or do that?" (1985, Vol. 1, p. 126). To be sure, Erickson's method of pseudo-orientation in time involved a very definite exception-based maneuvering which together with the distinct use of amplification proved to be very useful both in his own style of conducting therapy and in inspiring others to create new models. The union of exceptions-based thinking with the use of amplification essentially became the centerpiece of "solutions" thinkers like de Shazer and scores of others.

Two of de Shazer's books, *Patterns of Brief Family Therapy* (1982) and *Keys to Solutions in Brief Therapy* (1985), served an important function. They became foundational texts for many solutions thinkers. Exception-based by design, the models in both texts exemplified the Ericksonian reflection of the simple philosophical belief that *no problem happens all the time* despite the client's penchant to "universalize" a problem condition or situation, thereby implying no exceptions. Hence, creatively employed exception-based strategies represented a highly strategic counterpoint to a client's all-to-common penchant to generalize an unwanted, yet apparently pervasive, psychological condition. Exception-based strategies served the very crucial purpose of seeking chinks, however small, in the client's narrative armamentarium. Thus, exceptions to the client's script would generate the inroads for solutions to take place.

In the same spirit of exception-based strategies, de Shazer developed the miracle-question technique that became the key strategy of his solution-focused model. He had, in effect, integrated Erickson's "crystal ball" question technique ("pseudo-orientation in time") with Erickson's "utilization strategy." This powerful combination was the core of a very effective model, an important centerpiece on the table of solutions approaches.

The solutions-thinkers obviously shared many commonalities. They assumed a *constructivist reality*, an epistemological position which took hold in the 70s and flourished in the 80s. De Shazer in particular, who proceeded to write many books and articles on solutions approaches, based much of his research and practice on constructivist ideology (1991, 1994). Constructivism remains a central framework for the solution-thinkers. They all subscribe to the common premise that in any given society each individual *constructs* his or her reality; collectively, individuals also *co-construct* reality in a social context of common beliefs, attitudes, and feelings.

Both the various perceptions of the external world shared by all of us and the perception of the world as experienced within each one of us constitute different attempts at constructing our understanding of reality. Constructivists believe that despite our efforts to decipher reality, it remains incredibly complex not only because of its infinite number of components, but also because reality's components are contextually interrelated and intertwined *ad infinitum*, much like a limitless spider web. Since the human mind does not have the capability to understand infinity, it is incapable of divining reality in its totality. As a corollary, human speech or language, despite its obvious merits in the evolutionary chain of expression, also remains correspondingly limited, precisely because of this vast and overwhelmingly complex interrelationship that defines reality.

Again, our perceptions and understanding of both spheres, the commonly shared external world and our individual interior world, are semantically defined and described by human language, and they too are also subject to language's limitations. Admittedly, an individual can proceed only so far in the process of deciphering, or untangling, to make sense of the incredibly vast and detailed web of reality. Thus, it remains a constructivist premise that reality is incapable of being understood as an absolute because of the inherent limitations of human language and human thinking.

Reality, then, can only be understood, at best, in a way that approaches or approximates what reality appears to be according to the available data and information that we obtain and are able to process by our cognition and intuition. This relatively new Kantian epistemology confutes much of the Western world's prior epistemology. In antecedent thinking, dating back to the ancients such as Aristotle, it was generally assumed in philosophy that human language was essentially capable of fulfilling an Aristotelian "mirroring" of reality. However, with the advent of Hume and Kant, over two hundred years ago, the traditional Aristotelian perspective and its subsequent variations were shown to be limited and faulty.

The new Kantian position went on to describe more accurately not only our limitations in regard to how we learn, but also how we process our notions of reality and how we approach an understanding of reality. With the passing of time and the assimilation of this Kantian perspective, a slowly paced but marked revolution in epistemology began to take hold. Kant called his revolutionary philosophical innovation transcendental idealism. It meant that knowledge could only be a synthesis and a relative product of consciousness, *not* an absolute. The constructivist approach, a twentieth-century variation on the original Kantian epistemological matrix, stated that through the mind's ongoing processing of newly available information which confutes or confirms and enlarges our prior experiences, we interpret and continually give fresh meaning to the world around us. Understanding reality, then, is always subject to change as more information, hopefully more accurate than prior data, becomes available. It entails confirming or changing the meanings which we had previously ascribed to events and relationships of all kinds.

This, of course, implies the necessity of individual and collective willingness to subscribe to making those changes. Our phenomenological processes, which include our perceptions and ascriptions of meaning, could and would become an ongoing re-interpretation and development provided that there was a willing interest, a necessity and, particularly, a change in data. Yet perceptions, meanings, and interpretations are all embedded in the language we use to communicate. Hence, reality is posited as a reflection upon reality, *not a copy of reality*. It is an ongoing interactive process between the observer and observed phenomena, necessarily expressed through the medium of language. This Kantian position has had its admirers and advocates who went on to further develop and move in new directions in the past two hundred years. Generally speaking, however, the first half of twentieth-century psychology's assimilation of even the most fundamental Kantian epistemological positions was essentially slow. Yet, by mid-century that did change (Kelly, 1963).

Many other thinkers also helped set the stage for creating some of the underpinnings of today's modern forms of therapy. These forms presume some fundamental ideas regarding reality as process where systemic flux, human behavior, and cognition reflect *patterned relationships*. Through the efforts of philosophers like Alfred North Whitehead (1861–1947) and his philosophy of *organism*, which metaphorically described the study of the universe as a "patterned process of events," the concept of "process" as we use it today had its philosophical precursor. Likewise, Ludwig Wittgenstein (1889-1951), whose works in the study of language in the area of logical analysis, drew some important reactions. While he questioned many of humanity's unexamined assumptions and complacencies, he offered some useful tools for deconstructing language. De Shazer, a proponent of Wittgenstein's thought, made the latter's philosophical ideas available to the therapeutic community. For modern therapists, much of Wittgenstein's critical analysis of language has resulted in offering a greater sense of interviewing freedom and flexibility through the awareness of linguistic and logical anomalies.

In a very specific sense, beginning with Kant's initial work in epistemology, reality could no longer be looked upon as a mirrored copy, or in absolute, mechanistic terms. This was not because the truth didn't exist, as a nihilistic perspective might suggest, but because we can only approach the truth whose understanding improves only to the extent that new and more accurate information becomes available. Along the way to truth, reality becomes, in an interpretative sense, a "negotiable" entity both in social intercourse and in therapeutic settings. This is because language, no doubt the shared medium of expression in deciphering reality, is, in turn, embedded with idiosyncratic semantics of personal experiences and socially-driven ideological ascriptions of meaning dictated by any given culture at any given point in time. Thus, reality essentially consists of uncertainties and relative certainties.

Total agreement in any specific area on any specific thing or situation, if it indeed were to exist, would constitute the exception and not the rule. However, on the positive side, if a newly revised perception of reality and a freshly structured perception of the therapeutic problem present the client with emerging "negotiable" possibilities, O'Hanlon and Weiner-Davis argue that as therapists "one might as well negotiate a problem that is possible-even easy-to solve" (p. 55). This constructivist-inspired approach, based on an ultimately Kantian-informed position, though couched in deconstructive solution-oriented tactics, contains many powerful tools for achieving positive outcomes.

Armed with this new approach, one can begin to see how a purely "past-oriented" or excavational therapy has deluded itself all along into believing that simply devising unicausal patterns could effect a sustained therapeutic change. Many solutions practitioners who had the opportunity to practice both forms of therapy, future-oriented and past-oriented, have affirmed repeatedly that psychoanalytic *insight* presented only temporary usefulness at best. Essentially, psychoanalytic insight's major weakness was that it offered an explanation without a corresponding procedure to implement change. The benefits of experiencing insight in no way assured the client real and effective change in life (Snyder & White, 1982).

Since problems are embedded in language, which is part of a greater reality that is defined by multicausality, language may be used as a tool to *negotiate* a solution. For instance, when supportive evidence elicited from the client's own revelations in therapy seems to indicate the high probability of a different interpretation, such as alternative or "double" descriptions to a client's script (positive data that confute the client's negative script), the therapist may seize that opportunity to perform some very constructive maneuvers such as *reframing* old materials into a newer and more positive perspective. Even a failed but well-intentioned effort might be viewed and validated through *positive connotation* as valued and noteworthy. Naturally, *presuppositional questions* that by definition seek to empower and elicit positive responses may be used. The open-endedness of such questions as "What worked for you in the past?" and "What will work for you in the future?" seeks to encourage and promote strength.

Solutions ideology also emphasizes the notion that the client is the biographical "expert" on himself. Surely the client knows all the major and minor events in his life together with all their details. Assuring the client of his expertise in this precinct of reality is not only empowering, but also catalytic for the forward motion of therapeutic conversation. Because of this empowerment during the course of therapy, the client is more apt to utter all kinds of biographical data, which though seeming as offhand remarks, may yield important and often vital information. In particular, the client might unwittingly disclose behaviors, perceptions, or events that he has minimized or benignly neglected because they seemed apparently irrelevant. Yet much of that kind of client data presented might very well be "exceptions" to the client script. In the attentive ears of the therapist, such positive data emanating from the client could be the foundation for therapeutic opportunities to effect change.

In describing the major aspects of their solution-oriented therapy (pp. 26–50), O'Hanlon and Weiner-Davis present a useful composite of many prior and contemporaneous tactics and thoughts. While their premises incorporate many of de Shazer's ideas, the range of their strategies constitutes a uniquely conceived, broader base of therapeutic options within the realm of a solution philosophy. On the other hand, they also present outright confutations of many prevalent attitudes or theories in other modalities. Again, while employing many ideas from family therapy, they also point out their unacceptable differences. Of course, many considerations become a matter of emphasis or degree.

First, they have grave reservations in regard to the view held both in orthodox Freudian and psychodynamic thought and in some family/interactional approaches regarding their whole notion of symptomology and its implications. Those schools possess the common assumption that *symptoms* represent some "deep, underlying cause," much like the visible part of an "iceberg" represents a much larger reality beneath. The idea of symptom originated, in short, as a medical notion and implied as a corollary that it was not wise to treat the "symptom" unless one had an understanding of its underlying causalities (p. 27). This further implied for the therapist, then, the necessity of therapeutic excavation of sorts in psychoanalysis or in a family study of symptomology to derive "the source or true nature of the problem" (p. 27).

In effect, this conviction is reified, O'Hanlon and Weiner-Davis contend, both in psychoanalysis and in some family therapies because those schools believe that symptoms serve necessarily "some intrapsychic function" in the case of the former and some "family or interactional function" in the case of the latter. They also insist that those ideas seem to complicate and irritate the process of therapy even further. They argue that given those sets of beliefs, medical and familial symptomology, it follows that attempts at a scenario that include programmatic symptom removal without the proper care of handling its "function" would inevitably lead to new symptoms labeled symptom substitution (p. 28). O'Hanlon and Weiner Davis, therefore, do not subscribe to this situation as a necessary condition since it seems to indicate a lose/lose situation. According to them, that idea "serves no purpose" in therapy.

This, however, should not imply that there aren't "causes" or causal relationships. It simply means that causality in human relationships is often difficult to grasp and assess, and equally difficult to confirm even with an abundance of therapeutic time. O'Hanlon and Weiner-Davis view the use of symptom analysis and its related terminology as simply not useful. The coauthors cite the example of Alby Singer, the male lead character in Woody Allen's well-known classic film, *Annie Hall*. Humorously, Alby reveals to Annie that he's been in analysis for thirteen years, and he's still willing to give it seven more years. But if by then he doesn't get better, he'll be ready for Lourdes (pp. 10–11).

No doubt, this comic hyperbole was meant to depict the ineffectiveness and myopic qualities of endless psychoanalysis. Yet, this kind of psychological scenario, albeit extreme, was based on the medical notion of symptoms and on the search for their causes in the past, particularly childhood trauma. Obviously, there are many clients, especially those for whom money is no object, who do continue for many long years in psychoanalysis to little or no avail. One wonders why this occurs and to what purpose. Perhaps much of it may be attributable to the need for friendship in the guise of "going for analysis."

O'Hanlon and Weiner-Davis also take issue with the term: *resistance*. Taking their lead from de Shazer's work, they reiterate some very controversial solution-oriented ideas about the concept of client resistance. The term resistance, invented by Freud, had its day in the sun, but O'Hanlon and Weiner-Davis believe that many therapists, who still persist in its use both as a strictly defined Freudian term and as a broad *negative* mindset, make therapeutic practice all the more difficult for themselves.

While theoretically resistance once fit logically into the psychoanalytic paradigm, it has effected, since its inception, an inordinate influence on psychotherapy. In its original concept, resistance was to reflect the ambivalent condition of a patient's intrapsychic processes. Freud had proposed the paradoxical notion that the patient on the one hand wanted resolution to a problem and, on the other, opposed the change because of the anticipated anxieties that change would entail. Understood in this strict context, resistance made sense.

From their solutions perspective, the coauthors believe that today the concept of resistance as a mindset is not particularly useful in the newer, future-oriented therapies whose inspiration involves the concept of client empowerment. In essence, it is not a question of whether resistance exists or not. It is more a matter of focus, relevance, and usefulness. Admittedly, O'Hanlon and Weiner-Davis believe that if you, as a therapist, are focused and intent on seeking resistance, "you will almost certainly be able to find something that looks like it" (p. 29). In the solution-oriented models, the main focus lies in bypassing resistance, symptoms-search, and relinquishing the once obligatory journey to their respective meanings. While the therapeutic dialogue advances into areas involving the discovering of solutions, such a process leaves little room for resistance-talk. Thus, resistance is deemed unnecessary and counterproductive.

Because solution-oriented therapy is by design one of the briefest therapies, O'Hanlon and Weiner-Davis view every particular therapy session as potentially the last session for the client *if* during that session a satisfactory solution to the problem has been achieved. Taking their lead from de Shazer, their daring and innovating posture flies in the face of conventional wisdom in regard to treatment time.

O'Hanlon and Weiner-Davis point out that the reasons why the traditional approaches require longer treatment duration may be traced to the underpinnings of their strategies which were based on the "unsubstantiated" yet persistent notions that ultimately revert to the influence of the medical model and its emphasis on past trauma, "pathology and deficits" (p. 30). This suggests analogically that problems, and certainly deep problems, will necessarily require proportionately longer amounts of time. The unnecessary emphasis on medically-based premises also generated a scenario whereby many therapies unwittingly seemed to doom their efforts by their very notions. They become self-fulfilling prophecies of inevitable failure, exacerbating the course of therapy in the inordinate search for the pathological and the deficient. This scenario is based on general assumptions and not fact. Depending on the individual client, that assumption may become a powerfully insidious bias costing the client inordinate amounts of time and money.

Solution-oriented therapy does recognize the importance of exercising therapeutic flexibility, as in the case of many clients who come to therapy and insist on delineating their "pathology" as influenced by media cues, cultural influences, or prior therapeutic experiences. However, solution-oriented therapy does not invite or encourage the use of pathology-talk or problem-talk for extended periods of time.

The coauthors, in marshalling enthusiasm for their model, cite some historically relevant, well-designed, critical research dating back to the 60s dealing with laboratory rats (Burnham, 1966). In addition, they gleaned significant findings in the meta-analytical research of Rosenthal (1966) which included Burnham's experiments. Rosenthal's work dealing with the nature of experimenter influence confirmed consistently that "the experimenter's expectations influenced the outcome of the experiment" (O'Hanlon & Weiner Davis, 1989, p. 33). In a novel twist in interpretation, O'Hanlon and Weiner-Davis then asked: *What happens if* the implications of the results of experimenter *expectancy* research get extrapolated and applied to doing therapy? How could the condition of influence be useful to the therapist? What operative good or utility could be derived from that knowledge in the way one does therapy?

The coauthors now believe that much was derived from such research results. They cite many examples of their own work in psychotherapy and the work of many others in the medical/physical areas such as Achterberg's *Imagery in Healing* (1985) and Norman Cousin (*The Healing Heart,* 1983) at the Pain Clinic in California. They conclude from the studies that expectancy "biases" can be manipulated and become very useful for the client (O'Hanlon & Weiner-Davis, 1989, p. 33). "Since what you expect influences what you get, solution-oriented therapists maintain those presuppositions that enhance client-therapist cooperation, empower the client, and make our work more effective and enjoyable" (p. 34). Put succinctly, since what a therapist expects in the course of therapy influences what is obtained in the relationship with the client, solution-oriented therapists, in a real sense, help create positive self-fulfilling prophecies.

In the underlying body of assumptions, solution-oriented thinkers profess the operative belief that clients usually have the "skills and resources" to handle their problems. Caught in the immediacy of their problems, however, clients can often forget how to better manage their situation, or perhaps, they often cannot create the conditions for eliminating those problems. Now enters the therapist. His or her job consists of helping the client recall those needed talents and abilities. Whenever the client recalls some of his or her strengths, that moment empowers the client and moves the therapy forward. This also becomes a therapeutic turning point whereby client and therapist together begin the discussion of transforming the recollection of past strengths into future positive behaviors. Past actuality becomes shaped into future potentiality. Echoing in the background of this scenario is Erickson's work whose pioneering efforts influenced the creation of a body of research, literature, case histories, and follow-up studies (Coyne, 1985, pp. 60–61) to which O'Hanlon and Weiner-Davis subscribe.

Solution-oriented thinkers believe that change, as a general condition of life, is essentially a constant and ongoing process. Within any given span of time, change, unrecognized or not, is occurring all the time at different levels, and is sometimes more visible than others. Similarly, within the client's life, change and the opportunities for change often go by unnoticed or remain invisible to the client. Understandably, this kind of invisibility can occur easily. For one thing, clients are intent on the problem, its difficulties, and its implications. Depending on the nature of the problem, they may also be intent on the simple ontological problem of personal survivability in the process. These things usually furnish a certain aura of defensiveness and protectiveness around a client. Blind spots mushroom everywhere, making change evasive to the eye (O'Hanlon & Weiner-Davis, 1989, pp. 35–40).

Following the logic of the model, it therefore becomes the "therapist's job to identify and amplify change," very much in the spirit of Bateson's well-known dictum in regard to performing good therapy to search for a "difference that makes a difference." Solution-oriented therapy's philosophy emphasizes precisely that line of reasoning. "In the smorgasbord of information supplied to us by our clients, we think it important to focus on what seems to be working, however small, to label it as worthwhile, and to work toward amplifying it" (p. 37).

In regard to client information and to the therapeutic processing of that information for timely and positive outcomes, it is then not surprising that this model does not deem it necessary "to know a great deal about the complaint in order to resolve it" (p. 38). Similarly, "it is not necessary to know the cause or function of a complaint to resolve it" (p. 40). Together these bold statements represent two strategic principles working in tandem which serve to emphasize the quintessential search for positive change, however small, and then its amplification.

The vast amounts of time and energy once devoted by the more traditional therapies to past-oriented search, clinical excavation and retrospective exposition of client scenarios become transformed by solution-oriented therapy into exception-based approaches and their related amplification shaped into future-oriented, action-based scenarios. Clearly, if the focus of therapy is "mainly on problems and pathology, both therapists and clients perceive problems and pathology" (p. 39). By the same token, if "the focus of inquiry and discussion is on solutions and abilities, those images dominate" (p. 39).

Perhaps, to the practitioners of the more traditionally-oriented therapeutic modalities, one of the most challenging premises of solution-oriented therapy regards not only its exception-based design, but also its notion that only little change is necessary to begin effective treatment. Flying in the face of conventional wisdom and traditional inquiry that had usually focused on pathology and deficits, the solution-oriented approach finds its strength in reiterating Erickson's metaphor of the snowballing effect of change, even small change (p. 42). Also, citing three specific follow-up studies performed at the MRI, BFTC, and McHenry County, Illinois, Youth Service Bureau, the coauthors present a convincing argument that their solutions approach, which focuses on small change plus amplification, can be effective.

The design of the solution-oriented model, which encourages client empowerment, also includes the idea that it is only the client who can truly decide on identifying what is the goal for any given therapeutic treatment. Since family problems, rules, and values vary, solution-oriented therapists respect the uniqueness of the client's situation, the problem, and the goal desired by the client. In short, with few exceptions, such as in setting unrealistic goals, or in abuse situations regarding children, a spouse, or the elderly, solution thinkers believe that there isn't any one "correct" way to resolve a problem.

Similarly, while it is the therapist who prompts the ongoing process of eliciting pertinent information from the client, it is the client who offers the building materials, the exceptions, on which the solutions are built. In this respect, then, it is through the dialogue and the interaction that both therapist and client systemically "co-create" newer and more meaningful avenues that will lead to constructing solutions. In this solutions scenario the client is the "expert" on his problem and on the data that will lead to the solution. The therapist becomes the "expert" in facilitating that possibility.

Affirming their constructivist view of reality, which assumes a multicausal explanation of events and behaviors, O'Hanlon and Weiner-Davis boldly assert that "there is no one *right* way to view things" (p. 46). Since it is impossible to verify what is the "correct" or exact nature of events and behaviors, it becomes more important to validate each client's experience, then select those perspectives that seem more useful for the client's success.

While we do not think that there are any correct or incorrect points of view, we do believe that there are more or less useful viewpoints. That is, the views that people hold about their problems enhance or diminish the likelihood of solution. Useful views offer an escape from the psychological webs people weave. Views that keep them stuck are simply not useful. (p. 47)

Since the preliminary meanings that clients attribute to behavior often "limit the range of alternatives they will use to deal with a situation," (p. 48) the therapist needs to facilitate the emergence of newer meanings and interpretations in the ongoing dialogue in the search for solutions. Here again, once an alternative, or reframe, is found to replace an ineffective one, the change needed does not have to be a large one. For instance, in a protracted misunderstanding between father and son, often a small initial change in perception or in behavior on behalf of one of the clients can, in turn, change the whole nature of their apparently troubled situation.

Even in the most difficult situations, change can be realized if the process of therapy is addressed to the "possible and the changeable," rather than to globally "impossible and intractable." For instance, the coauthors are highly critical of the "current fads in therapy" such as the many overly subscribed psychiatric diagnosis of certain disorders like borderline personality disorder for which surveys have not found anyone "cured" of this disorder. Similarly, another abused and faddish psychiatric category, dependent personality disorder, is following the same confused course.

In sharp contrast to psychiatry's penchant for establishing disorders, syndromes, and new personality constructs, the coauthors reiterate one of their main solutions premises: goals must be "fairly well defined" and "realizable within a reasonable amount of time" (p. 49). Stated bluntly, O'Hanlon and Weiner-Davis do affirm what are the realistic, yet healthy, "limitations" of the solution-oriented approach. "To cure a borderline personality is beyond our ken, but to help a person get a job or make friends or have a satisfying sexual relationship or refrain from cutting herself is well within our abilities" (pp. 49–50).

In order to perform the model effectively, the coauthors emphasize those elements of the client's affect, behaviors, and cognition that "seem most changeable." Conversely, they eschew "psychological constructs not useful for change" (p. 50). Thus, traditionally founded personality constructs, such as personality types and disorders defined by psychiatry, serve only to initially assist the solution-oriented therapist in appreciating the apparent complexity of the problems affecting clients. In order to effect change, O'Hanlon and Weiner-Davis then assert that "a whole new set of constructs is needed to help people change" (p. 50). In sharp contrast to many models, having to create these new constructs and their related strategies to establish a shift in focus toward achievable therapeutic ends might explain why many opponents of solution-oriented therapy find it to be too radical a model.

Philosophically, the solution-approach origins and their seminal ideas remain tied to the constructivist view that de Shazer espoused as early as the mid-70s (1974, 1975) and then later in his *Keys to Solution in Brief Therapy* (1985). Eventually in 1991 in *Putting Difference to Work*, de Shazer developed, still further, the constructivist position in the area of solutions-based therapies. In short, the constructivist dictum, so essential to solution-thinking, states unequivocally that *"reality arises from consensual linguistic processes"* (1991, p. 44). Taking his lead from Wittgenstein, de Shazer approached the understanding of reality through the linguistic manipulations of language, how humans have employed it and how they continue to do so. Language, understood in its broadest sense, is the "currency" in the marketplace of reality. It is what humans share and what they learn to manipulate for their individual and collective needs. Humans have used and continue to use language to generate descriptions and interpretations of reality. As a quintessential premise of constructivism, de Shazer states, "Reality, or better, realities are invented rather than discovered; humans build the worlds in which they live" (p. 44).

This epistemological or constructivist posture has many implications. O'Hanlon and Weiner-Davis reiterate that in performing psychotherapy it is necessary to dismiss the medical model whose attendant analogies tend to equate a visit to a physician's office with that of a visit to a psychotherapist. Clearly, the coauthors view the two situations quite differently. For instance, in order to make a proper diagnosis and employ a treatment, a physician must first understand the symptoms. Without symptom assessment, proper diagnosis and treatment becomes impossible. Asking the patient specific questions about the illness or the infirmity *in a medical context* remains essential. The origin of the illness and the symptomology obviously represent the standard medical model. Unfortunately, the standard medical model has influenced the psychological interviewing model for decades in many detrimental ways. The former has readily provided much of the language, the metaphors and nomenclature for the latter. Yet the coauthors contend that psychotherapy, when examined in its essence, truly represents quite a different scenario. And here Thomas Szasz, a long-time advocate to depathologize mental problems, would most likely agree with O'Hanlon and Weiner-Davis views below.

Therapy is different. The complaints clients bring to treatment are not like broken bones or sore throats. As therapists we strongly influence clients' perceptions and experience of their situations during the interview process. What we choose to focus upon, what we choose to ignore, the way in which we word our questions, whether we decide to interrupt or remain silentCall help shape the picture of the client's situation. (p. 52)

Psychotherapeutic interaction functions are an interplay of *consensual linguistic processes. What* is said and *how* it is said become highly important components in the therapeutic dialogue. These remain especially crucial in the initial session where the client complaint is shaped as to its definition, its process, and its patterns. What the therapist says and how she or he addresses the client's complaint, no doubt, will lead "into a completely different realm of discourse" (p. 53). Right from the outset and in all subsequent sessions, *what* the therapist focuses upon in the interview, *what* is

202 • *Breakthroughs in Six Brief Psychotherapies*

omitted and *how* those choices become handled, all acquire the status of highly selective considerations that directly effect the direction and flow of the psychotherapy.

"Reality" is not a fixed, static given. It is influenced by our cultures and the interactions we have with one another. It is influenced by the language we speak, the words we use, the world views we share that are reflected in those words. It is with this in mind that we stress that therapy is like a little culture or society created in the session. This culture will, in our view, greatly influence the clients' feelings, thoughts, reports, and perceptions. (p. 55)

To reflect the reciprocal influence of psychotherapist and client, O'Hanlon and Weiner-Davis humorously ask a rhetorical question. Isn't it interesting that when a client leaves the office of a behavioral psychologist, the client almost always leaves that session with a behavioral problem? A client almost always leaves a psychoanalyst's office with issues unresolved from childhood, most likely oedipal. Obviously, therapy models, based on their own unique premises, create their own unique strategies and approaches. Regretfully, they also create their own pitfalls. Metaphorically, models in general create a kind of self-imposed limitation, a tunnel vision. Once again, one can almost hear echoing in the background the voice of Carl Whitaker whose caveat alerted us against the effect of being wedded to one's model (1976). He suggested, instead, a vigilant openness to changing strategy despite one's adherence to a particular model.

Generally, the act of adhering to a model does represent a healthy and desirable consistency, a positive attribute of performing therapy. Yet, the coauthors present the paradox that rigid adherence to a model's strategy, especially if the model is highly concentrated and structured, may unwittingly lead to further reification of the client's reality and thus his problem. The reiterative effect makes the problem become more concrete since the effect involves a surreptitiously tacit approval of the client's *perceived permanence of the problem.* It amounts to the therapist buying into the universality of the client's script. In effect, the problem becomes more increasingly "real" through the therapist/client interaction along this reifying vein. The counterproductive result of this reification, substantiated by the reiteration of client failures or inabilities, involves another terrible paradox of tacitly abetting the client in becoming, more and more, an "expert" on his own failures.

By contrast, solution-oriented therapy offers a way out of this dilemma. It contends that in minimizing the reification of client problems, the more favorable approach would involve emphasizing solutions strategies in the therapeutic interaction. This involves the way the problem is perceived jointly by therapist and client in their dialogic relationship and the way their ongoing interaction shapes and molds itself towards solutions, not towards reification of the problem.

O'Hanlon and Weiner-Davis suggest, both in the Introduction and in Chapter One of their book, the analogy between effecting good therapy and the ways of managing successful businesses. In their allusion to the business world, they reiterate the undeniable fact that one learns more by the lessons of business success than by business failures. It is a matter of nuance, but it is an important distinction. A person will learn more from reading about *how* highly successful companies have managed to realize much of their potential than from studying those companies that have failed (O'Hanlon & Weiner-Davis, 1989, pp. 6–11). Similarly, therapy can be briefer and more effective if therapist and client collaborate on the client's strengths and resources rather than focusing on the client's failures.

Thus, using the solution-oriented strategy of non-reification of the complaint, once the initial identification process of the complaint or problem is achieved, the coauthors have observed that invariably "different data also emerge during the assessment process, leading to different definitions of the problem" (p. 54). With a newer and less reified and a less embedded definition of the problem, it often means that an easier "negotiation" can take place in establishing a process towards a solution (p. 55).

As a corollary to the strategy of non-reification of the problem, solution thinkers do not care to search for the so-called "real problem," especially if that notion would imply any kind of permanence, suggesting fixed, static, categorical postures of feelings, thoughts and behaviors. They simply do not believe that such a condition "exists as a fixed entity" (p. 56). From a constructivist perspective, reality is perceived, instead, as "fluid" and in constant flux. If this crucial aspect of non-reification of client problem is actively pursued and incorporated into the therapeutic process, then the client's cosmos becomes a more "negotiable" situation establishing a new and positive interplay in the client and therapist dialogue, thus creating a new *system*. This new system consists not only of the client's presenting problem and the script of the client's experiences, but also of the newly emerging development viewed as a *co-creation* that will benefit the client.

According to O'Hanlon and Weiner-Davis, implicit in the overall design of solution-oriented thinking is the important assumption that it becomes easier "to negotiate a therapeutic reality that dissolves the idea" of the persistence and universality of the "problem" (p. 57). The solution-oriented therapist achieves this result essentially through an exception-based modality together with a broad-based spectrum of strategies where the therapist strategically develops and conveys the notion of *empowerment* to the client precisely through the client's positive revelation in the *exception* to his ostensibly negative script. By the kinds of quality questions the therapist poses to the client, the latter is assured and encouraged to search from within his strengths and abilities to deal with the problem.

The evolution of solution-oriented therapy consists of a broad spectrum of possibilities, incorporating many essential strategies from Erickson, many strategic notions from Haley and from the MRI, the Milan model, and, of course, many solution-focused ideas from de Shazer. Generally speaking, solution-oriented therapy presents a style of interviewing that is probably among the most fluid and protean of the modern brief therapies. Its approach is pragmatic and wholesomely inclusive of other modalities' specific practices that do not center on pathology and excavational strategies.

Exception-based thinking is grounded in the strategy of processing with the client the times when the problem or complaint did *not* exist, or at least appeared more manageable. In the solution-focused model, often referred to as the Milwaukee model (Steve de Shazer, Insoo Kim Berg and associates), exception-based thinking along with the miracle question constitute the inner core of this successful modality. While therapeutically flexible and applicable to many difficult problem areas including drug-use chronicity, this model is basically structured.

By contrast, the solution-oriented model as espoused by O'Hanlon and Weiner-Davis, while also being very effective and actually inclusive of the Milwaukee model, presents an interviewing style whose strategies present some notably different and somewhat less structured approaches. In addition to exceptions-based strategies, much of this model's efforts involve various approaches in the area of languaging, i.e., paying close attention to client wording and effecting change through a variety of language manipulation techniques.

Generally the interview begins by *joining* with the client. However, joining for solution-oriented therapists has a special meaning well beyond that of the traditionally immediate accommodation of the client. It also involves the use of *matching the client's language*, which is part of the *languaging techniques*. Once the client is accommodated, joining, in the sense of matching, becomes an immediately active stance implying not only the therapist's committed awareness of the client's specific use of language, but also the therapist's deliberate, linguistically empathetic involvement with the client's cosmos through the client's language style.

The concept of matching presents a strategy that places the therapist empathetically in a metaphoric "descent" into the client's cosmos, i.e., learning the client's feelings, cognition, and behaviors. It is a masterful strategy that vividly recalls many Ericksonian examples. In many ways, it is also reminiscent of Whitaker's innovative style, described as an experiential descent into "bilateral states of ego consciousness" (Whitaker & Malone, 1953). It was Whitaker who took pains to study the language of clients, particularly their use of metaphors, which led to the inchoate yet palpable vestibule of a client's cosmos.

For the solution-oriented thinkers then, after joining with the client, there ensues the process of identifying the complaint or problem where the initial key issue is to obtain a clear and specific picture of the complaint or problem. Generically generated descriptive labels and pathological labels will not do. Abstractions or labels of sorts often demonstrate little and prove nothing. At best, they are mild indicators, not descriptors. Thus, clients who present themselves summarily as depressed, borderline, phobic, sexually addicted, and the like, must re-address their sense of problem definition and must present a *behaviorally-specific* description. They must make an attempt to contextualize the nature of their complaint. It is only when specificity of the complaint is sufficiently clear that the therapist can begin to adequately relate to the client's complaint.

The solution-oriented model usually begins with the assumption that in the process of identifying the problem "it is possible to negotiate a therapeutic reality that dissolves" the notion that there is a problem. It has been a fairly common phenomenon in this model that a well-conducted assessment of the problem can often lead to a "problem dissolution" at a very early stage. This usually happens in the first session during the process of identifying the behavioral specificity of the problem (pp. 56–58).

This is most often the result of a combination of a very manageable presenting problem and of good interviewing that has involved, on the one hand, obtaining a clear problem-definition and, on the other, an effective use of interventive style questions. This process usually concludes when the client, in describing the problem's specifics in behavioral terms, suddenly realizes that there really wasn't any problem at all.

If the problem cannot be dissolved or resolved, the next phase involves negotiating a solvable problem. Once this is achieved, there begins the search for *exceptions* and their *amplification*. Whenever an exception is found, it implicitly involves examining the *differences* between the times when the complaint was present and those times when the complaint was either non-existent or simply more manageable. The exception-based strategy employed by solution-oriented therapists represents a very broad-based heading because within it are subsumed many other strategies.

At the beginning of exception-finding sequences, solution-oriented therapy usually includes questions regarding possible *pre-treatment changes*. These are defined as positive changes that the client recalls having taken place between the time that a final decision was made to seek therapy, usually indicated by a phone call for an appointment, and the client's arrival at the therapy session. From available research, it appears that changes do occur quite frequently for many clients during this pretreatment period. The research indicates that they are probably due to a variety of reasons, but usually center upon many clients' initiating proactive steps without the benefits of therapy. These steps may involve either beginning to resolve their problems or being able to manage them better, relieved, of course, that now an appointment has finally been made (Weiner-Davis et al., 1987). O'Hanlon & Weiner-Davis point out that this aforementioned study on pretreatment change had been corroborated by another study that preceded it just a year prior in Australia (Birch & Piglet, 1986).

Once exception-based questions begin, exceptions are sought first in the form of pretreatment changes and later in subsequent interviewing sequences. In the process of posing exception-based questions, the therapist employs two major, general strategies, *matching* and *presuppositional questions*. Each is "fluid," dynamic and non-prescriptive. In fact, these strategies are the unique, identifying characteristics of solution-oriented therapy. *Matching* represents the importance that solution-oriented therapy assigns to empathetically-based linguistic sensitivity. *Presuppositional questions* represent the importance that solution-oriented therapy assigns to *interventive postures* suggested by the questioning.

The strategy of *presuppositional questions* presents an effective *interventive approach* that in a subtle way propels the client's thinking into a future scenario where the problem hypothetically does not "exist" as such. In many ways, like the use of the miracle question or the "crystal ball" techniques, already discussed at length in Chapter 5, presuppositional questions invoke the imagining of a future time where the client might experience a sense of having "new space" wherein the problem is momentarily absent. In the form of a shortcut, presuppositional questions have embedded within them the assumption of a miracle-question scenario.

Especially for clients who are inextricably stuck with their old scripts, presuppositional questions metaphorically offer "new space," a temporarily "problem-free" environment for clearer and more positive thinking. It represents a new twist on the use and manipulation of language implicitly involving an imagined existence of *change* as *already having taken place* as, for instance, in a presuppositional question like "When the problem is gone, what would be the first sign you would notice?" The problem becomes subsumed as non-existent, and the client can begin to think about change as if it were a fact, not merely a wish.

In the internal interplay between two strongly related words "if" and "when," the question is posed so that the focus is not so much on *if* change will take place, but *when* change has taken place, what will it be like? A crucial component to this approach involves the point at which the client answers this and similar presuppositional questions. At that point, he or she is already *thinking and talking* in the language of "change," not doing problem-talk, but doing change-talk.

This represents a therapeutic posture that is the diametric opposite to the more traditional excavational approaches which usually operate with a "spiraling down" effect into the depths of the problem area, offering little or no redemption from the problem. Presuppositional questions, by contrast, seem to suggest the very opposite, a spiraling up effect that O'Hanlon and Weiner-Davis call a "benevolent spiral." Gingerich, de Shazer and Weiner-Davis had already labeled this phenomenon, i.e., talking along the avenues of change, as "change talk" (1988). It represents a posture that in turn utilizes to its advantage another phenomenon called self-fulfilling-prophecies. Gingerich and his associates had established in their 1988 behavioral study a positive correlation between presuppositional "change talk" questions and positive treatment outcomes.

The "change talk" strategy invoked by presuppositional questions represents the positive side of the coin whose opposite side, "problem talk" strategy, abounds with negatives. Studies, such as the one by Snyder and White (1982), presented a scenario that convincingly showed that depressed clients' unrelenting elaborative "problem talk" about their past trauma and pain only tended to make them more depressed in therapy. This represented another clear instance of the ineffective nature of past-oriented approaches. Indirectly, this study had the definite effect in lending more credence to those therapies that would focus on "change talk."

In essence, presuppositional questions employed in solutions therapy involve focusing on the very critical role that *expectations* play in our lives. To a significant degree, what one expects in life has an affect on what one ultimately receives. While one's expectations are not absolutes in themselves, they represent significant components in that part of one's mental life that deals with orientation and motivation toward one's goals. Solution-oriented therapists strongly believe that in therapy client expectations play a crucial role in effecting positive outcomes. Words represent the common "currency" in the interactive roles and relationship between client and therapist. How they are employed and how they relate to ideas, feelings, and behaviors represent the pivotal factor in fostering positive outcome expectations that in turn help pave the way to positive results.

If a therapist asks, "What will be different in your life when therapy is successful?", he or she is not merely seeking information but also implicitly introducing the idea that therapy will be successful. [However,] when one opens the therapy session with the question, "What problem can I help you with?" or "What do you see as the problem?", it is presumed that there is a problem…On the other hand, "What brings you here?" does not presume the existence of a problem. (O'Hanlon & Weiner-Davis, p. 61)

Presuppositional questions come in two basic kinds, both considered interventive in nature. First, there is one that immediately utilizes data already furnished by the client, an established exception to the client script, which reflects some kind of positive change as already having taken place. In this case, the focus of the presuppositional questions becomes one of *amplifying* a pre-existing change, or an exception-based episode, into a future context. This remains particularly useful since the pre-existing change becomes an immediate foundation, however small, on which to build new scenarios in the future.

The following represent examples where prior positive exceptions existed and the therapist poses presuppositional questions to amplify that condition in a future scenario. "What might *another small sign* be that would indicate to you in the coming weeks that things are finally changing?" "When you realize you're *doing more of the right things* next week, who will be the first one to notice those changes?" "When you see you're *progressing some more* next week, who will be your greatest admirer?" "How do you think you might feel next week when you *experiment some more in repeating some more profitable ventures?*

Secondly, there is the other kind of interventive questions where there appear to be no exception-based changes available to act as a foundation. Usually, this is the case where the client or client family simply feels stuck with nowhere to turn, unable to find, at this point, any exceptions, or positive episodes that confute their past scenarios. In this apparently difficult scenario, the therapist has no choice but to study the client's wording, particularly the descriptive nature of the problem and its embeddedness. The kind of client language employed in depicting the problem will then serve to offer *cues* suggesting what kinds of presuppositional questions the therapist might pose. This is useful because the therapist is utilizing not only the client's definition of the problem, but also the client's very treatment of his or her languaging, the choice of words, metaphors, and key expressions, not those of the therapist.

For instance, there may be a client who presents depression as the problem, and, additionally, remains adamant about there being no exceptions to that "eternal" condition. She apparently feels depressed all the time. Or, there may be a client family whose members have fought with one another so often over certain issues that they seem to view the antagonistic condition as hopelessly present and as "always" being there. Or, there may be a married couple that presents a problem scenario involving irreconcilable differences that started at day-one of their marriage and simply refuses to discuss the existence of a prior time that was happier.

Clearly, these represent examples where the clients admit to no prior positive behaviors to the therapist, and the therapist appropriately poses some suppositional questions. The therapeutic aim then becomes to simply move the clients from embedded positions by allowing, through the use of interventive questions, the clients to begin to think about change in a projected future that is free of the problem. This is also much like the scenario suggested by the miracle question technique. For example: "What kinds of things would you be doing in a world where *depression has left you and gone away?*" "What would the family be like when *everyone cooperates?*" "How would you know when your differences as a couple are *reconcilable?*"

As an integral part of presuppositional questions, the second strategy involves the use of matching the client's language, often simply called *languaging* or the use of mimetic language. In its original context in the plastic arts, the word "mimetic" basically referred to imitating and replicating, as an artist might, the reality that lay before him. Art in its most pristine meaning usually meant "reproducing" something else, a "creative" copy. Similarly, mimetic language refers to creatively utilizing language such as jargon, metaphors, and idiosyncratic meanings. Dealing with clients in this context, the use of mimetic language, or languaging, serves as a highly

212 • *Breakthroughs in Six Brief Psychotherapies*

effective and extensive kind of *joining approach*. This kind of joining, however, implies going beyond the therapist's traditional accommodation of the client with its warm and friendly greeting and its appropriate ice-breaking questions. Nor is it a *joining* that is limited to the first few minutes of a session in order to get therapy going. In solution thinking, joining remains an ongoing integral component of therapy in which the therapist is empathetically "with the client."

O'Hanlon and Weiner-Davis, in accordance with constructivist terminology, have aptly selected a specific phrase, *matching the client's language*, or, simply put, *matching* (p. 60). Ultimately, the metaphoric roots of this matching phenomenon are most likely found in Roger's approach since the term "matching" clearly implies a global, all-encompassing *empathy*. The therapist's matching represents an expansive empathy that attempts to reflect not only an understanding of the client's affect and cognition at the moment, but also the client's cosmos or perspective as immediately expressed in the client's choice of wording, especially in the repetition of key words or phrases, and in the choice of metaphors (Thompson, 1990, pp. 247–257).

O'Hanlon & Weiner-Davis present the frequently cited and extremely vivid example provided by Rossi (1980, Vol. 4, pp. 213–215) where the latter described a classic case involving Erickson and an apparently incomprehensible, unidentifiable patient in a psychiatric ward. For five years the hospital staff was not able to identify the patient. For many afternoons, Erickson visited the patient and was determined to enter the latter's cosmos. Erickson sat next to him and "conversed" with him. He sat assuming the same physical posture as the patient. He "joined" the patient, persistently *matching* the schizophrenic patient's "word salads" during the periodic interviews. It appears that gradually the patient warmed up to Erickson and began responding to him. In his word salads, the patient interspersed specific clues and occasional remarks that began approaching a "conversation." Eventually the patient reached a point where in responding to Erickson's word salad interaction in those regularly scheduled "interviews," the patient gradually revealed his name, identity, and other data, which for years had remained a mystery to the entire staff at the psychiatric hospital. Most counselors and psychiatrists cannot afford to spend the large blocks of time that Erickson spent with many of his patients. Yet the principle of matching, as exemplified by Erickson utilizing the patient's choice of words, phrases and metaphors, remains a very useful principle today.

In an analogous fashion, a divorced client who, two years after her failed marriage, says that she still feels "broken up," could be asked some very obvious and relevant "matching" questions: "How would you go about describing the feeling of being *broken up* to someone?" "What does being *broken up* mean?" "What do you think makes you use this phrase *broken up* today?" A therapist would be wise to follow along the lines of Erickson's matching principle and not change the idiosyncratic wording presented by the client. By contrast, it would be completely off the mark to ask the divorced woman the following: "How does it feel to be *depressed?*" instead of using the client's self-description of *broken up*. On the surface, the question using the word depressed may seem appropriate by most traditional therapeutic standards. Yet, a close examination reveals that it does not really allow expression of the meaning peculiar to the client's world within the parameters of the client-generated metaphor with its attendant semantic foundations. Depressed as a word choice is really the therapist's term, and its use in this particular instance constitutes poor matching of the client's language.

In short, instead of going with the flow of the client's language, the therapist is subtly coercing the client to describe *depressed*, a choice of words that is part of the therapist's frame of reference. This coercion biases the direction of therapy in that it caters to an agenda that reflects more the therapist's semantic base than addressing the discovery of what the metaphor "broken up" really means to the client.

People select particular words to reflect their experiences. The words chosen carry with them certain connotations for the speaker. To the extent that as therapists we match our client's language, clients typically come to believe that we understand, appreciate, and identify with their subjective experiences. Rapport and cooperation are built upon this belief. Clients often visibly relax when they sense that they are understood. (O'Hanlon & Weiner-Davis, 1989, pp. 61–62)

Matching, then, understood not just as a "joining" ice-breaker or as an initial accommodation tool, but more importantly, as an actively employed stance not limited to the initial session, can be extremely useful and effective in therapy. This is essentially a stance which allows not only a maximal amount of psychological "comfort," but also a therapeutic respect for the client's concerns being expressed in the client's own linguistic frame of reference.

Matching also provides a better foundation for a more effective utilization strategy, an allusion to Erickson's thoughts and practices, where a well-guided matching allows the therapist a freer hand to utilize those data far more effectively. The utilization strategy phenomenon becomes all the more apparent when, for instance, a client's frame of reference is brimming with unique expressions and meanings. In particular, those clients who typically use an abundance of workplace buzzwords, acronyms, computerese, legalese, or abstract terms represent unusually good candidates for being asked many "matching" questions. The therapist can achieve success in this area by simply utilizing terms typically initiated by the client, or by employing related terms contained in the jargon peculiar to the client, or by asking the client questions that clearly explain their meanings. For instance, an engineer, who presents his unhappy job situation as substantially described in the language of mathematical estimates and measurements, might be asked questions reflecting just that kind of parlance. *Scaling questions* would seem most appropriate and quite timely. The client could be asked questions on a continuum from one to ten where one equals no satisfaction on the job, and ten equals complete satisfaction, "Where are you now in terms of job satisfaction?" "Where were you a month ago?" "A year ago?" "Where do you see yourself a year from now?" Indubitably, this kind of approach will most likely appeal to the client as it matches his language, jargon, and frame of reference. Asked these kinds of questions, the client may likely feel understood since someone finally speaks "his language."

Obviously, different professions, vocations, and avocations, or lack of them, present interesting challenges to the therapist as far as finding an appropriate matching stance is concerned. The following are samples of questions that reflect good matching. A person in journalism, for instance, might be asked a series of questions as to how her present situation is affecting what she considers to be her *image*, both private and public. A religious person might be asked a series of questions that regard what might be *God's evaluation* of her present situation on Earth. A computer person could be asked a series of questions about what new *input* needs to be obtained to create a better *output* in his life. Just as there are literally scores of job-related questions couched in jargon or work-related nomenclature areas, there is also non-work related languaging. The same matching principle applies to individuals in off-the-job situations or to those who might be unemployed, retired, disabled, or convalescing. For instance, for someone unemployed who has experienced troubles interviewing because of nervousness, "When will you know that your interviewing is getting easier for you?" For someone retired who feels stuck at home watching TV all day and who appears unable to initiate new activities, "What will it take to get away from home and the TV and do something different?" For a disabled person having problems adjusting to the use of a new motorized wheelchair, "What will it feel like when you become more mobile with your new equipment?"

In addition to an innovative presentation of how good matching languaging has the quality of "magical thinking" in *The Structure of Magic (1975)*, Bandler & Grinder also wrote *Frogs into Princes* (1979). In the latter text, cited by O'Hanlon & Weiner-Davis (1989, p. 66), Bandler & Grinder deal specifically with the matching stance in regard to languaging on *sensory* descriptive levels, which often take on the form of metaphors.

And so, the five senses, which are frequently among the active components in creating metaphors, immediately take on new therapeutic meaning from the perspective of utilizing clients' language when they introduce *sensory data*. Based on the client's word choices, the therapist may aptly pose many sensory-related questions to elicit fresh information. For instance, a client focusing on scenarios where verbs tend to be "visual" in nature should clearly suggest that the therapist correspondingly generate visually-oriented questions.

A client, for instance, might say: "I couldn't *see* that tragedy happening to me. I'm so devastated that I can't *visualize* anything good ever coming my way." These two related statements clearly represent a significant opportunity for the therapist to *join* in that visually-informed scenario. The therapist might ask a series of related questions that "match" the visual description. "Who else would *see* it your way?" "What would it take to *visualize* other possibilities?" "What needs to happen for you to *see* it differently?" Sensory-approach questions, utilizing the five senses that correspond to the client's "sensory" statements, can obviously become a great source of interventive approaches spanning the broad dimensions of visual, auditory, tactile, olfactory, and gustatory realms.

A chef who speaks in metaphors or descriptions of flavors and tastes might be asked questions that rely on gustatory imagery. "What does it *taste* like in your present situation?" "How will you know when life starts acquiring a fresh new *flavor* again?" A woman who presents herself as clearly sensitive to smells and aromas by her choice of wording is a good candidate for questions involving examples such as in the following: "When things go well, what kinds of *aromas* might you imagine pervading your new life?" Or, "What would it take to get life *smelling* nice once more?" To a tactile person, "What feeling *touches* you most?" An auditory-oriented person, "Who will be *listening* to you when things get better?"

An intrinsic part of the matching stance involves not only mirroring the relevant components of the client's semantic world, but also employing useful presuppositional questions to ultimately enhance the interventive quality of the therapeutic interview. As the therapist proceeds to mirror pertinent linguistic elements from the client's statements in the form of questions, the therapist may also begin to "channel the meanings for those words in productive directions *or* use different words" (O'Hanlon & Weiner-Davis, p. 66). *Channeling* is a kind of *linguistic shaping*. Simply put, it means that after the therapist has been mirroring the language of the client and a linguistic beachhead has been established, it may be necessary to move on, deploying the client's energies and resources in a stance that is *moving away from the embeddedness of the problem* as defined by the language of the client. In other words, matching slowly and cautiously evolves into channeling where negative-talk moves toward solution-talk. Metaphorically, once the matching stance establishes a linguistic/empathic beachhead and the client is assured that the therapist is sensitive and aware of the client's problem, the therapeutic conversation must move forward. Like troops stuck on a beachhead, the conversation will most likely remain pinned down unless a breakthrough takes place allowing movement inland off the beaches into new territory. That new territory in therapy is secured by channeling.

Channeling, a particularly useful stance which allows movement away from the fixed positions embedded in the abstractions of *negative labels*, helps redirect and de-emphasize the negative labeling and moves "towards action descriptions found in everyday language" (p. 67). Channeling begins with a *deconstruction* of negative labels, terminology, and pathological descriptions. Then, a linguistic shaping ensues whereby the deconstructed labels and descriptions evolve into new and positive interpretations which have been co-created and co-constructed by the therapist and the client. The net effect of channeling amounts to a reframe, a broad-based *normalization* effect, a release from the stigmas and debilitating notions couched in solution-talk.

The client's initially problem-saturated language, which was at first the passkey for the therapist to gain access into the client's cosmos, is likely to contain *negatives* of all kinds that have become incorporated and embedded into the client's semantic frame of reference. Metaphorically speaking, through the proper use of channeling these negatives need to be linguistically "exorcised." Typically, these negative terms or labels, usually abstractions, represent self-descriptive phrases or metaphors employed by the client that have, in a sense, acquired a "life" of their own. Channeling is a stance that liberates the client from the embeddedness of the problem.

For instance, there are clients who, in addition to having been labeled by prior therapeutic experiences, pathologize their problem still further by perfunctorily identifying themselves with labeling in such phrases as: "I'm a borderline," or "I'm co-dependent," or "I'm sexually addicted." Unfortunately, the stigma and fixity caused by such labeling, which on the surface may appear quite innocuous, casts an unhealthy spell of universality and permanence to the condition *as if* suggesting that the condition cannot and will not ever be eligible for change. Thus, it becomes crucially important to begin to tear down this label, deconstruct the notion, as one might rip down a huge highway billboard ad from its lofty position of visibility. The first step means bringing down the label (abstraction) to its description in behavioral terms. Then it involves *deconstructing* it by asking what does that label really mean anyway *in its specifics* and how is it so. What are the connections at the cognitive level that have kept this notion alive? Thus, by fostering a dialogue wherein the client depicts specific content to an otherwise generalized form, its label or abstraction, and questioning its validity, both client and therapist now have the possibility of a new foundation on which to build or *construct* a solution.

Take, for example, the label of claustrophobia. Like all labels, particularly negative ones, it is limited and delimiting in knowledge. At the very best, the label "medically" represents a terminological expedient. Sometimes it may also represent a societal and conversational expedient such as in the statement: "This booth makes me feel claustrophobic." Solution-oriented therapy views both the medical term and the everyday label as obviously abstractions which serve no immediate purpose and have little efficacy for the purposes of creating change since without the knowledge of the client's behavioral description of that condition, claustrophobia is a vacuous term. As an abstraction it is static, smacking of a terrible sense of permanence. It also offers no clue as to its actual intensity, its quality, or its specific characteristics. In other words, how serious is it? To what extent does it affect the client in everyday activities?

Obviously, a fuller and more descriptive understanding can only come about by a series of highly focused, relevant, well-posed behavioral questions. Where do the person's experiences with claustrophobia take place? On a plane, in a tunnel, on an elevator? When does it happen most often? Under what conditions? Does it happen when alone, or does it happen even in the company of others? Labels by their very nature hide the specifics. It therefore becomes the purpose of most therapies to bring specifics to the forefront in clearly described behavioral terms. Surely, asking these behavioral questions is not the sole domain of solution-oriented therapists. However, solution-oriented therapy is different in that it employs the specific use of channeling to *deconstruct* the label and then build solutions.

To find a philosophical analogue that highlights the insidious nature and the delimiting quality of the label, it is appropriate to incorporate one of George Kelly's construct models (1963, pp. 156–157), in particular, his identification of the *preemptive construct*. In the array of constructs, Kelly posits the preemptive construct as one of the most treacherous. By its very nature, it both abbreviates and generalizes the temporal-spatial dimensions of phenomenon which act to preempt the possibility of considerations of other behavioral and cognitive specifics of an otherwise complex reality. Although in the following quotation Kelly does not use the word *label* as such, Kelly's definition of a *preemptive construct* describes very accurately how a label, especially a negative label, often functions to perpetrate and perpetuate a calculated disarray and misunderstanding.

A construct which preempts its elements for membership in its own realm exclusively may be called a *preemptive construct*...It can be exemplified by the statement, "Anything which is a ball can be nothing but a ball." In this case the construct is *ball* and all the things which are balls are excluded from the realms of other constructs; they cannot be "spheres," "pellets," "shots," or anything but balls. This is a pigeonhole type of construct; what has been put into this pigeonhole cannot simultaneously be put into any other...if a person is a schizophrenic, he is nothing but a schizophrenic...(Kelly, pp. 153–154)

This description comes very close to describing the battleground where solution-oriented therapists metaphorically fight one of their principal battles. The battle includes the problem's definition, its "construct" elements, the labels, and embedded thinking that have gone into the problem's definition and description. Often, there is the case where well-posed and well-chosen interventive questions through channeling can even dissolve the problem in the very first session by virtue of its deliberate deconstruction process.

The common scenario in solution-oriented therapy involves several sessions where extensive exception-based questions, presuppositional questions, matching sequences, and channeling are utilized to sufficiently create the conditions for finding a solution to a specific problem. The underpinnings of solution-oriented therapy involve a constructivist position which clearly does not assume a fixed reality. By contrast, because of many beneficial and useful reasons, human beings pursue their penchant for viewing certain elements of reality with a sense of permanence. Understandably, this penchant does serve, in fact, as a social and psychological expedient offering a source of comfort and security. However, permanence, like other abstractions, is a construct. In the absolute sense of the word, it does not exist in material realty. Yet this apparently useful and justifiably important need in humans to imbue reality with a sense of permanence through the use of abstractions can suddenly be jolted into the undesirable sense of impermanence by unexpected life events and tragedies.

Since permanence does not reflect the true nature of reality and existence, the condition that best describes reality might be identified as one of only *relative certainty*. This newer and more realistic perception of reality, employed by solution-oriented therapy, has the effect of opening up a whole new area that is immediately available to the therapist to be utilized for the client's benefit. Thus, whenever a client presents a problem, O'Hanlon and Weiner-Davis tackle it under the aegis and guidance of the relative certainty of reality. Solution-oriented therapists then proceed a step further by dividing relative certainty into helpful and unhelpful certainties. The problem is viewed as an *unhelpful certainty* (p. 73) since it is obviously not beneficial to the client. It is an area where:

Sometimes clients (and indeed therapists) talk in such a way as to close down possibilities and give the impression that nothing can change. If a client says, "I'll never get a job," when summarizing we might respond, "So far you haven't gotten a job...." This is different from...cheerleading. We do not say, "Of course, you will get a job," but we do speak in such a way as to keep the possibilities open for the present and the future. (p. 73)

Channeling as a process is a rich, wide avenue, where the use of languaging plays a key role in the movement away from pathology and problems. Clients whose use of verbs tend to universalize their unwanted condition in the present tense can be shifted by the therapist's languaging to the past tense as if to suggest the possibility that it may *not* necessarily reoccur in the future. For instance, in response to the example where the client says: "*I drink* a quart of hard liquor *every day*," the therapist could say, "So, *you used to do* a quart every day." Similarly, in response to the example where the client is already in the past tense and is universalizing his condition, and says, "*I used to drink* a quart of liquor every day," the therapist could say, "So, *for awhile* you did a quart a day." In both cases, there is a deconstruction which calls into question the implied universality of the behavior and an effort to minimize an unhelpful certainty in the client's mindset.

Clearly, reality's processes and structures are complex, but they are also negotiable, according to solutions thinking. Through channeling, a linguistic maneuvering involving a perceptual change, a client's problem may be shaped into dissolution or shaped into solutions in its journey from an unhelpful to a helpful certainty. The process involves calling into question a hurtful, painful, or negative behavior, which is deconstructed, normalized, and further shaped through change-talk on this continuum from unhelpful certainty toward helpful certainty. This therapeutic maneuver ultimately involves movement that calls into play the *possible* and the *achievable*. Goals must be specific and possible so that they are achievable. Solution-oriented therapists usually emphasize the selection of small, achievable goals. In the process, two major areas of the psyche, *freedom* and *possibility*, become tacitly invoked to help liberate the client from his problems. In short, if permanence is not the true nature of reality, and only relative certainty reigns, it follows then that, once the client feels liberated and given freedom from the embeddedness of an unhelpful certainty, the client can begin to sense the change. This newly found freedom creates the foundation for the ability to create anew, a renewal, a reframing. Freedom also makes possible a new reality making available an array of new choices.

To sum up the solution-oriented position, it is first of all a pragmatic modality. It uses what works in the Ericksonian sense. This posture is based on premises coming from constructivist philosophy which assumes a multi-causal view of reality. Thus, there are many ways to examine and approach a problem, and many ways to perceive and solve a specific problem presented in therapy. The use of languaging is crucially important since both perception and meaning are embedded in language. How a therapist opts to use language with the client will often help determine not only the course of therapy, but also the outcome of therapy.

Languaging necessarily involves the interaction between therapist and client, but unlike many prior modalities, solution-oriented therapists attempt not only to depathologize and normalize behaviors, but also to speak in an everyday language so that the interaction actually approaches a more ordinary conversation (O'Hanlon & Wilk, 1987). The process of solution-oriented therapy takes place in the naturalness of a "conversation" that is "coincidentally" therapeutic. A determined emphasis is placed on the avoidance of psychological "talk" and therapy and psychiatric terminology, unless, of course, deemed absolutely necessary by the context of the conversation. Otherwise, the therapist is encouraged to use ordinary language.

> A "fly on the wall" who did not know we were doing psychotherapy would not necessarily suspect what we were doing: he would see and hear only an ordinary conversation. What defines the conversation as psychotherapy is simply our goal in conducting the conversation. (O'Hanlon & Wilk, 1987, p.177)

Solution-oriented therapy, a unique brief therapy model, constitutes a major breakthrough in modern therapy by having created one of the most highly effective and pragmatic modalities available. Incorporating many excellent components from prior models, going as far back as borrowing some fundamentally powerful notions from Milton Erickson, it has incisively capitalized on promoting brief therapy by refraining from the traditional problematics of the problem-talk and by centering on securing solutions that are possible and achievable in a philosophical perspective that is described as future oriented. The process by which this is achieved employs joining as an ongoing empathetic stance, obtaining a specific and behaviorally-informed description of the problem, setting an achievable goal, deconstructing and depathologizing past behaviors, channeling, normalizing, seeking "exceptions" behaviors and amplifying them, using presuppositional, circular, and other kinds of interventive questions, and encouraging solution-talk.

Theoretically, solution-oriented therapy is positioned to introduce doubt into the client's semantic frame of reference, assisting the client to call into question those operative beliefs that have maintained the unwanted behaviors, freeing the client from unhelpful perspectives, introducing alternatives or exceptions to traditionally held scripts and scenarios, introducing change and change-talk, and embracing helpful certainties.

Chapter 6

The Constructivist Model

The foundations of today's constructivist-informed models in psychotherapy are traceable to their constructivist prototype found in the historical studies of the Italian Giambattista Vico (1668–1744). His ideas about how historical analyses are performed and how conclusions are drawn suggest thoughts that are relatable to many of today's brief psychotherapies. There is a connection between the two that is fundamentally constructivist in nature. Vico was the first modern thinker to propose the concept of viewing human history as interpretation (Collingwood, p. 65). Whether a historian studies history on a grand scale where large epochs are involved or his inquiries are limited to more modest eras, Vico concluded that historical studies and judgments derived from them in effect represent interpretations. Simplistically knowing the facts is not history. History, instead, is an interpretation of those facts. The following analogy may require some qualification, but from a general psychological perspective, we can approach a better appreciation of Vico's perspective by viewing historical studies like philosophical "reframes" of the past.

Vico professed that while the historian can never totally capture reality in all its fleeting complexities and details, the historian attempts to *construct* a view (Collingwood, pp. 64–71) that grasps its essence. While Vico's historical perspective heralded a more realistic and accurate way of assessing the complex nature of historical study, his innovation was too advanced for his time. To be sure, when Vico first presented his ideas about history as interpretation to early eighteenth-century intellectual circles, the philosophical community did not embrace his view initially.

228 • *Breakthroughs in Six Brief Psychotherapies*

Today, with the advantage of hindsight, historians have generally accepted his philosophical premises that history is a reappraisal, a reassessment, an interpretation of the past. An interpretation may at times be disturbing and at times edifying, but it is always an interpretation. Thus, Vico's sense of history is constructivist by nature since it is decidedly a mental construct.

For his constructivist model, Vico employed a time-honored dualism, characteristic of ancient Greek philosophy, encompassing the interaction between two major principles, the ideological and the material. Their workings are manifested through the continual dialectic or dynamic tension between a given society's ideology, such as its codes of behavior, aspirations, and operative myths on the one hand, and, on the other, its observable manifestations, such as its activities reflected in concrete accomplishments, in societal relationships, and its institutions. These two major realms continuously *interact* with each other and mutually *influence* each other in an ongoing *reciprocal process* which propels reality into a forward motion, thus leaving historical data in its wake which is to be interpreted by the historian.

While Vico never used the word "dialectic" in the Hegelian sense to describe the way the process of civilization works, he did propose its Hegelian precursor in his famous historic dictum of reciprocal influence "*verum et certum convertuntur*" (Vico, 1744). In essence, Vico proposed the idea that history as a discipline represents not only philosophically an *interpretation*, but also at its operational level, the reflection of the reciprocal nature of its *interactive dynamics*. This reciprocal nature, *convertuntur*, is involved in the *ongoing interactive process between civilization's ideals, verum,* and *its concrete activities and achievements, certum.* One area has effects on the other in a continuous, unrelenting manner. The ideology of a given culture effects its concrete activities, and its concrete activities in turn effect the culture's ideology. Since a historian cannot grasp all the particulars and complexities generated in history's intricate flow of events, he therefore forges a construct that can best explain what has transpired.

From the mass of data first compiled and then synthesized from both the ideological realm and the factual realm, the historian creates a viable interpretation that reflects an epoch's meaning and possible significance for the future. However, according to Vico, interpretation does not end here. With the passing of time and the input of new data, a newer interpretation will replace and subsume the prior one. This is part of a process, identified as a *becoming*, an evolution in time. Thus, history, viewed as mental construct, is necessarily never final, representing an ongoing *interpretation* of the past with each successive generation of historians rethinking the past as a whole, inclusive of the preceding interpretations of the past (Collingwood, 1956).

History understood in this manner remains, quite patently, a monumentally enormous, ongoing construct of the human mind. If Vico were a practicing psychotherapist today, he would characterize history as a remarkably complex and continuously evolving *reframe*. It would include the caveat that despite history's upward spiral, indicating his view of ultimate progress in history, the reframe would also subsume the negatives of human struggles and injustices. Vico would also view that *reframe* as a necessarily tentative interpretation. Because of the admitted complexity of history, new data and perspectives about the past could change the nature of preceding interpretations. Thus, history is never final.

As corollaries, Vico might also add that history as an interpretational construct is not admissible in the realm of absolute truth, but only admissible in the realm of *relative certainty*. Vico's exceptionally modern perspective has inevitably led many subsequent theorists to concur that Vico's writings and his model are prototypic of present-day constructivism (Simon et al., 1985, p. 69). In many respects, Vico must also be considered a visionary in that he not only antedates Hegel's triadic dialectic of thesis, antithesis, and synthesis, but also posited reality as an evolving process characterized by a spiraling, upward mobility into the future. A similarly related "benevolent spiral" appearing in O'Hanlon and Weiner-Davis' book, *In Search of Solutions*, is not surprising nor coincidental, but part of a future-oriented, processing mindset inherent in constructivism.

Vico's view of history as an interpretational construct engendered a fundamentally dualistic and an inherently interactive relationship between the major realms of *ideology* and *relative factual certainty*. It was the continual interplay between these two realms that explained *change*, the third triadic component, viewed as its resulting forward motion. More specifically, for any given historical period, it meant that its *ideology* was universally defined as consisting of that period's ideals, its operative beliefs, its moral goals and precepts, and its cultural aims and aspirations. By the same token, counterpoised to ideology, its dualistic partner, *relative factual certainty*, consisted of that period's activities and events as reflected and expressed in that epoch's observable achievements, its cultural artifacts, its moral deeds, its sociopolitical accomplishments, and its struggles. In effect, there are two major sets of data, one ideal and the other factual, that eventually become integrated into a resulting unified meaning which Vico and his modern counterparts have designated as interpretation.

The typical attitude toward history, as reflected in everyday speech and in the more common perceptions of history, simply does not acknowledge the more serious and more difficult side of history. To the contrary, in everyday parlance history typically becomes reduced, actually trivialized, and simply perceived as a "fund" of facts. The average person generally ascribes to the historian the capacity for good memory in the recollection of facts with the attendant talent for exercising a systematic ability to incorporate fact collecting into the enterprise. In short, an everyday perception of history typically reduces its importance to a huge factual repository. This simplistic view, where history is simply reduced to knowing and storing facts, may become admittedly a sufficient source of enrichment for some, but it inherently misses the significance of history, the ability to achieve an understanding of historical change.

In Vico's view of history as interpretation, history necessarily involves embracing and understanding an intricate dialectical process reflected by

The Constructivist Model • 231

ideologies on the one hand and concrete activities of cultures on the other. It involves a willingness to shoulder premises and processes that inherently demand focus, thought, and a synthesizing imagination. In addition, Vico's philosophical suppositions also invite many other important considerations to come into play. They may appear as history's unsettling and disconcerting side, rife with hatred, cruelty, injustice, and genocide. To be sure, Vico's idea of history as interpretation joins the serious ranks of those dualistic theories that require the historian and the student of history to have, among others things, an intuitive and an imaginative sense for operational dynamics and interactive scenarios.

On another note that is equally important, history, as a discipline, categorically does not function in the same way as do the hard sciences where the experimental method establishes unvarying laws, such as in physics, chemistry, biology, and botany. Indeed, in the hard sciences, a law must be replicable and remain true all the time. It must account fully for any and all apparent irregularities. Otherwise, it remains a theory, a hypothesis yet proven.

In Vico's constructivist perspective of history only *operational precepts* exist (Collingwood, pp. 63–64). Unlike the laws of the hard sciences, operational precepts behave like *integrating principles* that guide and take into account both ideological notions and the myriad of historic factual data. History does not use the methods of the hard sciences. It remains, instead, a kind of expanding knowledge, based on new data, that takes the form of highly *interpretative constructs* that rely heavily on intuition, creativity, and ultimately the perspective and value system of the historian as interpreter.

Admittedly, readers often find this view of history as unsettling and even unnerving because history as interpretation does, in a sense, undermine humanity's easy and relentless desire to view historical reality as fixed and permanent. In this wishful and often wistful scenario, many of our very basic affective and intellectual needs in categorically wanting to know what is "true" or what is "certain" become thwarted and frustrated. Worse yet, some of our most cherished ideas and beliefs regarding a given epoch or a given personage from the past may be challenged and even assaulted when confronted with newly derived information and/or perspectives.

Nevertheless, because we are all "historians," to one degree or another depending on the breath and depth of our historical frame of reference, we are all affected by our own self-imposed historical constructs and cultural influences. Whether we are considering history in the universal sense or in an immediate autobiographical sense, our historical perspectives do affect us. This leads us to the proverbially overwhelming question: what is truth? What is truth, especially if historians sometimes view historical data in radically different ways from previous generations of historians or even from their contemporary peers. Then, where or how does truth exist?

Does it mean that everything is relative in the sense that studying history becomes a disheartening and futile effort in attempting to find some position of certitude? Does it mean that "all is relative" in the worst possible sense such as in nihilistic relativism where nothing really matters anymore? Is history a lie? Those seem hardly the answers we would hope for. Additionally, these concerns would clearly indicate all the more that the perennially simplistic, everyday notions of historical truth would also not suffice.

Perhaps the best way to address the epistemological issues of "how do we know what we know" involves addressing them in the same way Kant (1781) addressed them. Kant's epistemological studies revealed that knowledge surely does exist provided, of course, that we keep in mind a very important caveat. That caveat involves two basic ideas. First, we can only *approach* the truth; it is impossible to know it completely or to know it in any absolute sense. Second, the reason why an absolute sense of knowledge is impossible to achieve involves two considerations: the inherent complexity of all phenomena and the inherent limitations of the human intellect.

Therefore, to bridge the gap between our "finite" mental faculties and the unending complexity of nature, civilization and culture, Kant introduced the term *phenomenological* as explaining the way we necessarily piece together, or *construct*, the complexity of external data with the mind's finite processes. His model, dualistic and constructivist like that of Vico, posited the existence of the mind's innate cognitive categories on the one hand, and, on the other, external sensory data that become integrated by the mind's cognitive processes. This dualistic process, which produces phenomena, is analogous in many ways to the historian's interpretation of the past. It is never complete and, of course, it remains phenomena in that they are subject to change based on the incorporation of newer and more accurate information.

It follows from Kant's model that the reasons why we rethink and reinterpret phenomena involve two ideas. First, the process is precipitated by the discovery or recovery of new data previously not included in prior data. Second, since our minds are constantly generating new ideas, those very ideas may be applied to the process of re-interpreting something that we once thought of as essentially understood and acceptable. Put in psychological terms, this could easily be called a broad, ongoing reframing. The observer employs new constructs to re-interpret older constructs, thus creating new ones.

Going one step further regarding both Vico and Kant, today we have inherited the burdensome contents of an overwhelming paradox. Neither Vico's sense of history, viewed as interpretation, nor Kant's view of cognition, viewed as phenomenological events, assert or reflect the existence of a fixed or knowable *absolute reality*. To the contrary, they perceive an *ongoing process of change*. As far as history is concerned, it exists in the mind of the historian and also, collectively, in the minds of readers who subscribe to that historian's interpretation. Thus, it is the historian's interpretation or construction of the interplay of historical data, both abstract and concrete, that creates the historical evaluation, narration, and ultimate interpretation. Clearly, history is *not* the recorded data of historical events themselves as many would like to think. Recorded data are merely the artifacts of history.

234 • *Breakthroughs in Six Brief Psychotherapies*

Similarly, the perception of reality is in the mind of the perceiver, as in a person's view of one's history and one's personhood. The perceiver constructs his own reality, and his interpretation of his place in the world is found in his mind. In no way does this present a nihilism of sorts. It simply asserts that one's personal assessment is analogous to that of the historian assessing history. It is an interpretation based on information/data and one's *viewpoint*. Again, we have returned to psychology. We are dealing with behaviors reflected in the information, data, and activities on the one hand, and cognition and affect reflected in our constructs and perspectives on the other. Once more, there is a reciprocal relationship which when viewed in broad existential strokes, shows how cognitive and affective areas influence behaviors, and how behaviors influence cognition and affect in ongoing sequences.

For the sake of specificity, if we momentarily leave Vico's world which deals essentially with history, and we enter into the everyday epistemological realm of the individual, the Kantian perspective affirms that the individual, any individual, is constantly and uniquely interpreting and re-interpreting the world around him. Paradoxically, there may be as many interpretations as there are interpreters for any given situation. While Kant's innovative view was surely radical for his time, he ironically marveled not as much at the fact that so many interpretations could exist for any given observable situation as much as at the fact that agreement between interpreters was actually so common.

Kant was principally responsible for having critically confuted nearly two millennia of Western epistemology which essentially had posited cognition as a "mirroring of a reality that exists independently of the observer" (Simon et al., 1985, p. 67). Kant's revolutionary confutation of that traditional point of view helped bring about the more modern notion that "any statement about reality is primarily a statement about the observer" (p. 67). Kant's constructivist legacy, which he labeled phenomenological, has indeed influenced Western epistemology with particular emphasis in such areas as physics (e.g., Heisenberg's twentieth-century

"Uncertainty Principle"), biological ecology, psychology and its phenomenological, systemic, and cybernetics areas.

Many modern constructivist thinkers, such as Auerswald (1968, 1972), von Foerster (1981), von Glasersfeld (1984), Maruyama (1974), and Maturana & Varela (1988), have advanced constructivist ideas whose origins ultimately may be traced as far back as Vico and Kant (Simon et al., pp. 67–70). Their aggregate achievements have generated many theories and effected the practice of psychotherapy, particularly in the last four decades. Thus, most brief therapies have by now subsumed many of these constructivist dimensions and are clearly approaching psychotherapy from a more meaningful, useful, and practical perspective. Reminiscent of Vico's image of history as "spiraling up" couched in an existential becoming, modern brief therapy similarly speaks of a "benevolent spiral" in depicting the process of therapy where the outlook is positive and health oriented along the lines of Milton Erickson's ideas on "iatrogenic health" and Maslow's modern concepts regarding "wellness."

Von Glasersfeld's work, for instance, echoes a quintessential Kantian premise when he states that an individual can never "mirror" reality as such, but can only construct a "model that fits" it (1984). To varying degrees, because every client in therapy creates his own specific cognitive model of reality through the unique use of mental constructs peculiar to his experience and his ongoing interpretation, it therefore becomes the modern therapist's task and responsibility, while working collaboratively with the client through the interviewing process, to decipher aspects of the client's constructs. It may mean, on the one hand, *deconstructing*, in collaboration with the client, those data and aspects that are detrimental to the client's welfare and that are thwarting the client's growth and mental well being. On the other hand, it may mean *reframing* useful data into newer and more useful perspectives, offering mobility and opportunity out of once embedded situations. For example, in posing questions in an eliciting stance, the modern therapist aims at deciphering the client's semantic frame of reference for eventually laying the foundation for deconstructing useless or negative components. In a subsequent "probing" stance the therapist might create a "reframe" where the client's useful outcomes from the past experiences or present strengths are reconstructed into a new perspective. Thus, a client who is experiencing a problem that he has labeled as depression might be able to redefine or positively relabel this condition through a therapist's reframing suggestion, as merely a temporary condition, a "detour" from what are essentially non-depressive scenarios in his life.

Auerswald, from his constructivist perspective, chose to focus much of his attention on the systems of the "ecological" panorama. By ecological he meant focusing on the interactive influences of related systems that surround the client much like concentric layers around a focal point. He emphasized how their interactive relationships influence and effect change. He focused his attention, for instance, on the relationships between a small system, such as the family, and those of larger societal systems, such as community organizations, religious, and cultural influences. In varying degrees, their reciprocal influences do effect changes in affect, cognition, and behavior. For example, a Muslim family living in a Christian or Jewish society cannot help being influenced to some degree by the latter's influences. Societal influences abound, and how their influences may be utilized for the client's benefit are the part of the therapeutic conversation that Auerswald considers important. In short, he and other constructivist thinkers have enriched psychology and have laid the foundation for a host of contemporary therapeutic methods, approaches, tactics, and techniques. Constructivist influences were spawned in the early family/strategic and family/systems areas dating back to the 50s. These influences have since grown in a consistent and dramatic manner as reflected in the six breakthrough models discussed in this book.

As an aside, more recently in a different but related area, in the realm of cognitive/behavioral psychotherapy of the 80s and 90s, many of their representatives have finally emerged espousing constructivist views also, and their number seems to be growing (Carlsen, 1988; Efran, Lukens, M., &

Lukens, R., 1990; Mahoney, 1991; Mahoney & Lyddon, 1988; Neimeyer, R. & Neimeyer, G. 1987). In these cognitive/behavioral modalities that have recently embraced constructivist foundations, their major commonalities involve activity on a continuum that is steadily moving away from their once strictly empirical (positivist) view of treatment toward treatment approaches that operate within the reality of personal meanings (constructivist) that the clients have created for themselves (Mahoney, 1993). This movement within the cognitive and behavioral therapeutic communities represents a truly significant and much needed shift in their orientations.

By comparison, the realm of brief therapy, starting as early as the late 50s and throughout the 60s, based on family/systems, cybernetic thought, and strategic therapies, had already integrated many constructivist notions to varying degrees and were well on their way developmentally. It is principally because of these early advancements and seasoned foundations that when Terry Real's 1990 article, "The Therapeutic Use of Self in Constructionist / Systemic Therapy," appeared, it was apparent that he had realized one of the major crowning achievements of constructivist-inspired models. His particular model reached high levels of integration and refinement in the wake of a relatively long legacy on the trajectory of family, family/systems and strategic models. Real creatively synthesized the best components of many prior models into one highly effective model. Real's approach included a clever choice of stances which encapsulated a systematic thoroughness while offering a great sense of therapeutic flexibility.

The mobility and malleability ensconced in the synthesis of five stances is permeated by Real's principles that convincingly espouse the quintessential importance of the therapist's ability to exercise *multiple engagement* of self in therapeutic conversations. The latter serves to underscore the constructivist perspectives that culminate in the importance of a therapist's "I-thou" active participation and collaboration "with each member's perceptions and experiences." Whether there is only one client present or whether there is an entire family present in session, the

238 • *Breakthroughs in Six Brief Psychotherapies*

therapist "facilitates change through participation" with each person, i.e., through the "system" created by their presence. It, therefore, remains crucial from an operational point of view that the therapist's engagement is viewed "*as positioned within rather than as acting upon a system*" (Real, 1990, p. 255). This perspective is thoroughly constructivist.

The position of the therapist's multiple engagement also fits closely with helping to achieve second-order change, a topic already discussed in detail in the MRI model, where change is viewed as effective *only if* it effects a significant impact in the "systemic" cosmos of the client, not just the implementation of a behavioral reversal. Real espouses multiple engagement as an integral and actively employed component in the therapeutic interactive process precisely because it helps insure "systemic" change. The questions the therapist chooses to ask or not to ask, how therapeutic questions are posed, what client data the therapist chooses to discard and what data are kept and integrated into the dialogue all become crucial considerations in the process of operationalizing the principles permeating the five stances that constitute this highly mobile, flexible, and inclusionary model.

In keeping with the constructivist view, Real reiterates that "*Multiple engagement stresses the relational perspective over the extremes of pure interventionism or pure facilitation*" (p. 255). In simpler words, while the therapist should not ignore either interventionist or facilitative aspects, the focus should be placed on *relational perspectives*. The therapy session should, in effect, reflect an emergence of a therapeutic "conversation" where the therapist and the client remain cybernetically collaborative participants of a newly evolving system defined by the session and its unfolding conversation. Ideally, that kind of therapeutic conversation should approach the essential qualities and demeanor of an "active I-Thou encounter between all persons engaged in conversation, including that particularly important person, the therapist" (p. 260).

One of the obvious premises of constructivist therapy employed in this model involves the idea that we do not live in a universe with one meaning, but with a "multiverse" of meaning. This echoes a Kantian thought that there exist as many descriptions and observations as there are describers and observers. In brief therapy, and particularly in constructivist-informed therapy, the client together with the therapist deliberately expand and stretch the "relational" aspects of the client's cosmos so that embedded explanations, indicating narrow and self-defeating causalities, are abandoned in favor of liberating, alternative explanations. This rather innovative constructivist characterization of human cognition, more immediately reminiscent of Bateson's ideas of "double descriptions," includes the hopeful expectation of ultimately managing, improving, and eliminating the existence of problems presented in therapy. Unlike many models that dwell and focus on the embeddedness of problem situations, constructivist-informed therapy has achieved favorable outcomes by necessarily allowing the client to experience in the therapeutic process newer perspectives and more meaningful and helpful possibilities.

Before embarking upon an illustration of his constructivist model, Real takes some time to discuss its background, interpreting the development of family/systems and strategic thinking. The decades of the 70s and 80s were the major era in the consideration of the present model under discussion. For all practical purposes, Real views its evolution, with its attendant disclaimers of model overlaps, as essentially a three-phase formation. First, the "expanded" *strategic* phase typical of the 1970s, second, the Batesonian or *information-based* phase typical of the 1980s, and third, the constructivist phase, which he calls the *constructionist* or *language-based* phase (p. 256), typical of the late 1980s.

In the first phase, the therapist is "the chief therapeutic agent," who through the revolutionary dynamics of *circular questioning* and *positive connotation* is then able to create an intervention at the end of the session. The purpose of the intervention involves assigning the family in therapy a task or ritual to be carried out between sessions. Its specific aim is to help generate the necessary foundation for the family dialectic to dissolve the

240 • *Breakthroughs in Six Brief Psychotherapies*

problem. This 70s systemic approach was found to be very functional and is directly attributable to the Milan school.

However, Real views this initial strategic phase as moving in a natural evolution towards an 80s information-based phase. This phase clearly demonstrated that a "fuller articulation" could be achieved by operationalizing an enhanced circular questioning. The enhancement involved focusing more intensely on the process of creating timeline *differences* and *patterns* at the informational level. By contrasting time intervals and the *differences* a problem pattern presented, therapists noticed that this approach made an immediate effect in the quality of response from clients. Often the dissolution of the problem occurred in the therapy session itself. This "information-based" Batesonian interviewing process no longer made it necessary to rely on the post-session intervention, once viewed as a primary tool. This new process apparently created successful therapeutic sequences of "smaller micro-interventions" in the therapy session itself, thus the accelerated therapeutic process and its effectiveness. In practice, this shift inevitably occurred when the successful process of questioning, based on Batesonian principles, obtained primacy over the more end-of-session intervention. Suddenly, therapy had grown and had become closer to what might be called a healing "conversation" without the necessity of post-session interventions. This was possible because the nature of therapy was viewed differently.

The third stage, the constructionist or language-based phase, evolved from the second phase. While it kept what had been learned from the two prior stages, it also took on a radically different focus, going many steps further. Instead of simply working with Bateson's "double description," whereby alternative views begin to warrant the client's willingness to consider other explanations of an apparently embedded situation, the third stage focuses intensely on more radical epistemological innovations that deal mainly with changes in perspective. Alluding to von Foerster, Real sums up the third phase as the therapeutic relationship where the focus shifts from "observed" to "observing" systems (p. 257), where everything is interpretation that emerges from the newly created system defined by the therapist and client in their conversation.

In essence, Real's model more accurately expresses the heart of the constructivist orientation whose influences had existed during prior decades. Constructivist thinkers professed many tenets for decades and indeed many principles were incorporated in various models since the late 1950s. But Real's model is unique in that so many constructivist tenets become actualized and operationalized in one model. All the more interesting is the fact that his model also incorporates the most recent adaptation and orientation that has often been called radical constructivism. Reminiscent of Kantian philosophy, Real proposes the idea of the drastic "eradication of the idea of objectivity" (p. 257). Human cognition, because of its finite qualities, cannot really suppose that it can think in terms of creating a "representational" view of reality whereby a "mirroring" of a reality takes place. To the contrary, constructivism posits that human cognition does not mirror external reality at all, but rather, an observer's internal reality interpreting an external one. In fact, all reality is ultimately a construct of the mind. It is constructed not only individually, but also and perhaps more importantly, it is constructed collectively "through social discourse, through language" (p. 257). Thus, language, the medium of verbal expression and mental constructs, becomes a key player in this scenario. Linguistic sensitivity and languaging, the choice of words and expressions become crucial in psychotherapy.

While Bateson was a constructivist thinker himself and in his day was considered radical, it now appears that he was not radical enough. Bateson made many significant moves *away from positivism* which had posited an empirical "scientific" view of the world containing things "possessed of intrinsic qualities" (p. 258). Bateson had countered the positivist view in a relatively powerful way by pointing out that an entity can only be truly defined "with reference to…what surrounds and contextualizes it." He said this with much conviction because he believed that an entity that is attempting to be defined through "intrinsic qualities" inevitably would

242 • *Breakthroughs in Six Brief Psychotherapies*

fall short of meaning because of its inescapable emptiness in the world of abstractions.

In exemplifying Bateson's bold epistemological thoughts, which again are traceable to Kant, Real cites the simple example of defining a chair. For instance, in the process of attempting to abstract the empirical quality of a chair, Bateson would say that there is no such thing as the abstraction "chairness." By its very nature, this abstraction rings hollow.

> For Bateson, a chair, for example, is defined not by some intrinsic quality of "chairness." A chair can only be defined with reference to the "not-chairness" that surrounds and contextualizes it-the floor it rests upon, the empty space around it, the sofa it is not. If the world were comprised of one large chair, we would have no way of apprehending it. For Bateson, "things" are mutually defined, existing only with reference to the surroundings that give definition. We live in a world not of things but of patterns of relationships, of "information." (p. 258)

As if Bateson's beliefs were not radical enough in his *de-emphasis of scientific measurability and objectivity*, the more radical constructivists believed that Bateson's world of "things" that mutually defined themselves apparently did not go far enough. Indeed, in the more recent radical constructivist vision, all objectivity is abandoned. This radical pronouncement, again, is based on the incisive, constructivist notion that human cognition does not "discover" reality, which implies certain objectivity; rather, human cognition *continually constructs its reality* both at the individual level and at the collective level.

Radical constructivists, in asserting the primacy of language as the medium of expression and cognition, insist that "reality is not discovered through objective means, but is *consensually agreed upon* through social interaction, through conversation." In essence, things *are* "what we agree to call them" (p. 258). Indeed, if this perspective more closely reflects reality, then one can begin to see how Real's reiteration of cybernetic differentiation

The Constructivist Model • 243

between first-order and second-order change acquires even more importance. In the first-order instrumental change, the agent therapist is viewed as "acting upon the system in the way a doctor acts upon a patient or a mechanic upon an automobile." Clearly, there exits and operates a decided bold division between what is acting and what is being acted upon. However, in a second-order cybernetic perspective, a constructivist outlook, the agent therapist is necessarily posited "as positioned in potentially useful ways *within* the system" (pp. 258–259) defined by the therapeutic conversation. Obviously, the "system" that is being referred to is the one immediately shaped by the therapist and client interaction in their therapeutic conversation. In a constructivist scenario, the therapist's role of multiple engagement of self is decidedly that of "participant-facilitator," consciously relinquishing the role of "expert" and first becoming a willing listener and learner while entering into the depth and breadth of the client's cosmos. Behaving more like a curious traveler in a foreign land, the therapist must first learn the terrain and landmarks of this new place before challenging the client's meanings of what constitutes his world.

Real's constructionist model attempts to avoid the extremes of pure facilitation, non-instrumentality, and the opposite, pure interventionism, instrumentality. In sum, the therapist has only himself as a tool and the use of words, the common currency of their "conversation" with which to work. It is within this context, so challengingly described, that the therapist attempts to achieve the fullness of a "self-in-system perspective" which will hopefully approach the level of a "healing conversation" with the client.

Given the limitations of time and space, the only behavior directly accessible to the therapist's control is the therapist's own behavior. Therefore, how he moves through the conversation, how he speaks, the questions he asks, how he places emphasis on his wording, how he employs body language, how he totally communicates, is the only major tool available. It is not surprising then that this approach aspires to achieve an "active I-Thou encounter" to characterize the relationship between the

244 • *Breakthroughs in Six Brief Psychotherapies*

therapist and a client, or, between the therapist and an entire family "engaged in conversation." In this context, Real invokes some of his champions such as Silverstein, Goolishian, and Anderson, who have served as examples of refining the art of therapeutic conversation. In sum, the engaged "conversation" requires two important qualities of the therapist. The first quality is a special commitment that suggests a certain humility of spirit. The second, the responsibility that likewise suggests a shared "common sense" with the client, an attitude that has decisively moved away from any implied arrogance of a unilateral know-it-all or upmanship attitude that sometimes professionals might unwittingly or deliberately bring to the therapeutic session.

> As a participating system member, the therapist need not necessarily agree at all times with his own. But he is always respectfully *engaged* with multiple realities that greet him. Such a constructionist conversation demands at one and the same time the humility of a self-in-system perspective, the common sense to take personal responsibility for oneself within the system, and the political sense to acknowledge that social discourse is indeed social, and merely idiosyncratic. (p. 260)

As a prelude to a discussion of each of the five stances, Real submits a typically constructivist caveat to the reader. It includes the idea that the "set of stances that follow are offered as illustrations of, not prescriptions for, the operationalization of a constructivist-systemic therapy." Real suggests that there is a multitude of "stances one might take to further therapeutic dialogue," but those aspects that remain essential are "the therapeutic activities, therapeutic positions, or uses of self, which taken together may serve to guide the therapist in his participant-facilitator role" (p. 260).

Real's constructivist model consists of five modular *stances*. In general, because the term "stage" implies steps and a necessary chronological sequence, it is noticeably avoided and only used in some specific instances where deemed necessary. Stances, however, which reflect the overall design of this model, provide a definite modular flexibility and mobility. In effect, the therapist, necessarily viewed as a "participant-facilitator" in the process, may maneuver between stances enhancing the ever-constant goal to expand the "positioning" of the client-therapist relationship, offering an ever-widening panorama of options, new opportunities, and new perspectives in viewing the problem situation. The five major stances that are suggested and elaborated as essential tools consist of the following: *eliciting, probing, contextualizing, matching,* and *amplifying.*

Operationalizing the *eliciting stance* involves the assumption that the therapist takes a deliberate "one-down" position with respect to the client. The "mantle" of therapist expertise is quickly cast aside. Particularly in this stance, the client *is* the expert in all the aspects of his or her world with all of its failures and all of its strengths. The immediate purpose of the therapist's activities involves understanding and appreciating the client's cosmos, *not* the diagnostic categorization or pigeonholing of client deficits and pathologies.

The therapist is to take nothing for granted. Any client intake data or prior therapy experiences may become open to possible discussion, welcoming fresher and more meaningful interpretations. The therapeutic stance of "not knowing" is mightily respected so that the therapist begins at ground zero in deciphering the client's world. Unassumingly asking the client what brought him to therapy, the therapist is a full-time active listener. When the client presents the problem situation, the therapist asks the client for different ideas, theories, or past therapy explanations about the "problem." The therapist is careful not to counter the veracity of either a client's apparent display of contradictory views or of a client's apparent disarray of informational sequences; nor does the therapist suggest new ideas or alternatives or, worse, offer remedies for the situation. Instead, "incomplete" information and /or apparent contradictions are best handled by relevant questions, couched in a healthy curiosity, that indicate the therapist's genuine concern in attempting to understand the client's cosmos.

Maintaining a position of curiosity, not preconceived notions, should be the guiding principle in relating to the specifics of the client's problem area. The therapist resists the invitation to "rule" on one correct version of reality from varied versions that a client might present. Instead, the therapist shows respect for competing constructs, whether within the client's individual script or within couple or family scripts. It is especially important in the beginning session that, metaphorically speaking, all client data is viewed in a state of flux, not fixed but simply open and subject to more curious inquiry in regard to both specificity of the unique meaning the clients attribute to elements of his affect and cognition and the unique meaning the clients attribute to the familial and social influences.

In the eliciting stance, the therapist maintains a "both-and" position in the client's presentation of competing or contrasting scripts. The therapist does not employ a "but" position, implying the acknowledgment of apparent contradictions in client narratives. Differing client opinions, contradictory views and interpretations should not be pointed out to the client. From a constructivist perspective, confrontation would imply at the outset of therapy that the client is wrong or that he is simply not telling the whole "truth." In an effort to avoid that kind of scenario, positions which seem to present deliberate or inadvertent contradictions are "neither judged nor countered." However, this is not to suggest that the therapist is being passive and unresponsive. To the contrary, the therapist is actively listening and absorbing as many client constructs as possible. Contradictory constructs, and especially those constructs that might have "received only scant attention" and are mentioned off-handedly, become prime candidates for discussion as the eliciting stance moves forward in soliciting greater specificity of the data.

In actuality it is the therapist's acute listening skills that help create the necessary foundation for asking illuminating and challenging questions that make the therapeutic conversation flow in a wholesome and revealing manner. Equally important is the style and manner in which the questions are posed. The therapist's best posed questions are usually characterized as

The Constructivist Model • 247

relatively short, direct and without prefatory or introductory remarks, which typically would seem to include a bias of sorts or inadvertent clues as to the direction in which the question should be answered. Ideal questions are short in length and open-ended, offering ample space for client elaboration. The following are examples:

"So what is your view of the origin of the problem?
"How did you come by that view?"
"What do you think made you see things necessarily that way?"
"So what happened that made it possible?

Once client elaboration takes hold, the therapist should also pursue specificity in those areas that are laden with conflicting information. This line of questioning also helps to break through the inevitable "monologing" tendencies that many clients have usually created for themselves in the pre-session rehearsals of their position. Questions of specificity, inherently encouraged in the eliciting stance, offer new and challenging possibilities to the client. What would have been an otherwise dried up, flat narrative can suddenly become freshly inspired alternatives to once embedded scripts. This is accomplished very naturally out of curiosity and specificity, not pre-conceived diagnostic categories.

This can be especially true of a client whose remarks might have appeared at first as off-handed or "secondary" to the main ones presented. Often, the therapist's effective pursuit in realizing in-depth specificity in "off-handed" client remarks or in metaphorically-laden client expressions can immediately bring to life those situations. This kind of strategy can become more effective and redeeming, saving time and energy, because the therapist may often obtain quicker access to the client's world. In the brief excerpt below, one can infer many possibilities of questions based on following the "internal" logic of a simple metaphorical expression, an *ego, a mile wide*:

Th:	So how do you think you have a problem with your supervisor?
Cl:	He's my boss, and he's got an *ego, a mile wide.*
Th:	*A mile wide* is kind of big. What makes you say a *mile wide?*
Cl:	He's really envious of me.
Th:	What is *his ego* envious of?
Cl:	I just created a new patent for the company's portfolio.
Th:	And, what about his *mile-wide ego?*
Cl:	He wished he had gotten the patent.
Th:	How does this *mile-wide ego* get reflected in your dealings with him?

In the process of obtaining more specific information about the meaning of the client's presence in therapy, the therapist's line of questioning should begin to expand the possibility of new meanings. This procedure is called amplifying. When used effectively in the eliciting stance, this can lead to other directions, moving away from the embeddedness of the client's stock answers while moving toward newly created rationales and explanations regarding the nature of the problem perceived by the client. This is achieved by relevant questions posed by the therapist that widen the search for meaning that exists within the client and must be elicited, always of course, in a collaborative manner with the client.

In the eliciting stance, questions are usually inspired by information coming from the client. It becomes the therapist's responsibility, then, to ask relevant, effective, and curious questions. Enhanced by the art of specificity and the art of knowing when to desist from pursuing inconsequential client data, the eliciting stance can be a powerful tool. In this stance the focus is on the client's "meaning" world, the semantic frame of reference that gives value and importance to what the client feels, thinks, and how he acts. Especially in difficult problem scenarios where the session may encounter difficulty in getting started, a firm adherence to eliciting the client's "meaning" world makes good therapeutic sense, being a safe and practical place to begin.

Real offers a case illustration of a couple in therapy where a properly developed eliciting stance became highly effective. A couple came to therapy with a history of fighting. The wife described her husband as "oversexed and exploitative," and not surprisingly, the husband described her as "frigid and angry." Yet it wasn't until the second session, still in an eliciting stance, that the therapist noted the husband making a remark that turned out to be pivotal. The husband commented that, in essence, it wasn't so much that he was interested in sex all the time. What he really wanted was a deep sense of "reassurance" of her love. For him, having sex was his way of getting reassurance, albeit short-lived. It further emerged in the eliciting stance that his wife had had an affair two years prior. And, even though they agreed that it had made the marriage stronger in some ways, it also left the husband with a great sense of insecurity. Sex, however, was one area in which he felt relatively competent.

After this particular interchange of information in their therapeutic "conversation," the therapist asked the husband a key question: would he be less demanding *if* he felt in some way more special in his wife's eyes? The question was auspiciously followed by both husband and wife reminiscing at length about the time they met. Two weeks later this episode, in which the husband revealed his feelings of insecurity and the therapist challenged them with the key question, apparently inspired the wife to "spontaneously" attempt "a radical new response" at home. She made unrehearsed and apparently sincere declarations of her love for him and her commitment to the marriage. After that event, it appeared that the problem ended, and therapy terminated in the eliciting stance.

In conclusion to this therapeutic scenario, Real points out some key ideas as semantics that were most likely operational in this particular situation and would help explain its resolution. When the wife originally viewed her husband as simply oversexed and exploitative, "she had only two options: to give in and degrade herself, or to withhold and deprive herself." When as a couple they were offered an opportunity through a cleverly devised eliciting question and, thus, afforded an *alternative explanation* through a deeper and different expression of the *meaning* of their interaction as husband and wife, the latter's new perspective of her husband as understandably "insecure," rather than oversexed and exploitative, in turn offered fresh options for changes to take place. Clearly, an apparent change in meaning had effected a change in attitude and behavior. Because the eliciting stance deals with the important "meaning" layers in one's affective, behavioral, and cognitive areas, a change in meaning in any one of these areas effected during the eliciting stance may be all that is necessary to make change take place in the other areas. Eliciting easily becomes a powerful tool when used wisely and effectively.

The second stance presented is called *probing*. In this stance, the therapist takes an active role in *creating a specific recasting of highly select client data* and presenting it as an empowerment tool, usually a compliment or reflection of a new perspective. It may take the form of a question, a statement, or simply a genuinely felt response that is potentially empowering to the client. A statement or question made in this probing stance simply reflects the fact that the therapist has taken a select portion of unmodified client data and has repackaged, re-ordered, and reshaped it into something new that has the effect of challenging one or many of the prior, seemingly ineffectual perspectives that had once circumscribed part or all of the client's cosmos. It represents a "creative" challenge to the client's old ways of looking at things.

While probing shares some commonalities with the eliciting stance, it is essentially very different. Probing shares one major commonality with eliciting in that it still continues the same drive in the search for meaning. Like eliciting it is semantically based. While the probing stance may naturally follow eliciting, it is different and should be implemented only under special conditions. When at a given point in the eliciting process the therapist decides that he has gathered sufficient client data for an area of inquiry, he could be in a position to enter into a probing stance. Probing may consist of a therapist's question, statement, or a brief series

The Constructivist Model • 251

of statements that presume the provisional or experimental establishment of a new perspective based on client data.

There are caveats to this process. First, basic client data cannot be modified or altered. The only thing that should appear different is the resultant or emerging perspective, representing in essence, only a re-arrangement of the original data. After creating a probe, the therapist inserts it into the conversation and observes the client's responses. The probe's qualities may be described in many ways. Often, it is called an "alternative description," a new interpretation or a new perspective of the client data. Some therapists prefer the term *reframe*. When the client seems amenable to a probe, this allows the therapeutic conversation to move forward, expanding and exploring the many consequences and opportunities afforded by this new outlook. If the probe is indeed accepted and it moves actively into an expansion and an exploration of newer and greater meaning presupposed by the probe, this newer phase would be more aptly called *amplifying* the probe. As in eliciting, whenever the therapist's line of questioning elaborates a given theme, affect, idea, or behavior in an effort to elucidate a point, this constitutes amplifying.

The second caveat involves the fact that the client may disagree with the new and challenging perspective. If this is the case, the therapist should consider returning to the eliciting stance and continue the search for more data and related meaning. However, before returning to eliciting, this interval may serve as an opportunity for the therapist. The therapist's curiosity in regard to the quality and content of a client's dismissiveness may present an important feedback opportunity for gathering more incisive client data. For example, after a client disagrees with a probe, a therapist might ask: "How would you see it?" "or change it? "or correct it?" In essence, a probe is only a temporary testing of the waters whereby a new perspective, or an "alternative description," or reframe is posed and presented via the dialogue. In no way is it etched in stone.

The third caveat involves the idea that a therapist's probe is a phenomenon that should not be construed as being effected by an expert revealing the "truth." A probe in a therapist's office is simply an attempt to re-order a perspective by a "member," in this instance the therapist, of the "system" as defined by the evolving conversation. In some ways it is like friends who, outside of a therapy session, might ask questions or make statements throughout a conversation which challenge the speaker's views in their discourse. However, in order for a probe to be effective in therapy, it must represent a co-creation, an agreement that is accepted as true by all the communicants in the conversation. In essence, there are two basic possibilities in probing, the client's agreement or disagreement toward the probe. If there is disagreement, it invariably pays to invite explanations of the client's position.

The fourth caveat involves a probe being confused with psychoanalytic "clarification." A probe is radically different from clarification. A probe attempts to effect a co-created agreement for a change of outlook. Psychoanalytic clarification, instead, with its underpinnings of diagnostic categories, pathology and deficits, is coming from a totally different orientation. The goal of psychoanalytic "clarification" involves the assumption that an "underlying" content is assumed to exist such as a deficit. While linguistically it might be argued that both a probe and a clarification attempt to find a better answer to a previous explanation, they are indeed two different phenomena.

The fifth caveat involves Weingarten's notion of exercising "tolerable discrepancy" when creating a probe (1987). Alluding to Weingarten's work on language-based systemic therapy, Real reiterates the importance of observing the guideline of "tolerable discrepancy." Put simply, it means that whether one calls the probe an alternative description, a new perspective, or a new interpretation, the therapist should follow the guideline which suggests that the "alternative description must be discrepant enough from preexisting descriptions so as to be useful, but not so wildly discrepant as to be offensive and, therefore, rejected out of hand" (Real, p. 262).

In a sense, the probing stance does involve some form of experimentation in that the probe which creates a new outlook is an attempt. In developing a probe, the therapist is cautioned to be in tune with clients' "feedback and deal sensitively with the information derived from their response." Modifying client data specifics or creating outrageous scenarios just to offer a new perspective might even anger a client. Just as one can visibly detect disapproval on a client's face when a therapist makes an untimely or perfunctory compliment to the client, so too clients have their own sense of wisdom and can quickly detect adulation or an inappropriately created probe.

In short, probing is an attempt to help loosen up rigidified patterns at the meaning levels of affect, behavior, and cognition. It is not meant to serve as an "explanation" that deciphers everything that has been presented in therapy. A probe's purpose, instead, is much more modest. It might be compared to applying a little solvent or paint thinner to loosen up some paint that has apparently solidified. A probe is geared, first, to move the conversation forward and, thus, to expand the meaningfulness of the conversation. Second, it may assist in deciphering certain aspects of the complex interactions in the web of causality in the client's interpretation of his being, the world and surrounding people.

Real offers a case illustration of a couple "on the brink of divorce." The wife is a homemaker with children. She views her husband as "a refrigerator" and "a block of ice who wouldn't know a feeling if it fell from the sky and landed on his face" (p. 263). The husband is "the CEO of a computer company," and he is, not surprisingly, "fed up" with her constant complaining. At one point in the session, the husband begins to talk about his feelings and about his prior attempts at expressing them. He recalls that, one night, while driving home, he wanted to express how much he loved his wife and their children. Upon entering the house and hearing the clamor of the children and seeing the clutter, he described himself as "shutting down." Believing this information as useful, based on the flow of prior information being consistent with the husband's apparent attempts at expressing feeling, the therapist ventured into a probing stance by exclaiming to the couple: "*This is no unfeeling man!*" And, the therapist added: "This man feels passionately. It isn't that he does not feel but that he cannot express what he clearly feels so deeply!"

Naturally, as one can see from this probe, it implies taking a risk while definitely containing "tolerable discrepancy." The probe may fail, and the risk is clear. It may mean that the husband may disagree for some reason unforeseen by the therapist, but, more importantly, it may involve the wife as possibly reacting very unfavorably, thinking the probe as reflective of tacit alliance between husband and therapist. This unfortunate event could quite possibly alienate her still more in her efforts at making the marriage work. However, when the husband responded in tearful emotion, "It just goes away," to describe the immediate withdrawal of his feelings, the therapist followed up brilliantly with questions in *computerese* to match the language with which the husband was so familiar. Regarding the husband's inability to express his emotions, the therapist asked, attempting to specify and at once reframe the nature of the problem: "Do you think we're dealing with a *storage* problem or a problem with *access?*" The timely idiosyncratic reframe offered in the form of a question in computer jargon, not only matched the husband's repertoire of expression, but also zeroed in on the problem by reframing the problem situation in a "language," in this case, computer jargon, to which the client clearly related.

In effect, two probes or reframes were presented sequentially.

The first probe seemed to debunk the notion that he was an unfeeling husband. The second probe seemed to create a shift from the notion that his strong feelings for his family were merely withdrawal to a problem of obtaining "access" to them. Once the two probes were accepted, i.e., agreed upon by the communicants in the system, the wife, husband and therapist, newer and healthier options became immediately available. For instance, if as a couple, they accepted the two probes, they could begin to challenge each other to explore new areas of cooperation rather than disagreement.

The Constructivist Model • 255

Now, no longer looking at her husband as unfeeling, the wife could concentrate her efforts on "helping" him, indeed, encouraging him in whatever possible way to express himself. Now, no longer viewing his wife as a complainer, the husband could also focus his attention on new ways to express his love for her and the children. As a couple they might decide to create evening settings at home that might include more of a "quiet time" for the children so dad could unwind from a day's work and, perhaps even specify family time for play and fun after dinner. As a couple, they might decide to plan to spend more time with each other, discuss family matters, and get involved in functions that are mutually agreeable.

In sum, probes or reframes offer new possibilities because the meaning ascribed to a former problem situation has changed. In this particular case, the couple could opt to leave the tyranny of old ways of interpreting things in favor of more liberating, alternative ways. Once change in meaning is effected through a change in perspective, it offers potential shifts to alternatives in behavior, in affect, but mostly, in cognition where more changes in ascribing new meaning avert ineffectual and useless ways. Put succinctly, "new frames produce new options for change" (p. 262).

The next major stance is called *contextualizing*. Real aptly points out that this stance is quite different from the two prior stances especially in one major regard. Both eliciting and probing focus very heavily on the meaning levels, i.e., an individual or family "members' beliefs and ideas" and how these beliefs and ideas in turn might effect their behaviors, their affect and cognition. These stances have been described as having a semantic frame of reference, the meaning of things for the client. The contextualizing stance, while not shunning meaning, instead does focus on affect, behavior, and cognition and their effects "out in the interactive field, connecting it to the meta-domain of overall pattern" (p. 264). The shift in emphasis necessitates seeing the three broad aspects of psychology, affect, behavior and cognition, from *social interactive* perspectives. This obviously involves other people and social interactive patterns. Alluding to Bateson's work (1972), Real succinctly expresses the orientation of the third stance in simpler terms by describing it as one where there is a language shift away from the individual's interior space toward "the pattern that connects" people to one another. The emphasis is on behavioral transactions and all the constituent elements of any given transaction. For instance:

Th:　　When your daughter shoplifts, who gets most upset?
Mom:　My husband.
Th:　　What happens when he gets upset?
Mom:　He goes into an absolute rage.
Th:　　And then what happens?
Mom:　For days no one can talk to him. My other children who did nothing to deserve this treatment, have to walk on eggs and be careful not to show their faces to him. Frankly, I'm afraid he'll do something violent one of these days.

Alluding to the work of Keeney & Ross (1985), Real denotes the prime importance of the contextualizing stance as emphasizing the "political" aspects of "behavioral interaction" (Real, 1990). The term "political" means "power," i.e., any kind of "power" exercised in social transactions. Power may be overt or covert or both at the same time. Power represents a force or a pressure in affirming and furthering of one's ends. Like any force or pressure, power may be exercised for positive or negative ends. In particular for the therapist, recognizing the power factors in social relations and interactions and how they are transmitted into the structures of social transactions represents an important first step in realizing the formation and posing of pertinent questioning sequences. The attentive recognition of power and power structures allows the discerning therapist to precisely follow the flow of the energies, the resistances, and the struggles through the use of relevant and meaningful questions.

In this regard, Real calls into play the example of depression. When presented as a problem in therapy, depression is most naturally referenced to a person's "interior space." And so, in the eliciting and probing stances a therapist understandably will spend some time on its "meaning," the relevance of the depression. The third stance, which deals with contextuality and its dimensions in social interactions, therefore shifts the focus from the "interior space" of the client to the external field exhibited by social activities and exchanges at all levels. Working hand-in-hand with the use of circular questions and focusing on the *differences of transactional sequences contrasted in time*, Real emphasizes their use in the contextualizing stance. These questions do *not* inherently presume a unilateral perspective, but rather a *systemic*, multilateral investigation of social transactions.

The therapist's circular questions inherently deal with socially interactive patterns. The therapist first elicits the different ways in which members of any given system (e.g., family members) interact with one another or the different ways by which they react to the problem situation. For instance, in the following interview excerpt, the sequence of events and reactions are the key elements in establishing an interactional pattern:

Th:	When your husband comes home drunk, what happens?
Jill:	We argue.
Th:	Who is most upset by this?
Jill:	I am.
Th:	Who is the least upset in the family?
Jill:	My three-year old, Joey. He doesn't understand yet.
Th:	Who else gets upset?
Jill:	My ten-year old, Tracey.
Th:	What does she do?
Jill:	She usually runs away and hides.
Th:	How does that work for her?
Jill:	Not well…and not for long.
Th:	How's that?
Jill:	My husband goes looking for her.

Th:	And then what happens?
Jill:	When he finds her, she cries and runs away again.
Th:	And what does he do at this point?
Jill:	He comes in the kitchen and takes in out on me.
Th:	What happens?
Jill:	When I don't answer him, he gets even angrier.
Th:	And then?
Jill:	He goes in the garage. He probably drinks some more. He usually has more liquor in the trunk. He usually falls asleep in the car. The other morning, he came to the bedroom and apologized. Then, he went down to the kitchen, made himself coffee and toast, and went off to work.

In circular questioning, contextualized sequences are then enhanced. This process involves describing the problem's qualitative *differences in time* and *in meaning* by creating a timeline, usually between the present and the past, as in the following excerpt:

Th:	How is this episode different from prior episodes?
Jill:	It's basically the same routine. He drinks and then feels sorry. Then, for the next few days, he doesn't talk. He crawls inside of himself like a snail in a shell, and he won't come out for anybody.
Th:	So, were there any detectable differences this time, however small?
Jill:	Well…maybe, there was one.
Th:	What's that?
Jill:	He usually comes to the bedroom to apologize and then runs off to work after his coffee and toast. This time, instead, he also kissed and hugged Tracey before going to work. He never did that before. Tracey told me he hugged her real tight and seemed to have tears in his eyes.

Th:	Does this change have any special meaning for you?
Jill:	I don't know. It might…
Th:	How's that?
Jill:	Well, he could be a sensitive man.
Th:	Is that so?
Jill:	He just has trouble getting it out…
Th:	Getting what out?
Jill:	His feelings.
Th:	And so, you think he has trouble expressing feelings?
Jill:	I think he needs to learn to talk about what's going on inside of himself.
Th:	So, how do you see his kissing and hugging Tracey *this time* as having special meaning?
Jill:	Maybe he's trying.

In addition to emphasizing the use of the Milan school's systemic inquiry, whereby behavioral sequences display the relational connections of the problem area over time, Real also advocates the use of the Milan school's substitution of the verb "to show," or equivalent demonstrative verbs, for the verb "to be." Shifting the verb from a "to be" scenario to a "to show" scenario helps to downplay the implied "universal" or permanent quality that clients usually like to ascribe to their condition. For instance, a client's opening statement, "I've been depressed for quite some time now," seems to imply a long duration, yet it contains a wide spectrum of possibilities including: since I was a child, two years, one year, six months, four weeks, etc. By countering this mindset with the use of verbs that demonstrate conditions, the linguistic maneuver helps to identify the meanings and purposes of social behaviors and their consequences.

This clever shift compels the client to make calls on the paradoxical underpinnings of a selectivity process that implies an unspoken yet operative hierarchy of needs and values. The choices that the identified client makes, for example, in making the problem behavior "visible" to *some* people, yet *not to others*, contains a definite meaning because it ultimately entails different consequences and related payoffs. How consequences and payoffs function and for what reasons usually raise more interesting questions and elicit many useful answers towards expanding the systemic interpretation of the client's cosmos. For instance: "To whom do you usually show your depression?" "What generally happens when you do show your depression?" "Who else gets to see your show of depression?" "How is the reaction different when you don't show your depression?" "To whom do you specifically *not* show your depression?" "How does that person normally deal with you when you don't show it?" "What would happen if, all of a sudden, you were to show your depression to that person?"

Regarding the "show" factors and their related consequences and payoffs, Real aptly cites Olga Silverstein's important work on contextualizing, especially in elucidating the connections of probable causation. Since there are often connections between displaying specific behaviors and having a targeted audience in mind, Silverstein investigates the area of "the negative social consequences of change" and, correspondingly, on the "positive function of the system as it is organized around a symptom" (Real, p. 265). For instance, in dealing with these two aspects, respectively, she could ask, "What might happen if you did show your depression to someone you had originally not wanted to see it?" Or "How is it helpful that only certain persons get to see your depression?" Both aspects of Silverstein's sustained line of questioning dealing with positive and negative consequences, help elaborate and expand the possibilities in the "contextualizing process," a source for useful information for expanding the systemic range of the client's world. This process helps clients to "connect the dots" in the relationship between their behaviors and their consequences and related payoffs. When a client can visualize the causal factors between behavioral sequences, it can often speed up the process of dissolving the problem. The ensuing sequence illustrates the importance of inserting "show" as a useful verb substitution in the contextualizing process of the "symptom," the problem behavior. The second portion of this excerpt illustrates the tracking of the behavioral sequences of the initial appearance of the depression. Time differential plays a key role.

Q: To whom do you *show* your depression the most?
A: My husband.
Q: How's that?
A: I'm usually home most of the time now.
Q: Are there times when you don't *show* him your depression?
A: No. He sees it all the time when he's home.
Q: Are there perhaps times when he doesn't see it?
A: No. Never.
Q: How about your children? Do you *show* them your depression?
A: No.
Q: How's that?
A: Both are away at college.
Q: If they were to come home, would you *show* them your depression?
A: No. I'd try real hard not to.
Q: How's that?
A: I don't want them to worry about me when they leave.
Q: How would that be helpful to you?
A: I'd know that they could study better...not worrying about me.
Q: How about your folks? Do you *show* it to them?
A: No.
Q: How is it that you don't?
A: They're both sick and getting old. I'm afraid they'll get worse. And I don't want them to die on me.
Q: How would their dying affect you?
A: It would make me more depressed.
Q: How is your husband handling your depression?

A:	Sometimes, very supportive. Sometimes, not very well when it deals with our sex life and social functions.

(later in the session)

Q:	How far back can you trace your depression?
A:	Last Christmas.
Q:	Do you know what triggered it?
A:	I'm not exactly sure. It was around the time when I lost my job. My husband usually does no traveling for his job, but this once he went away on business. When he returned, he mentioned that he had a good time at the conference. Then he started getting phone calls...at home. I suspected they were women he had met at the conference. For a while I got real angry with him...for several weeks...then the anger just went away somehow.
Q:	Which came first? Losing the job or his trip?
A:	His trip came first. I lost my job about a month later.
Q:	How did it happen?
A:	I starting taking off too many days. I was already feeling down and getting worse by the day. I couldn't work the way I used to. I didn't want to tell them about it.
Q:	How was it different for you when your husband talked about these women?
A:	I got real angry. I sensed something was seriously wrong. And then, all of a sudden, I seemed to get over that episode with my husband...as if it had never happened. That's when I started getting depressed. Then I started faltering at work.
Q:	Who was the first to notice when you showed your depression?
A:	My husband.
Q:	When you showed your depression, who was the person who noticed it the most?
A:	My husband.

Q: Who is most affected by showing your depression?
A: My husband.

From the overall sequence of contextualizing questions, it becomes evident that the client's depression is presently being directed at the husband. Additionally, the onset and apparent disappearance of her anger at her husband six months ago and the ensuing depression and their possible interrelationships are areas that need to be expanded upon. Thus, the use of demonstrative verbs, *showing* and *not showing*, when discussing the client's depression, represent valuable and effective approaches for delineating the beginning and development of the problem. These strategies add dimension and quality data to the contextualization stance whose purpose entails expanding the client's appreciation and understanding of her problem, its causal relationships, and possible approaches to the problem's dissolution.

The next major component of the constructivist model is the *matching stance*. It involves achieving certain ends which may have powerful effects on the therapeutic process, but on face value they may appear typically unassuming and modest in nature. Matching involves implementing the psychotherapeutic process called "mirroring" which is technically described as someone accurately rephrasing affective, behavioral, or cognitive data. Mirroring has its roots in Rogerian therapy, its concept of empathy, and its related qualities of warmth, genuineness, respect, and the therapist's nonjudgmental posture towards the client. In Real's model, mirroring deals with the therapist's being able to descriptively replicate the client's affective, behavioral, and cognitive data and the client's meaning of that data. Inherent to the concept of mirroring is the importance of the therapist avoiding the temptation to add "any input extraneous to the emerging material itself" (Real, p. 267).

Unlike the probing stance where the therapist attempts to insert a change in perspective within the judicious limits of "tolerable discrepancy," the matching stance does not attempt to react at all to "the pattern or tensions within the system." It merely tries to replicate those patterns or mirror tensions with appropriate words, careful, of course, not to contaminate the client's original scenario, especially those areas involving client affect and meaning.

Real distinguishes between two kinds of matching as operative at two different levels, *the individual level* and *the level of overall pattern*. Real associates *empathy* as matching "the pattern exhibited by an individual system member." Therefore, the use of empathy quite simply represents a therapist's mirroring the data of an individual client, a one-to-one correspondence. Citing Keeney's work (1983) regarding the now classic case of Milton Erickson which in turn was based on Rossi's writings on Milton Erickson (1980), Real alludes to one of psychotherapy's famous examples of matching *at the individual level.* It regards Erickson's long and arduous treatment of an institutionalized schizophrenic patient with whom he spent many sessions engagingly mimicking the patient's word salads and actively paralleling the client's speech patterns. [When the patient was initially brought into the hospital, he bore no personal identification. For a long period of time, the staff literally knew nothing about him, including his name or his origins.] Through a time-consuming and steady use of the method of matching as empathy, Milton was able to create the initial pathways that led to the patient's eventual recovery and release from the hospital.

Dealing with the concept of empathy, Real also points out an important therapeutic principle applied in the constructivist model. The principle regards the usefulness of employing empathy and its possible uses and implications: "*If you want to reinforce or entrench a position, counter it. If you want to liberate a position, then join with it*" (Real, p. 266). In short, therapeutic movement often comes about more speedily when the clients "are witnessed and accepted" nonjudgmentally in their plight, in their efforts, and in their struggles.

Thus, focusing on effectively *joining* the client's cosmos represents not only a good first step, i.e., in the traditional first-session sense of joining, but also a strong and powerful tool throughout therapy (O'Hanlon & Weiner-Davis, 1989, p. 68). Coincidentally, this general posture of *joining* the client throughout the session also helps to explain in great part why effective constructivist therapists, and solution or future-oriented therapies, typically do not have to deal with so-called "countertransference" problems as do many traditional practitioners (pp. 60–74).

When matching deals with systems greater than one client, such as in couples or family therapy, Real labels this as matching *at the level of overall patterns*. He uses this term interchangeably with *reflecting*. This scenario is more complicated for the therapist as it entails not only the "mirroring" of a "two" or a larger-than-two-client system, but also the processing of complexities usually inherent in an "overall pattern." Thus, reflecting becomes intrinsically more difficult to handle because matching the nature of a larger system may contain more pitfalls due to the complexity of the patterns. For example, as is most often the case in couple therapy, the conflicting scenarios of both individuals may make reflecting more easily prone to a biased mirroring. The possibility of a perceived, yet unintended, alliance between therapist and one of the two clients may, all to quickly, become an unfortunate reality.

Real offers one such illustration of a couple in therapy. The session was conducted with a team format, i.e., in addition to the therapist conducting the interview there were two other therapist "team members" listening and observing attentively behind a one-way mirror. At one particular point of the interview, the couple's session was greatly stymied by the husband's and wife's mutual accusations of "heavy drinking." This was complicated by their initially presented problem that dealt with a two-year hiatus of sexual intimacy. When the therapist attempted to clarify what was the main issue amid the welter of the couple's denials of drinking and mutual "accusations," only greater ambiguity seemed to ensue. At this point the two team members exited from behind the one-way mirror and deliberately began "to argue in front of the couple."

266 • *Breakthroughs in Six Brief Psychotherapies*

Citing Sheinberg's critical and novel treatment of this approach called the "debate" technique (1985), Real illustrated its use whereby each team member intentionally takes an opposing view to the problem virtually mimicking the positions as presented by the couple, and they overtly "debate" the issues. One team member argued that drinking was in fact the main issue to be addressed. The other team member, by contrast, argued that the drinking problem was nothing more than a "red herring" and that intimacy was the real problem that needed to be handled first. The debate technique in effect achieved a clever matching at the level of overall pattern. The two team members imaginatively mimicked for their intended "audience" the deadlocked position into which husband and wife had put themselves. As an aside, this staged "debate" most likely also reflected or mimicked, not only the deadlock in the session itself, but also to a significant degree, the last two years of the couple's style of communicating.

After five minutes of this "debate" and its related animated presentation, the two team members "thanked the couple for putting up with them and retired behind the one-way mirror." The effect which the team had hoped for involved creating a visual and moving presentation mimicking a "play-within-a-play" theatrical routine used by writers such as Shakespeare in his tragedy *Hamlet*. The purpose, of course, was to exhibit unequivocally the dilemmatic situation, the deadlocked position which had become the problem or issue at hand.

After the team had its "debate" and returned behind the one-way mirror, the wife reacted "dramatically" exclaiming that the drinking *was* indeed the heart of the problem and still is! Addressing her husband, she said, "You know that we drink too much. We always drank too much. For Christssake, we met in a bar! You know that I'm an alcoholic and I'm not so sure about you either" (Real, p. 267). The wife's action brilliantly exemplified the reaction that the therapists had sought by employing the *matching* sequence through the "debate" technique.

This effective non-impositional "debate" technique reiterated the importance of matching, or mirroring, at the overall level of pattern.

Correspondingly, this approach also illustrated the wisdom of therapists resisting "the temptation" to side with either one of the two clients, but simply feeding "the tension back into the system." In this case, the tension had been created by the deadlocked situation. Feeding the tension back into the system, which was the style of the couple's communication, escalating the tension, represented mirroring at the level of overall pattern.

As a conclusion to matching, it is important to reiterate the importance of mirroring being effected accurately. Whether at the individual level or at the level of overall pattern, the therapist and/or the therapist team members must be careful not to impose their affect and/or their cognition on the client(s). If they reflect an affect, it should mimic the dominant affect as originally expressed by the clients. Similarly, if they reflect an impasse at the cognitive level, e.g., which raises the question of what is really "the problem:" the drinking or the lack of sexual intimacy, the reflection should also mimic the deadlocked position as originally expressed by the clients. Mirroring usually becomes more sophisticated and complex at the level of overall pattern. Thus, how accurately an affective or cognitive pattern is reflected with as few therapist biases as possible remains crucial to keeping *matching* respectful and non-impositional (Andersen, 1987).

The next and final stance in Real's model is the *amplifying stance*. It involves the use of a systemically-guided elaboration of a specific affect, behavioral sequence or idea, or combinations of them. It is assumed any amplifying is aimed at effecting growth and understanding in the therapeutic conversation. Amplifying easily lends itself to elaborating areas in the model's four stances: eliciting, probing, contextualizing, and matching. Thus, anytime the therapeutic conversation moves in the direction of "evoking" an elaboration of client information, however small, that process represents amplifying.

On a larger scale, where many stances are used collectively, amplifying may also deal with *thematic developments* of particular areas of the client's cosmos. Ideally, an amplification should rest on information that is

268 • *Breakthroughs in Six Brief Psychotherapies*

"available as a resource within the system" and then systemically proceed to expand it (Real, p. 267). Real cites examples from de Shazer and Lipchik's elaboration of "exceptions" in a solution-focused model (Lipchik, 1988; Lipchik & de Shazer, 1986) and an example from White's elaboration of "unique outcomes" (1988) in his narrative techniques model. Similarly, in the following excerpt, a husband and wife have already revealed an "exception" or a "unique outcome" in a past situation where they demonstrate how they had acted in a positive manner. This action clearly indicated that they had at least once challenged and countered their dominant negative behavioral patterns. The therapist's use of amplifying this unique behavior is pivotal and becomes the foundation for *working thematically* with the client. The following illustration may elucidate the process of the *amplification of a theme:*

Th:	You said that *last night* was *a specific time*, in fact, the first time in two weeks, *where you could have fought with each other but didn't?*
Husband:	That's right.
Wife:	Yes. That's true.
Th:	To what do both of you attribute that?
Wife:	It's hard to pinpoint. I imagine the fact that he came home early…I should say, on time…made me happy.
Th:	So you think that helped in your resolve *not* to fight?
Husband:	I'd say a strong "maybe." I'm not sure that's it.
Th:	Was there anything else happening?
Wife:	Well, for the first time in months, he brought home some flowers…I know that took time and effort.
Th:	So, is that how you found the strength *not* to argue?
Wife:	I don't know if that's it. I just felt his coming home and having dinner together…and flowers…a lot of things…made it different, very different.
Th:	When has this happened before?

Wife:	It used to happen all the time when we were first married ten years ago.
Th:	How's that?
Wife:	Having dinner together, flowers…happened very often. I'd say dining together was the rule. And he brought flowers home at least once a week without fail.
Th:	What changed?
Wife:	The kids came along…I got focused on them. Tom got promotions at work. We drifted.
Th:	And so, how do you see last night's flowers and dining together?
Wife:	Well, I wouldn't go as far as saying it changed everything. This is only once in six months. I don't need flowers every night, but once in a while…
Husband:	I had to defer some work to make time for us. I also had to make time to come here tonight.
Th:	Did you ever defer your work to get home to have dinner with Susan?
Husband:	I used to…all the time. Now I'm a supervisor, and things changed. It's not easy managing 50 people doing around-the-clock service and repairs on business computers. I have to manage my time very carefully.
Th:	How did you manage to reach this decision to make time?
Husband:	I'm not sure. During the day I'm so wrapped up in my work I really don't know how I decided to get home early.
Th:	And you also got the flowers. How did you do that?
Husband:	I'm not sure. I just allowed myself time to pick them up before coming home.
Th:	So, you allowed yourself time. Sounds like there's the influence of good time-management for your marriage.

Thematic amplification may proceed for an undetermined period of time. It is the most difficult of the amplifications as the strategy entails the process of systematically and *systemically* developing client "exceptions" or "unique outcomes" and how they can be integrated for generating problem dissolution or creating solutions. By working thematically with client "exceptions" or "unique outcomes," however small in nature, the therapist together with the clients may amplify past strengths and resources to create new meaning, significance, and alternatives for the clients. Thus, thematic amplification, perceived as a process, can last a whole session and, of course, may dominate stylistically in the ensuing sessions.

The amplifying stance, of course, also aligns itself with other more specific therapeutic stances such as eliciting, probing, contextualizing, and matching. The amplification's duration may vary from very brief inquiries to highly strategized lengthier sequences. For example, the amplifying stance may align itself with an interviewing sequence occurring in an eliciting stance. A therapist may want to elaborate an affective, behavioral, or cognitive sequence. Since eliciting, by definition, has semantic underpinnings, it may tend to focus on amplifying the meaning of affect, behaviors, and cognition. The following begins with amplifying the client's cognitive interpretation of the client's newly found salaried job. This then develops into the job's meaning at an affective level through *amplification in an eliciting stance:*

Th:	So, what does going out to work mean to you now?
Harriet:	Right now, it means just about everything to me. It's like a new world to me.
Th:	Could you say some more about that?
Harriet:	Well, I don't have to rely on *anybody* for my things…especially my ex. The kids are all in school, and I'm doing something for myself for the first time in years.
Th:	Sounds pretty powerful. What else does it mean?
Harriet:	I can buy the clothes I like and not wear hand-me-downs.

Th:	What does that feel like?
Harriet:	I finally feel that I can be myself.
Th:	What is that feeling like?
Harriet:	It's really hard to describe. I just know that I like it a lot. It's all so new to me…I haven't felt this way since I can't remember when…maybe when I was sixteen.
Th:	Could you share one specific instance of what that must have felt like at sixteen?

Similarly, amplification may also be used in a probing stance. By definition, probing naturally involves selectively reframing some of the client data and then creating from that data a new perspective. The new perspective usually entails something important that the client has forgotten or has benignly put aside. The reframe represents an attempt at changing the client's old or embedded point of view by introducing a new perspective generated from once forgotten or discarded data. But since it is in fact an attempt, it may or may not presently be amenable to immediate client acceptance. Assuming, then, that the reframe or probe is being generally accepted by the client in the following scenario, the excerpt represents, first, the probe and then a sequence constituting an amplification of that probe. Specifically, the probe involves establishing a perspective in which the client is viewed as "artist." The client's presenting problem of depression becomes defused for the moment by the probe. The amplification of the probe involves beginning with the client's initial talents as a youngster. This excerpt concludes at a point in development where the elaboration could continue quite easily to amplify more of the client's growth as an artist. The following is an *amplification in a probing stance*:

| Th: | You happened to mention that you've done portraits and sold them consistently for quite some time now. |
| Leo: | Just about ten years. |

Th:	So, you're twenty-five now. That means you've been painting since you were fifteen.
Leo:	That's right…. Actually, I started before fifteen.
Th:	When you come right down to it, you're really an artist! (probe)
Leo:	I guess you could say that. Yet, right now, that's the farthest thing from my mind. I forgot.
Th:	I'm curious though. When was the first time you knew you had artistic talent?
Leo:	I was twelve…in middle school. I'd doodle a lot and make cartoon sketches in class.
Th:	Who were the cartoons about?
Leo:	I'd make cartoon sketches of all my teachers.
Th:	What were they like?
Leo:	I'd really exaggerate their features. If they were fat, I'd make them fatter. If they were skinny, I'd make them as skinny as a rail.
Th:	What about your favorite teacher?
Leo:	I exaggerated her features too. I'd put a great big smile on her face.
Th:	Who was this person you liked?
Leo:	My math teacher. I hated math, but she was organized, explained everything. Even the slow kids did okay. And she always had a smile for everyone, talked to everyone, and liked everybody.
Th:	How did you sketch her?
Leo:	As attractive…I gave her sexy features. And, she was different…she had unusually short hair. And so I deliberately made her hair look real spiky, more than what it really was.
Th:	So, you were good at embellishing hairdos and bodily features?
Leo:	I was.

Th:	What did all that early start do for you?
Leo:	For one thing, I used to have a lot of fun doing that. I was popular. I had lots of laughs with my friends.
Th:	I'm really intrigued by this story. Could you tell me some more about what you did with all that talent?

Amplification may also be used with great effectiveness in a contextualizing stance. Contextualization, with its emphasis on social transactions known as behaviors in the "external field," can yield needed information in a very effective manner. Additionally, since behaviors ultimately involve semantic foundations, behaviors will often indicate the way of understanding a client's belief system and motivation. Thus, the therapist's effective use of amplification in a contextualizing stance encourages, in the client's perceptual range, an ever-broadening formation in an effort to associate and interrelate the affective, behavioral, and cognitive components. In this particular excerpt, the client, who has had a history of dealing with her controlling husband, is asked to show the difficulties she has encountered in her more recent attempts to challenge his controlling attitude. The therapist also calls into consideration the behavioral and cognitive aspects of other members of her cosmos in regard to the control issues. The following is an *amplification in a contextualizing stance:*

Th:	So, you didn't know about his controlling mannerisms before you got married?
Mary:	Well, it's difficult to figure out some things unless you've lived together. But, after the honeymoon, I knew.
Th:	And how long have you been married?
Mary:	Just about a year.
Th:	And could you talk about a recent example?
Mary:	Well, he's starting all over again about my needing to switch jobs.
Th:	Switch to what kind of a job?

Mary:	One where I can make more money…for him.
Th:	How did he first tell you?
Mary:	In a real smooth way.
Th:	What makes you say "smooth?"
Mary:	It was about nine months ago. It was toward the end of dinner at an expensive restaurant. Right when everything was so perfect, the food, the music, the flowers on the table…
Th:	Well, how was it for you?
Mary:	I got angry when he started on the subject I thought we had dropped a week before. He ruined the entire dinner!
Th:	How's that?
Mary:	Because everything was great until that point.
Th:	What happened?
Mary:	I said I wasn't interested in switching. Yet he just kept right on insisting, ignoring what I said. He kept repeating that we'd need more money if *I* wanted the finer things. Well, what about *his* sports car? Does he need a sports car for work?!
Th:	Then what happened?
Mary:	I told him that I had given it some thought. We had discussed that just a week before. I thought it was really a dead issue. I had told him that I enjoyed my job teaching computer science in high school. Again, he insisted that I could easily double my salary if I just worked in industry and didn't waste my time teaching a bunch of morons in high school.
Th:	Who else in your families would agree with your view?
Mary:	Probably his mother. She *too* had to go along with her husband all of her life and has come to resent it. He drags her all over the place wherever he wants to go, and she never gets to do what she would like.

Th:	Who else would agree with you?
Mary:	My mother, definitely!
Th:	How's that?
Mary;	My father has been a hospital administrator for years. And, at times, he really gets to be impossible, demanding everything from her. And I know she resents him a lot for that. For instance, sometimes after she comes home from a day's work at the office, she ends up cooking for a house full of people she doesn't even know. Meanwhile, he thinks he's such a big shot. She's told me this. She's grown to hate his bossiness, his selfishness.

Contextualizing the theme of control as illustrated in the client's own marriage and in that of the marriages of her parents and in-laws makes available for the client a broadening recognition of the apparent nature and pervasiveness of control issues in the immediacy of her own world. This recognition, brought about by appropriately positioned therapeutic questions and sequences, serves to expand the client's ability to understand the pattern of controlling behaviors, their repetitive qualities, their pervasiveness, their apparently ongoing and inconclusive nature when left unchallenged and unchecked. The amplification, as expressed in the relationships in the client's cosmos, will hopefully invite the client to consider fresh ways to deal with her husband and new ways to think about her marriage.

The amplifying stance may also be employed in conjunction with the matching stance. The matching stance, reminiscent of Rogerian strategy, stands as unique in Real's constructivist model in that the therapist genuinely attempts to *mirror* what is presented by the client(s). Thus, when the amplifying stance is aligned with the matching stance, it almost always means expressing and maintaining a very sustained kind of "joining" that goes beyond the usual joining in the first few minutes of the introductory session. In this stance the therapist does nothing to manipulate "the pattern or tensions within the system," but merely replicates them by

276 • *Breakthroughs in Six Brief Psychotherapies*

employing empathy and, of course, amplifying them. Amplification of matching, like the matching stance itself, may be effected at two different levels of expression. It may be effected either with an individual client, or with the overall pattern suggested by two or more clients.

With an individual client, the technique of mirroring is characterized by the therapist's use of a pronounced empathy with the client situation. When there is more than one client, however, mirroring necessarily entails being empathic not with one client, but with the overall pattern suggested by the system. The aim is to avoid coalition with any individual client member. For instance, in the former scenario, suppose we have an individual client who presents as a problem experiencing a tormenting sense of deep isolation and alienation due to grief. In this kind of situation, after some relevant introductory questioning sequences, a therapist might easily respond with a strategy that would include empathy and its amplification for achieving greater effectiveness. In the following excerpt, a woman of 35 who has lost her husband in a boating accident describes her pain and the complications surrounding his death. The following is an *amplification in a matching stance with the single client*:

Th: The pain you just described seems beyond the normal limits of human endurance.

Lucy: I've been crying on and off since they buried him 25 days ago. I still can't believe it.

Th: I can sense that you've been through an unbelievable amount of pain and anguish. Your suffering is so overwhelming.

Lucy: I'm still in shock…

Th: I can sense the strain of that shock from the tremble in your voice, from the look in your eyes. It's so strikingly clear to me how deep your pain must be.

Lucy: You can imagine the horror of going downtown…to identify the body: and, I had just seen him alive a few hours earlier…

Th:	Just a few hours earlier...I'm sure that was painful.
Lucy:	It felt like I had been jolted. My brain and my body felt numb...shocked...then, at one point I suddenly wanted to run away from everything as fast as I could. I felt like I just wanted to jump out of my body...escape, run away as far away as possible never to return to that...sight.
Th:	So, you were in a tremendous shock and felt like fleeing as fast as possible. And, you felt like jumping out of your body. The sight was so powerful and overwhelming.
Lucy:	After that...when I went home, I felt totally isolated and alone. I felt as if at once I was alienated from myself and as if I was lost in a foreign country where suddenly, it got late...and I had no shelter and I had no one to turn to. It was just a strange and ugly place I could not understand.
Th:	So, you felt alienated, alone and lost, as if in a foreign land...having no shelter, no one to turn to.
Lucy:	When we moved to this city just eight weeks ago, we felt pretty isolated. It was just the two of us. Now, I'm alone. It's as if I have the weight of the world on my shoulders.
Th:	So you feel immensely burdened and isolated in a strange town.
Lucy:	Very much so...
Th:	How has the isolation been particularly burdensome?
Lucy:	We have no children. And so, when we moved here for his new job, we knew no one...and I still don't know anyone real well. We had both lost our parents early in life...and I have no sisters, no brothers...my husband was everything to me. We had been married for over twelve years, and I knew him for two years before that.
Th:	So the isolation is complicated by the fact that you have no children, no parents, no siblings to turn to. Your husband,

> in effect, was everything wrapped up into one person for
> the last fourteen years.
>
> Lucy: I guess you can say that's pretty close to how I feel.

Obviously, the particulars of a matching amplification sequence can hardly be predetermined as the client offers that information. What the therapist offers is a deep empathic posture that reflects and rephrases those particulars accurately. As is often the case when the presenting issues are those dealing with intense grief, listening to a client vent and then mirroring a client's cosmos can go on for as much as an entire session and sometimes even more in extreme cases where tragedy plays the major role. A genuinely engaged therapist, invoking the idea of therapeutic flexibility, must accordingly forget and forgo the inherently "self-imposed rigidities" due to shortsighted allegiance to a therapeutic model, in fact, any model. It makes more sense choosing "to be with the client" in collaborative, "conversational" sequences which often are best brought forth by employing a matching amplification. In this respect, Real's constructivist model might rightly be proclaimed a remarkably flexible, universal model. It can be especially beneficial for beginning therapists since it has many useful flexibilities brilliantly structured into its five comprehensive stances. The matching stance properly includes many positive lessons learned from Rogerian practice and theory dating as far back as the 50s regarding empathy, genuineness, and positive self-regard for the client.

Matching amplification, of course, may also be employed beyond the purview of one client. It may deal with a couple, or a family, or an intergenerational situation. In these sets of relationships, which contain more than one client, the constructivist therapist must switch gears from employing empathy with one client to that of empathy at the level of the overall pattern. In Real's constructivist model, the term *reflection* has been designated to describe therapeutic situations where there is more than one client in therapy.

In brief, reflection represents the therapist's position that mirrors a purposefully inclusionary view of the whole situation or overall pattern as presented by the clients collectively. The therapist does *not* focus empathically on the position of any one client which might incur a detrimental effect on the whole situation. By its very nature, reflection is obviously more difficult than mirroring with one client. To be effective, it must gingerly avoid bruising the personality of any member of the client group while attempting to focus empathically on the group's pattern.

In the following excerpt, there is a fairly typical situation involving a single, head-of-household mother and her children. She has three teenage children, two girls and one boy, who are apparently very angry and resentful of her for "forcing" Dad to leave the house. The two teenage girls have already expressed their feelings about why they think they are in therapy today. Collectively, they seem to express essentially not only sadness, but also a definite resentfulness toward their mother. At this point, the excerpt begins where the male adolescent, who is the oldest of the three, is being asked to reply to the question of why he thinks he is there in therapy. The following excerpt is an *amplification of matching at the overall pattern.*

Th:	Bob, now that we've had an opportunity to talk with your younger sisters, why do you think you're here today?
Bob:	Well, I don't see why Mom is getting on my case about keeping my room clean and helping out with the chores.
Th:	Well, what about the room and the chores?
Mom:	Well, it's not just the household chores. It's something very different. It's a feeling I'm talking about, and it's hard to express...suddenly, every little thing has become a very big deal, a problem. It's a feeling, that's all.
Th:	Could you describe this feeling?
Mom:	Well, it seems that every time I ask you to do something, you always have an angry look on your face. And, you don't even look at me the way you used to.

Th:	So, what kind of feeling do you experience?
Mom:	I feel alone, isolated…like I'm not getting the respect I used to get when I asked someone to do something.
Th:	Bob, what do you feel is happening?
Bob:	I'm not angry with you, Mom…
Mom:	I'm not too sure about that. You always look pretty angry lately.
Bob:	That may be true…but that doesn't necessarily mean I'm angry with you…
Mom:	Well, it just seems I can't talk to you anymore. This all began when your father left.
Bob:	He didn't just leave…you wanted him to leave.
Mom:	Bob, we've had this conversation before. Your father drinks too much and he won't change. I've begged him a zillion times to stop drinking. And, that's why he had to leave. I had reached the point where I…
Bob:	Well, maybe there's more than that.
Mom:	What is that supposed to mean?
Bob:	Well, he wasn't violent or anything like that. He never hit you. He never hit us. He doesn't carry a gun…So he drinks a little. No one has gotten hurt, and I feel bad he's not home with us.
Mom:	How do you think I feel? Married sixteen years, and it's always the same story every weekend. You're fourteen, and he's been drinking heavily from before you were born. It's not as simple as you make it. He's become an alcoholic. I guess I'm the only one that sees that. No one sees my side.

During considerably more interviewing, all the client members have had an opportunity to express their feelings and perceptions with depth of meaning. Correspondingly, the therapist has consistently validated their feelings and perceptions throughout the process. To conclude this

The Constructivist Model • 281

particular amplification with its focus on feelings, the therapist might synthesize all those feelings by garnering collectively the impact of the individual feelings into one thematic whole as contributing to the overall pattern. The therapist in this particular case concludes the amplifying by offering a recapitulation of the preceding interviewing sequences all under the thematic presence of sadness.

Reflection, here at its conclusion, becomes like an empathic summary of the major sequences suggesting sadness as an appropriate *unifying theme that has affected all of them*. It might be expressed in the following manner:

Th: In most of our discussion today, I sensed great pain in each of you. And yet, while each person's pain is truly unique and different, I also sensed a certain deep sense of sadness that seems to be affecting all of you. It's almost like the kind of sadness that one experiences when something is coming to an end. It's a kind of grieving. It is a profound sadness that is often difficult to express. It seems to be a deep sadness that reflects, on the one hand, how one is frightened by losing someone whom one loves and, on the other, how one is also frightened by all the many unknowns that lie ahead for everyone involved. I was wondering what could be done in the coming days with all that sadness that seems to be weighing so heavily on everyone?

In achieving a shift in affect from the clients' initial anger to sadness at an overall level, the therapist has aptly chosen matching amplification as the vehicle that allows for more "space" in the subsequent conversations and sessions. Sadness indeed had touched all of them, and its identification as a therapeutically useful dominant feeling in a reflection creates an egalitarian quality which will hopefully allow the clients to begin expanding and stretching the boundaries of their entrenched positions, that have been characterized by a persistent monologing.

282 • *Breakthroughs in Six Brief Psychotherapies*

Since sadness was a major affective commonality, a common denominator among the clients' affect, it served as a unifying theme in developing and relating it emphatically at the level of overall pattern in the family system. As long as "the therapist tries to avoid any input extraneous to the emerging material itself," the question of "fit" is overcome, and the therapist is justified in this kind of movement.

In sum, the amplification stance, like the other four stances, is quite important because of its obvious synergistic quality. In a sense, it remains the most protean of the stances as Real's constructivist model requires a systemically ongoing and expanding view of relationships, both from within the therapist-client system and from without, as in the "ecologically" peripheral systems. Amplification becomes a most useful and meaningful stance in developing thematic sequences and elaborating any given stance. The amplification process makes the growth and development of "interior space" possible as well as that of relationships in behavioral interactive areas.

Real cites Tomm & Lipchik's work (1987) in which the former openly speaks of a client couple who in the opening of an interview subsequent to the initial session seemed most eager to pursue a conversation about their progress from the last session. Tomm, who because of his more traditional training as a therapist employed a pathology-oriented approach at the time, disregarded the couple's enthusiasm by responding: "Well, what problem would you like to work on today?" Naturally, in compliance with the therapist, the couple immediately reverted to their problems from their prior session. For Tomm, this example served as a realization of how, unfortunately, therapists may unwittingly amplify clients' problems instead of amplifying their progress.

As a fitting closure to the presentation of Real's five-stance constructivist model, it is important to reiterate the importance of his model as a major breakthrough, consisting of a brilliantly devised synthesis of decades-long constructivist developments. His culminating model includes a well-positioned and studied synthesis, incorporating the "multiple engagement" posture of the therapist, characterized as an "I-thou" relationship with the client. By following the principles of an "open curiosity, sensitivity to feedback, and respect" and a sense of utility, the engaging therapist becomes an active participant both with the immediate client-therapist system and the circumscribing client systems. When properly exercised and performed, the five stances function synergistically, offering an effective and remarkably reliable model both for established and beginning therapists. Adhering to a do-no-harm, nonconfrontational philosophy, Real's model is flexible operationally, providing a foundation for alternative therapeutic approaches, experimentation, and ample allowance for a therapist's unique individual style. The model's conceptual design offers the willing and engaging therapist the necessary tools to create a deep rapport with clients in order to jointly generate the conditions within which clients will co-create answers, resolutions, and solutions to their problems.

Chapter 7

The Narrative Techniques of White & Epston

Michael White and David Epston rank among the most prominent psychotherapeutic innovators in recent times as they have realized many extremely resourceful ideas, perspectives and techniques in dealing with client problems. Knowledge of the effectiveness of their brief therapy techniques was so widespread that it has taken little time for them to achieve worldwide recognition. Their innovations are thematically identifiable in the title of their bestselling book, Narrative Means to Therapeutic Ends (1990). Their genius is revealed in their innovative uses of narration in psychotherapy. These uses involve three highly related and interwoven ideas: reauthoring client stories, externalization of the problem, and relative influence questioning.

To those unfamiliar with White and Epston's narrative techniques, the resulting approaches derived from these three fundamental ideas may seem, at first blush, contrary to "common sense" approaches in dealing with problems. Yet outcome results have shown their success rate as remarkably high. Patients who had been dismissed by the psychiatric community because they were identified as no longer able to be helped by more psychotherapy actually went on to find ample and more meaningful levels of therapeutic progress with therapists employing narrative techniques. In some ways, the model's surprising success story is reminiscent of the MRI model of the 60s and 70s whose problem-focused approach, also deemed similarly "uncommonsensical" in its day, proved to be far more effective than its rival models.

288 • *Breakthroughs in Six Brief Psychotherapies*

Before embarking on an examination of the background and foundations of the narrative technique development, it is beneficial to briefly view the model's basic design and purpose. White and Epston developed the narrative approach so that it was not only therapeutically brief, but also effectively long lasting. The model's interviewing process becomes a vehicle for clients to reauthor their stories, their life scripts. This means that therapeutic activity in White and Epston's model literally involves helping clients to reauthor their lives. It is a storied therapy which essentially employs a right-brain focus that challenges the appropriateness of left-brain activity typified by its logico-scientific mode (Bruner, 1986). Narrative techniques begin by defining the problem and then *relabeling* it in a special way so that the relabeling becomes immediately useful because the stigma and embeddedness of the problem are minimized. This is part of a maneuver called *externalization of the problem*. During the subsequent interviewing activity, clients are encouraged to retrieve from their past experiences events and situations that particularly served to "contradict the problem's effects in their lives and in their relationships" (White & Epston, 1990, p. 56). Those specific moments, exceptions that defied and challenged the problem and its influence, are identified as *unique outcomes*. Separate and distinct, unique outcomes represent positive aspects that may have been forgotten or discarded by the client.

Once those positives have been accessed, the therapist then encourages the clients to reauthor their life scripts according to these newly rediscovered aspects and their new meanings, thus creating a freshly devised and more useful narration. This process is obviously based, and must be based, on the client's own truths, which may have been put aside but are now incorporated into a newly evolving amalgam, forging a fresh and innovative narration, a newly devised script. This narrative process is achieved by the use of a highly developmentalized series of formative questions called *relative influence questioning*, which prompt the clients to specifically articulate their powers, strengths, and, generally speaking, their fighting spirit in having resisted, defied, and challenged whatever subjugating forces prevailed at the time. The entire process serves the function of being a source of empowerment for clients.

If one now recalls the constructivist thinkers, many of whom have been discussed in this book's prior chapters, their outlook on psychotherapy essentially utilized interviewing as a systemic elaboration and expansion of specific areas of a client's past, making room for newer and more comprehensive explanations. These preferred explanations were characterized as being multi-causal. In fact, they constituted, metaphorically, a growing web of causalities whose recognition by the client now served to liberate the client from previously held simplistic, unilateral, and delimiting explanations of the client's past. The major tools for achieving this positive ongoing effect, named *negentropy*, are *reframing, circular questioning,* and *exceptions.* The whole purpose of the circular interviewing process was to expand the client's ability to find more comprehensive and therefore more liberating explanations for their lives while plainly dismissing hackneyed, unilateral explanations, namely, one-sided, simplistic, and reductionistic rationales that only served to undermine the client's prior efforts to find solutions to problems. By the client actively recalling and embracing old, forgotten positives from the remote and recent past, called exception-finding examples, a new freedom occurs which creates fresh pathways for the client.

While the narrative techniques model of White and Epston in some respects is similar to established constructivist models, it would be erroneous to equate the two as being the same. Let us look at some of their basic similarities and then elaborate their differences. Both models are similar in that they depend on the client's ability to expand the notion of his past. Both models involve a reshaping of the past, particularly in regard to its "rediscovery" of newly introduced past information. Both models depend upon an engaged client/therapist relationship that is actively and deeply involved, participating in selectively reshaping portions of the past as a co-creation.

However, there are many basic differences. Established constructivist models heavily depend upon *circular questioning, reframing,* and *exceptions.* Exceptions and reframes are relatively brief in nature and are intended to serve as a basis for widening the range of the therapeutic conversation so that thematic developments can take place through circular questioning. The purpose of circular questioning is basically to allow thematic expansion of the client's perception of the problem's multiple causality so that the totality of the evolving picture becomes ultimately broader and more liberating to the client. Narrative techniques, instead, focus on actively seeking *unique outcomes* that generally do *not* fit into the client's dominant version of his past stories. Once accessed, unique outcomes serve as a foundation for *relative influence* questioning, a series of formative questions. The first in the series consists of *unique account* questioning, followed by *unique redescription* questions, and *unique possibility* questions. Each stage of this process helps to solidify and validate the original unique outcomes of the clients by narratively developing *revisions* of their strengths and their relationships with themselves and with others (White & Epston, 1990, p. 41). Ultimately, their cumulative incorporation of these revisions into the ongoing narrative sequences evolves into the reauthoring process.

Narrative techniques also employ a new technique called *externalization of the problem.* Unique to the world of psychotherapy, it involves creating a special *personification* of the problem so that the problem, in a metaphoric sense, acquires a life or an identity of its own, separate and distinct from the client. This special effect involves perceiving the problem *as if* it were "outside" the client. The personified problem is thus perceived as existing and objectified as *external* to the client. Despite the maneuver's apparently uncommonsensical status, bearing the familiar trappings of an apparent stratagem or artifice, it possesses the capacity to deliver effective and powerful results therapeutically. It achieves this wholesome function because the client, now divested of self-blame, guilt, and shame, is free to discuss without fear and is immune from retaliatory ploys. Once the problem is thus externalized, the process of *relative influence* questioning ensues whereby the client's recognition of the times he or she resisted or defied the influence of oppressive agents is validated. By design, these and other narrative devices effect a new and empowering version of the client's life story. Ironically, while the externalization of the problem process may seem to suggest a wholesale, indiscriminate refutation of the client's ownership of responsibility, it actually validates and encourages the emergence of a more responsible client.

The purpose of this evolving narrative process involves inviting the individual client, or any client system consisting of two or more persons, to ascribe new meaning to their fundamentally important, unique outcomes. This invitation, however, is not seeking in any way an overall "normative" response in the societal sense, a caving in of sorts, but actually one that is unique and personally liberating to the client system so that the individual client or family members may allow themselves to move on in life. This positively employed, sustained psychotherapeutic narrative activity allows the client to refrain from any new investiture of energy in the old array of self-defeating, embedded, delimiting explanations and interpretations. More importantly, after the client begins viewing his past differently and reaches the point where those perceived differences become significant, he will feel receptive to the oncoming feelings of empowerment. Thus he will be better able to face the future in a less problematic manner.

Once clients have initially defined and described the problem, White and Epston's approach of reauthoring completely bypasses the whole psychological gamut of psychoanalytic excavational issues by deftly deflating and defusing the old *problem-saturated* dominant story line. It focuses, instead, on the positive aspects inherent in "unique outcomes," those things forgotten, discarded or simply neglected in time by the clients. When the client is afforded the opportunity to revisit these forgotten "victories" of the past, therapy gathers momentum, moving more rapidly toward possible solutions and resolutions. Those roots are found in the reification of past strengths and their revivification through amplification and integration processes of the newly emerging narrative; *not* a movement towards a reification of the dominant, and obviously negative, story line. When the latter happens, as in so many other traditional therapies, the process tends to spiral downward more and more into the problem area, and it appears that the client unwittingly becomes more and more an expert on his failures with each subsequent visit to the counselor.

Instead, in the process of reifying strengths in White and Epston's model, the client is recreating and reauthoring a new story which focuses on success, not failure. In the narrative approach, it is not so much that past failures or inadequacies are denied as much as they are shaped, subsumed, and submerged into a broader, more liberating and expanded client account where success is the focus in the new story line. From this perspective then, the overall effect of a client's reauthored life history, based and focused on "unique outcomes" from the past, amounts to having expanded upon the client's own native ability to create and amplify more positive explanations and alternative interpretations of what were once problematic affects, behaviors, and perceptions.

This new and rewarding development in the history of brief therapy called narrative techniques obviously did not happen overnight. While the finished product is new and unprecedented, it was ultimately based on many prior critical influences, both immediately and distantly philosophical. Reauthoring the client's life deliberately counters the Western world's pre-Kantian epistemological views, which fostered the promotion of wholesale, *unilateral truths*, asserting the existence of one and only one scientifically-biased truth. Now in retrospect, Kant's new view of phenomenological reinterpretation of "truths" allows reauthoring life scripts as epistemologically sound. However, White and Epston's advancement of reauthoring stories takes its more immediate inspirational lead from two major sources, Michel Foucault and Gregory Bateson. White and Epston built many of their ideas not only on Bateson's basic work on "double descriptions," but also on many constructivist thoughts and developments that began with the MRI and its influence on subsequent brief therapy models. White and Epston also based their theoretical background on

Foucault's scholarly work and his challenging approaches to both psychology and sociology from a culturally idiosyncratic view of history (Foucault, 1980, 1982).

Let us first discuss Foucault. The content and striking results of Foucault's work reflect a deeply penetrating scholarship imbued with minute and alarming detail regarding the injustices and violations perpetrated against those of humanity's less fortunate and more vulnerable societal classes such as the imprisoned, the poor, and the institutionalized. As such, Foucault's basic operational premise regarding his theory of knowledge and power bears an irrefutable tone of emancipatory crusading (Sheridan, 1980). The author's style became controversial since it was difficult for many critics to reconcile the emancipation-of-the-oppressed tonality with the operational position taken by Foucault's self-description as an "historian of systems of thought." Thus, it is not so much that his scholarly revelations and results are not revealing and well documented as much as the difficulty in accepting both the logic of his premises and the lack of other perspectives to understanding history more equitably. Moreover, it is not that no one believes that power and knowledge *can* and *do* corrupt, as much as one understands historically and more objectively that power and knowledge are tools. Like all tools, power and knowledge may be employed for good or evil.

Thus, in order to appreciate Foucault from a broad, historical perspective, we must reincorporate into our thinking one of the useful lessons learned from constructivist thought, namely, the thoughts of Maturana and Varela (1987, pp. 46–49). They indicate that individuals and institutions alike are all posited as biased by their own cause and perpetuation of self. Maturana and Varela have identified this cybernetically as *autopoiesis*, where any system and its subsystems operate in an ongoing, reciprocal relationship mutually defining each other while striving for self-perpetuation. In short, autopoiesis echoes one of Hegel's historical corollaries to his triadic synthesis: entities or systems are poised to maintain and perpetuate themselves. Hence, while Foucault's work is painfully profound and useful in the application of its documented information, his work focuses essentially on the "insurrectional" aspect of history. It leaves little room for other points of view which might obviously include how developments in the knowledge of the sciences for the same time frame were correspondingly *not* the cause of oppression, but liberation and succorance to humanity. This latter aspect is apparently missing in Foucault. Hence, as a general rule, historical studies depicting a specific aspect of history can only be valid when they fully recognize that the results of their inquiries came about through scrutiny employing only one major lens. In fact, while White and Epston obviously admire Foucault's contributions to scholarship and to a warranted countercultural reaction to sociology and psychology, the coauthors readily admit that "it is clear that Foucault does not propose any alternative ideology, any other ideal unitary knowledge around which we can organize our lives" (White & Epston, 1990, p. 26).

However, in the general reaction to established culture and particularly its power structures' frequent abuse of their lower echelons, Foucault's work offers invaluable information which White and Epston view as immediately applicable to their therapeutic theory and practice. In strong agreement with Foucault's depth and perception of the misuses of power and knowledge, White and Epston developed the underlying principles of their therapeutic model as being frankly opposed to a good deal of Western society's positivist traditions and belief systems. They were especially against how psychotherapy, especially psychoanalysis, had been so repressively practiced in the past by the controlling agencies, powers, and approved knowledges of the time. By contrast to many prior models, the spirit of White and Epston's narrative techniques model is in many ways countercultural. White and Epston have generally aligned themselves in strong opposition to the more recent trends of the soft sciences, the so-called "normative sciences" such as sociology and psychology. Like Foucault, White and Epston view these disciplines as essentially organs or *agencies* of the "approved" and favored knowledge of the time. In that respect, they represent the "erudite" and "expert" knowledges in

The Narrative Techniques of White & Epston • 295

the hierarchy, and thus wield their time-specific, operative mythologies prevailing as "the truth."

In unanimity with Foucault's theory, White and Epston view *as insidious* many of today's normalization and socialization processes in Western civilization's cultural, ideological, and academic institutions (White & Epston, 1990, pp. 18–27). The coauthors' powerful countercultural position apparently drew much of its drive and animation from Foucault's in-depth studies of abuse. For example, in his *History of Sexuality* (1984), Foucault examines how the institutional hierarchies of religion, government, and academia exploit that area of behavior. He points out how they abuse their power status, their prevailing position of knowledge and wield their "truths," their so-called "normalizing" truths, to ultimately *disempower individuals positioned in lower hierarchies* (Foucault, 1984).

Similarly, through a parallel and related development in the classic text, *Sex by Prescription*, its prominent and controversial author/psychiatrist, Thomas Szasz, who like Foucault, also reproaches those in power status positions who alone presumably "know" the supposed truth. Szasz shows how easily they misuse power and knowledge and have the effect of disempowering the individual. Out of many examples that Szasz offers in this work, Szasz cites with peculiar equanimity two striking cases, that of St. Augustine (354–430) and that of today's practitioners of sex therapy. According to Szasz, though these two examples represent the mindset of historical epochs quite disparate in time, they share an all too common thread of power abuse. When compared, they blatantly exhibit the misuse of power in an ironic authoritative twist in values, actually a reversal or polar opposites of each other.

> To the Great Doctor of Christianity in the fourth century, sexual desire was a disease; to the great doctors of coitus of today, lack of sexual desire is a disease….Doctors of theology and doctors of medicine, clerics and clinicians, have much in common, especially when it comes to sex. What they share, above all else, is an arrogant certainty that they

and they alone know how God or Nature intends us to enjoy ourselves...Hence, they have always been, and apparently always will be, not great teachers...but great meddlers. (1980, pp. xi–xii)

Like Szasz, and of course like Foucault, White and Epston bear a similar oppositional and countercultural spirit representing philosophical positions that are particularly critical of any institutional abuse of power which typically produces negative side-effects, those perniciously promoting the disempowerment of its more vulnerable societal individuals. With Foucault's scholarly research as foundational, White and Epston indict any institution where power is wielded abusively. The institutions impeached are surely not limited to church, state, and academia alone. In a genuinely true spirit of egalitarianism, White and Epston are critical of any and all hierarchical powers who abuse their position, including smaller societal entities that are neither as prominent nor as visible. By contrast to other therapeutic models, especially those *not* in the realm of family/systemic models, the narrative techniques model proposes the liberating viability of therapist and client collaboration in reauthoring a client's life during the therapeutic process. It is presented as a humanely restorative and a genuinely emancipating experience offering the individual new avenues leading to an eventual recapturing of more of one's "space." This is particularly true of one's "inner space," irrespective of the past or presently approved, time-sensitive knowledges, power systems, and mythologies.

With an understanding of Foucault's background and its role in the development of narrative techniques, one can better understand and appreciate much of the energy that drives the narrative techniques model. Foucault's importance lies in two basic ideas. The first deals with the various kinds of knowledge that exist and persist in a given culture; and, secondly, the crucial importance of detaching the individual person from those knowledges that clearly act to subjugate the individual. Foucault asserted that this area is discovered by studying the effects of the conflict between the dominant knowledge of a culture, which he generally assumes as abusive, and the subjugation status of its individuals. Hence, an in-depth *deconstruction* of this area defined by relationships, both past and present, can generate new interpretations and could effect an entirely new interpretation for an individual reauthoring his or her narrative development.

This deconstructed reality is characterized by conflict. On one hand, there are the hierarchically superior and oppressive forces which oversee the "erudite knowledge," those controlling "truths" that subjugate and disempower; on the other hand, there are those "local popular" or "indigenous" knowledges that have been "exiled from the legitimate domain of the formal knowledges and the accepted sciences," (White & Epston, p. 26), which display the elements of *narrative reactions to the subjugation*. Foucault saw tremendous importance in the inquiry and retrieval of the latter kind of information, especially because it did not have to conform or comply with any formally "erudite" requirements from above. Foucault called these "naive knowledges, located down on the hierarchical power scale and beneath the required level of cognition or "scientificity" (Foucault, 1980). These *unique knowledges* became for White and Epston *unique outcomes* that in newly revisited narrative context contradicted both the existence and the visibility of the dominant forces in their subjugating actions. Unique outcomes are, obviously in some ways, like *exceptions to the rule* as seen operating in the approaches of some other therapeutic models. However, here unique outcomes acquire special significance as exceptions since they call into play a hierarchical continuum of power, the prevailing powers and their subjugation of the lower echelons, and naturally the latter's resistance to and reactions against the former. After unique outcomes are collaboratively processed into unique accounts and then into unique redescriptions, they finally evolve into a discussion of unique possibilities, a convergence of all the new forms of knowledge uttered. The client has in effect created a new narrative, a new perception of self by having established a new narrative for oneself.

From Bateson's work on systems (1972, 1979), White and Epston employed, among other things, his theories regarding *restraints* and *double description* (White, 1986a). These ideas necessitate and involve the use of Bateson's stochastic theories. Bateson argues brilliantly that the interpretation of reality in any given situation or event involves the individual's selection of *what appears to be relevant at that moment in time.* Accordingly, it follows that the unique consequences of that interpretation have implicitly discarded or have allowed many alternative explanations *to go unrecognized.* Bateson identifies the forces that discard and disallow other explanations from coming to the fore as "*restraints.*" These forces may operate at affective, behavioral, cognitive, or relationship levels, and they effectively hold back or restrain the individual from making alternative, often more beneficial, choices.

According to White and Epston, the therapeutic search for multiple descriptions, or specifically, a *double description,* which is a previously unselected alternative choice in a retrospective scenario, may indeed hold the key to unlocking antecedently unacknowledged yet meaningful data. That data could alter the meaning attributed to any given "event," internal or external to the client. Locating and then therapeutically processing a double description has the uncanny effect of testing and challenging the negative influences once exercised by the restraints in the client system (Bateson, 1979).

Bateson's idea of a double description indubitably contains theoretical underpinnings which, again, involve his constructivist ideology that views reality as being perennially subject not only to interpretation at any given point in time, but also to multiple interpretations all the time. Bateson maintained that it is through the recognition and acceptance of multiple descriptions, rather than through singular descriptions, that the individual is able to break out of a unilateral view of the world and move on to a systemic or multi-level view of the world.

Bateson called any multiple view a "double description" and he metaphorically compared its effect to the use of binocular vision. With its use there is a new depth perception, previously missing, which offers an enhanced dimensionality. He deduces from this newly enhanced view "that the combination of diverse pieces of information" defines a new way of approaching "patterns which connect" (1979, p. 68) and helps create a richer and much better way, a systemic way, of understanding phenomena.

In short, the client need not be shackled or limited to believing and rehearsing useless, old scripts, much of whose content had been imposed by influences from without. By contrast, the therapeutic "retrieval" of alternative explanations previously discarded precisely constitutes the new liberating energies generated in the creation of reauthoring a client's life script. These liberating narratives become possible because the scope of one's narrative patterns and the relationships have been expanded to more accurately reflect the complexities and the alternatives of reality. White and Epston, of course, reiterate the importance of the Batesonian constructivist perspective and the existence of multiple truths. In one of the early pages of their book, they succinctly state that since "we cannot know objective reality, all knowing requires an act of interpretation" (White & Epston, 1990, p. 2). This echoes many of Vico's related thoughts as developed in Chapter 6. Constructivist premises implicitly contain the idea that reality is, in its essence, a multiverse of individual and collective perceptions and constructs.

After the general idea of reauthoring, the second basic idea of the narrative model deals with one of the major tools employed in the reauthoring process, *externalization of the problem*. It involves a new development that White discovered as recently as the early 80s. Both its initial formation and subsequent developments became topics discussed and published at different occasions (White, 1984, 1985, 1986a, 1986c), well before the 1990 bestseller. It is a specific technique which plays a major role in reauthoring a client's story. The metaphoric maneuver switches the problem originally viewed as "internal," or residing within the client or a relationship, to one viewed as existing "external" to the person or to the relationship. In effect,

300 • *Breakthroughs in Six Brief Psychotherapies*

it creates a "personification" of the problem as if the problem had a life of its own.

> "Externalization" is an approach to therapy that encourages persons to objectify and, at times, to personify the problems that they experience as oppressive. In this process, the problem becomes a separate entity and thus external to the person or relationship that was ascribed as the problem. Those problems that are considered to be inherent, as well as those relatively fixed qualities that are attributed to persons and to relationships, are rendered less fixed and less restricting. (White & Epston, 1990, p. 38)

Externalization is a collaborative process between the therapist and the client/narrator It is a process whose purpose involves *identifying* and *deconstructing "knowledges," discourses,* and *narratives* that have oppressed the client/narrator. Once this is achieved, the oppressive entity is then deliberately *separated* from the person of the client/narrator (White, 1993, pp. 22–61). It is a therapeutic process in which a client is involved in an "objectification" of the problem as if it were *external to the person or relationship that was ascribed as the problem* (White, 1990, pp. 38–76). In a specific sense, externalization of the problem might be considered like poetry's rhetorical device called personification in which inanimate things are attributed human qualities like thoughts and feelings, thus metaphorically acquiring a life of their own.

> I have argued that the practices associated with the externalizing of problems may be considered counter-practices to cultural practices that are objectifying of persons and of their bodies. These counter-practices open space for persons to re-author or constitute themselves, each other, and their relationships, according to alternative stories or knowledges. (p. 75)

The Narrative Techniques of White & Epston • 301

In particular, externalization of the problem as a technique, requires decisive operational efforts on behalf of the therapist and the client. First, the individual client, or, in the case of a family the family members present a description of the problem. The therapist carefully notes the family members' choice of "wording" and their apparent beliefs and opinions about the problem. After this description is achieved, the therapist, in collaboration with the family, redefines the problem. With everyone's agreement the process is concluded by assigning the problem a new name that is appropriate for the externalization process. After this crucial preliminary portion, the therapist then "objectifies" the problem as if it were a physical entity, an "external" tyrant, essentially an oppressive force. He then treats the newly renamed problem *as if* it were something or someone residing outside of the minds and bodies of *all* the family members.

For instance, if in the preliminary discussion of the problem the therapist notes that the family members all seem to be saying, in one way or another, that it is Dad's depression that is the problem, the therapist might simply "externalize" Dad's depression as "depression," not *Dad's* depression, as the problem. Similar is the case of a blended family where all the members, including the parents and the children, fight blaming each other for the family problems and family disharmony. The therapist could feasibly externalize "blaming," *not* the blaming of each other, as the problem. Again, in the case of a married couple, where continued verbal abuse of one another is presented as the problem, the therapist might externalize *verbal abuse*, not the verbal abuse of *each other*, as the problem.

The therapist's externalization of what is perceived to be an appropriate name or choice of wording for the problem offers many possibilities. The therapist's interpretation of the presenting problem may be externalized as an "objectified" oppressive job, lifestyle, habit, attitude, career choice, hobby, sport, addiction, etc. The ultimate purpose of this maneuver involves creating a new mindset for perceiving the problem and a new identification name whereby the therapist's questions treat the "identified client" as no longer stigmatized by the problem. Now, the identified

302 • *Breakthroughs in Six Brief Psychotherapies*

client, relieved of that burden, can become more like all the other members of the family since the problem has been "externalized" and not "located" inside the identified client. He can now shed his scapegoat status and can begin to speak more freely about how the problem has effected him too.

Consider the example when the father's depression is presented as the problem and it is subsequently externalized and simply labeled as "depression." Each member of the family, including the father, may now be asked a variety of questions without the therapy session potentially becoming an "assault" on the father as the discussion on depression emerges. The following questions, directed to all the family members, inherently have the effect of treating the father with impunity and immunity from blame. "How has the depression held you back?" "Have there been times when you fought off the depression with some success?" "Were there times when the family as a whole fought off the depression with some reasonable success?" "Who seems to be the most proficient in the family at fighting off the depression?" "Why is that?"

This strategy, which at face value seems to defy a "common sense" approach, has been shown to be very effective in dissolving rigidified client positions and embedded narratives. Ironically, it appears that one of the reasons for the advent of externalizing the problem strategy came in response to helping clients who, for one reason or another, had experienced either no progress or severe difficulties in acquiring mental well-being from more conventional psychiatric and counseling modalities. This rather critically important category of clients, unable to find even minimal help and satisfaction in prior therapeutic efforts, includes especially those people who have experienced problems of chronicity such as addictions.

In the late 80s it became very clear to many psychiatrists and psychotherapists that White and Epston had discovered a unique and invaluable psychotherapeutic breakthrough. This became obvious in their articles published prior to their 1990 bestseller. It seems that many therapists who had reached an impasse with certain clients, discovered that where they were previously unable to make any inroads with certain kinds of clients, they were able to achieve success in many cases using White and Epston's approaches (Tomm, 1993, pp. 62–64).

White and Epston's idea of reauthoring life scripts was obviously inspired by Bateson's seminal idea of double description, whereby an alternative view in a client script offered new meaning to an otherwise hopelessly embedded situation. However, White and Epston are credited with abundantly developing the search for alternative or "second descriptions" in the narrative presented by the client. Once a baseline narrative was established, the evocation of a double description or alternative explanation then served as a gateway, a breakthrough in finding unique outcomes or positive outcomes that were previously discarded.

The unfolding of a second description, which is inherent in "unique accounts," defies and contradicts elements in the problem-saturated dominant account. When properly enacted and processed in the therapeutic conversation, the second description can be used to generate client liberating opportunities, moving away from embedded and problematic situations (White & Epston, 1990). The notion of therapeutic questioning whose sequence moves from the initial "unique outcome" to "unique accounts," to "unique redescription," to "unique possibilities" was a field of inquiry which White had already published in 1988. White and Epston call this overall process *relative influence questioning*.

Whenever a client recalls in the interviewing process a "unique outcome" from his past, this represents an effective and meaningful starting point for reauthoring a life script. In short, any new narrative sequence generated by a client's "unique outcome" describing the affect, thoughts, or behaviors that *contradict* or bear the appearance of an anomaly in regard to the dominant story line, constitutes a significant starting point. The subsequent developments, originally made possible by the initial emergence of "unique outcomes," involve their being processed through the network of relative influence questioning.

304 • *Breakthroughs in Six Brief Psychotherapies*

With the development of each additional "unique outcome," the client ascribes not only newly assumed importance to the meaning of the "unique outcomes," but also new meaning to the client's past in general. As a corollary to this phenomenon, this change, large or small, in turn begins affecting and influencing in positive ways the client's subsequent conversations. In other words, on the one hand, the process heightens the importance of a "unique outcome," originally defined as what defied and contradicted elements in the problem-saturated dominant account, and now has the effect of making the dominant story, previously deemed as oppressive and problematic, less intense and potent. The overall results of this process involve the realization of a new client narrative, the ostensive co-creation of the client with therapist collaboration.

In order to operationalize this inchoate development, White and Epston created a range of questions in *formative sequences in four distinct categories*. They include unique outcome, unique account, unique redescription, and unique possibilities questions that invite the client to elaborate in-depth alternative explanations in each of these four categories. While the idea of double description obviously goes back to Bateson's work, much of the inspiration for molding the specific nature and quality of unique accounts, unique redescription, and unique possibilities questions was based on Bruner's work which was replete with topographical metaphors and descriptions (Bruner, 1986).

In order to develop an all-inclusive example of the four distinct formative sequences called *relative influence questioning*, let us take the case of a young adult female who has first visited a psychiatrist. After an ample amount of interviewing time, the psychiatrist determined with some certainty that the depression was not organic or cyclical but situational. He then suggested that she visit a psychotherapist for counseling while she remains on a relatively mild anti-depressant. Upon visiting a psychotherapist, the client relates her immediate past history to the counselor. The early portion of the session is devoted to her describing, with some detail, the dimensions and quality of her depression. Let us assume that the therapist and client have decided to *externalize the problem* and plainly call it depression.

Once externalization of the problem is achieved and the client understands the ramifications of that tactic, the therapist may then go on to pose questions in and around the whole idea of depression and its specific effects. The mode of questioning begins with the search for unique outcomes, the initial step in relative influence questioning. In the aforementioned case it involves searching for times when there was less depression, or when there were times when the client actively fought off the depression with some success. If, instead, this had been a family in therapy, the same manner of questioning would clearly be applied to all the family members. "Unique outcome questions invite family members to select out those intentions and actions that contradict the problem-saturated description of family life…This [process] redefines the family members' relationship with the problem" (White, 1988, p. 41). The search for unique outcomes also sets the tone in that it involves the search for good intentions and positive actions that have been discarded or forgotten. The following are examples of various unique outcome questions:

-Can you recall an occasion when you could have given into the problem but didn't?

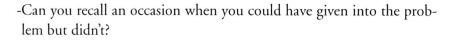

-Can you recognize an occasion when your determination to escape the problem was such that you nearly managed to free yourself from its hold on you?

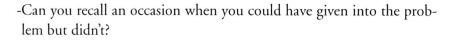

-Can you identify an incident during which your relationship felt fitter and stronger and nearly didn't buckle under the weight of the problem?
-Are you surprised to discover that you have been able to escape the grip of your mood in this meeting and respond to some questions? (pp. 41–42)

306   • *Breakthroughs in Six Brief Psychotherapies*

Let us assume that at one point during the interview the client evokes from her memory a unique outcome, and it is clearly identified as differing from the more dominant problem-saturated story line. Once established, the therapist would then be able to move forward and be in a position to begin asking, first, "unique account" questions, then "unique redescription" questions, and finally "unique possibilities" questions, all part of relative influence questioning.

Let us view the nature of *unique account questions*. "Unique account questions invite family members to make sense of the unique outcome by locating it within a pattern or class of events that are linked in time and place" (p. 42). The following examples of unique account questions are samples based on White's questions (pp. 42–43):

"How did you do that?"
"How were you able to make things change?"
"How did you manage to turn things around?"
"What did you do that made the difference?"
"How did you get that to happen?"
"What made you come up with that great idea?"
"What were you telling yourself?"
"What do you think you did right that day?"
"Where do you think you got the notion to try something new?"

Unique redescription questions, which ensue the development of unique account sequences, have more of a semantic or "meaning" base to them. "Unique redescription questions invite family members to ascribe significance to unique outcomes and unique accounts through redescription of themselves, others, and their relationships" (p. 42). Again, the following examples of "unique redescription" questions are samples based on White's questions (pp. 43–44):

"What does this say about your abilities?"

The Narrative Techniques of White & Epston • 307

"What did you learn about yourself?"
"What new image do you have of yourself?"
"What new quality about yourself do you want others to know about?"
"How has this view of yourself changed how you view yourself as a person?"
"How has this new perspective changed how you look at your family members?"

Unique possibilities questions deal strictly with future contexts. "Unique possibility questions invite family members to speculate about the new personal and relationship futures that are attached to the unique accounts and unique redescriptions" (p. 44). Examples of "unique possibilities" sequences might begin with one of the following of White's questions (pp. 44–45):

"What difference will knowing this about yourself make in your next steps?"
"What difference could this new understanding of your relationship make to its future?"
....
"Since you find this picture of yourself appealing, in what ways could you enlarge it by siding further with it?"
....
"If you were to side with these new discoveries about yourself, what do you think your next step would be?"

The steps in the overall formative sequences just described, collectively called "relative influence questioning," illustrate how this process functions. This small sampling of formative questions from the various stages obviously is an abbreviation of a much longer process that adapts itself according to the clients' unique circumstances and feedback. The brief sampling serves to suggest many other questions of developmental consequence that are operationalized thematically in the therapeutic dialogue between therapist and client(s) through systematic and systemic forms of amplification.

The following three observations serve to round out the significance of the process of relative influence questioning. First and fundamental to the entire process, it involves finding alternative descriptions or double descriptions for aspects of the presenting problem. It amounts to finding an instance, an exception, and an event that contradicts the client's problem-saturated account where the problem was initially presented and described.

Second, it involves bringing to the fore the influence of the problem on the lives of those affected as evidenced in the discussion of the problem. Correspondingly, it also involves bringing to the fore the influence of the family members on the problem as evidenced in the discussion of unique outcomes.

Third, the overall process of relative influence questioning inherently involves inviting the client(s) to reconstruct and reauthor new descriptions of old stories. These are now viewed through a new prism of once neglected and discarded "truths" that have come to replace the dominant, more suppressive "truths." It calls into play the redefinition of the problem and its entire relationship to the client's life. It suggests a resolution of, or solution to the problem by systemically bringing into play new client-based information in the form of unique outcomes that were once discarded.

In sum, many outcome studies have revealed that this brief interviewing modality has commonly achieved "instantaneous remissions" where remissions were recorded as occurring even with a limited amount of "relative influence questioning." The surprising effectiveness of this model has been known to quickly reverse therapeutic situations as if the problem suddenly became a non-problem. Those whose therapeutic goal is psychotherapy through reauthoring lives cannot emphasize the centrality of the synergistic effects of relative influence questioning and externalization of the problem enough. The process begins with a general description of the problem. Once the actual "objectification" of the problem takes place and the problem is thus externalized, it is this subtle network of structured questioning sequences that then serves as the basis and foundation for reauthoring client scripts.

Moving on to creating and asking relative influence questions based on the client's past, the therapist seeks "unique outcomes" by asking unique outcome questions. This involves discovering specific times when that negative influence of the problem did *not* have as much effect and where the client *did something different* that resisted and/or overcame the negative influence. In other words, to counter the negatives of the influences on the problem, the client is asked to recall the times from the past when he/she handled it positively by either being able to resist or being able to *not* succumb to the problem at all. Strengths are focused upon, and in many ways this strategy is the complete opposite of Freudian "excavation." In the latter the client often repeats and seems to reify negative influences and thus becomes, ironically and painfully, more "expert" on how he or she did *not* succeed in the past. To the contrary, White and Epston's model, which also deals with the past, has an approach that is radically different. Once a unique outcome is established, specific questioning sequences, unique accounts, unique redescriptions and unique possibilities create a conduit for change where positives from the past are amplified. Together, the positive materials generated from the unique outcomes are thematically woven and couched in narrative sequences which systemically represent an inevitable unfolding characterized by a new narrative, a reauthoring of the client's life script.

In an aesthetic and practical manner, White and Epston have brought the methods of psychotherapy a full 180-degree turn away from the original psychoanalytic and inferential orientation of one hundred years ago. By respectfully utilizing the intellectual harvest from the Kantian constructivist revolution in epistemology, together with Bateson's stochastic ideologies, Foucault's idea of resisting repressive ideologies and the developments of many other thinkers clearly documented in *Narrative Means to Therapeutic Ends*, White and Epston have created a unique and outstandingly effective model of psychotherapy. Their model is in tune with the complexities of the physical universe and the multiverse of meaning which more closely reflects the multi-causal reality in which we live. They have creatively utilized the complexities of reality in tandem with stochastic perspectives to liberate the client in a more effective and respectful manner. Empowerment, effectiveness, and genuine respect for the client are among White and Epston's most outstanding characteristic qualities in their perception and practice of psychotherapy.

References

Achterberg, J. (1985). *Imagery in healing*. Boston: New Science Library.

Ackerman, N.W. (1937). The family as a social and emotional unit. *Bulletin of the Kansas Mental Hygiene Society, 12*(2).

————. (1958). *The psychodynamics of family life*. NewYork: Basic Books.

————. (1967). The future of family psychotherapy. In N.Ackerman, F. Beatman, & S. Sherman (Eds.), *Expanding theory and practice in family therapy* (pp. 3–16). New York: New York Family Association of America.

Adler, A. (1927). *Understanding human nature*. New York: Greenberg.

Andersen, T. (1987). The reflecting team: Dialogue and meta-dialogue in clinical work. *Family Process, 26*(4), 415–428.

Anderson, H., & Goolishian, H.A. (1988). Human systems as linguistic systems: Preliminary and evolving ideas about the implications for clinical theory. *Family Process, 27*(4), 371–393.

Ashby, W.R. (1952). *Design for a brain*. London: Chapman & Hall.

————. (1956). *An introduction to cybernetics*. London: Chapman & Hall.

Auerswald, E.H. (1968). Interdisciplinary versus ecological approach. *Family Process, 7,* 202 215.

————. (1972). Families, change, and the ecological perspective. In A. Ferber, M. Mendelsohn, & A. Napier (Eds.), *The book of family therapy* (pp. 684–706). New York: Science House.

Bandler, R., & Grinder, J. (1975). *The structure of magic*. Palo Alto: Science and Behavior Books.

————. (1979). *Frogs into princes*. Moab, UT: Real People Press.

312 • *Breakthroughs in Six Brief Psychotherapies*

Bateson, G. (1936). *Naven: A survey of the problems suggested by a composite picture of the culture of a New Guinea tribe drawn from three points of view.* London: Cambridge University Press.

————. (1972). *Steps to an ecology of mind.* New York: Ballantine.

————. (1979). *Mind and nature: A necessary unity.* New York: Dutton.

Bateson, G., Jackson, D.D., Haley, J., & Weakland, J. (1956). Toward a theory of schizophrenia. *Behavioral Science, 1,* 251–264.

Bateson, G., & Mead, M. (1976). For God's sake, Margaret. *The CoEvolution Quarterly,* Summer, 32–43.

Beck, A.T., & Weishaar, M.E. (1989). Cognitive therapy. In R.J. Corsini & D. Wedding (Eds.), *Current Psychotherapies.* Itasca, IL: Peacock.

Becvar, D.S., & Becvar, R.J. (1993). *Family therapy: A systemic integration.* Boston: Allyn & Bacon.

Bell, J.E. (1975). *Family therapy.* New York: Aronson.

Bellak, L., & Small, L. (1978). *Emergency psychotherapy and brief psychotherapy.* New York: Grune & Stratton.

Berg, I.K. (Therapist). (1994). *So what else is better* [videotape]. (Available from Brief Family Therapy Center, 6815 West Capitol Drive, Suite 300, Milwaukee, WI 53216).

————. (Therapist). (1995a). *Irreconcilable differences* [videotape]. (Available from Brief Family Therapy Center, 6815 West Capitol Drive, Suite 300, Milwaukee, WI 53216).

————. (Therapist). (1995b). *I'd hear laughter* [videotape]. (Available from Brief Family Therapy Center, 6815 West Capitol Drive, Suite 300, Milwaukee, WI 53216).

Berg, I.K., & Reuss, N.H. (Therapists). (1997). *Solutions step by step* [videotape]. New York: Norton.

Bergman, J.S. (1985). *Fishing for barracuda.* New York: Norton.

Bergson, H. (1911). *Creative evolution.* New York: Holt.

Bertalanffy, L. von. (1968). *General systems theory: Foundation, development, applications.* New York: Braziller.

Birch, J., & Piglet. (1986). Clandestine courage training: Discovered. *Dulwich Centre Newsletter*, Spring, p. 10.

Bloom, B.L. (1990). Managing mental health services: Some comments on the overdue debate in psychology. *Community Mental Health Journal, 26*(1), 107–124.

————. (1992). *Planned short-term psychotherapy: A clinical handbook.* Boston: Allyn & Bacon.

————. (1997). *Planned short-term psychotherapy: A clinical handbook* (2nd ed.). Boston: Allyn & Bacon.

Bochenski, I.M. (1957). *Contemporary European philosophy.* Berkeley: University of California Press.

Bodin, A.M. (1981). The interactional view: Family therapy approaches of the Mental Research Institute. In A.S. Gurman & D.P. Kniskern (Eds.), *Handbook of family therapy* (pp. 267–309). New York: Bruner/Mazel.

Boscolo, L., Cecchin, G., Hoffman, L., & Penn, P. (1987*). Milan systemic family therapy: Conversations in theory and practice.* New York: Basic Books.

Bowen, M. (1966). The use of family theory in clinical practice. *Comprehensive Psychiatry, 7*, 345–374.

Bowlby, J.P. (1949). The study and reduction of group tensions in the family. *Human Relations, 2*, 123–138.

Brammer, L.M., Abrego, P.J., & Shostrom, E.L. (1993). *Therapeutic counseling and psychotherapy.* Upper Saddle River: Prentice Hall.

Breunlin, D.C., Schwartz, R.C., & MacKune-Karrer, B. (1992). *Metaframeworks: Trascending the models of family therapy.* San Francisco: Jossey-Bass.

Briggs, J.P., & Peat, F.D. (1984). *Looking glass universe.* New York: Simon & Schuster.

314 • *Breakthroughs in Six Brief Psychotherapies*

Broderick, C.B., & Schrader, S.S. (1981). The history of professional marriage and family counseling. In A.S. Gurman & D.P. Kniskern (Eds.), *Handbook of family therapy* (pp. 5–38). New York: Brunner/Mazel.

Bromberg, W. (1975). *From shaman to psychotherapist.* Chicago: Regnery.

Bronfenbrenner, U. (1979). *The ecology of human development.* Cambridge, MA: Harvard University Press.

Bruner, J. 1986. *Actual minds, possible worlds.* Cambridge, MA: Harvard University Press.

Bullock, A., & Woodings, R.B. (1983). *Twentieth-century culture.* New York: Harper & Row.

Burnham, J.R. (1966). Experiment bias and lesion labeling. Unpublished manuscript, Purdue University.

Cannon, W.B. (1932). *The wisdom of the body.* New York: Norton.

Carlsen, M.B. (1988). *Meaning-making: Therapeutic processes in adult development.* New York: Norton.

Collingwood, R.G. (1956). *The idea of history.* New York: Oxford University Press.

Cooper, J.F. (1995). *A primer of brief psychotherapy.* New York: Norton.

Corsini, R.J. (Ed.). (1981). *Handbook of innovative psychotherapies.* New York: John Wiley.

Cousins, N. (1983). *The healing heart.* New York: Norton.

Coyne, J. (1985). Book review of *The process of change* by Peggy Papp. *Family Therapy Networker*, March/April, 60–61.

de Shazer, S. (1974). On getting unstuck: Some change initiating tactics. *Family Therapy, 1*(1), 19–26.

———. (1975). Brief therapy: Two's company. *Family Process, 14,* 79–93.

———. (1979). On transforming symptoms: An approach to an Erickson procedure. *American Journal of Clinical Hypnosis, 22*(1), 17–28.

———. (1982). *Patterns of brief family therapy: An ecosystemic approach*. New York: Guilford.

———. (1984). The death of resistance. *Family Process, 23*(1), 11–17.

———. (1985). *Keys to solution in brief therapy*. New York: Norton.

———. (1988). *Clues: Investigating solutions in brief therapy*. New York: Norton.

———. (1991). *Putting difference to work*. New York: Norton.

———. (1994). *Words were originally magic*. New York: Norton.

Efran, J., Lukens, M.D., & Lukens, R.J. (1990). *Language, structure, and change*. New York: Norton.

Encyclopedia of psychology. (1973). Guilford, CT: Dushkin Publishing Group.

Erickson, M.H. (1954). Pseudo-orientation in time as a hypnotic procedure. *Journal of Clinical and Experimental Hypnosis, 2*, 161–283.

Erickson, M.H., & Rossi, E. (1979). *Hypnotherapy: An exploratory casebook*. New York: Irvington.

———. (1983). *Healing in hypnosis*. New York: Irvington.

Erickson, M.H., Rossi, E., & Rossi, I. (1976). *Hypnotic realities*. New York: Irvington.

Eysenck, H. (1952). The effects of psychotherapy: An evaluation. *Journal of Consulting Psychology, 16*, 319–324.

Federn, P. (1943). Psychoanalysis of psychoses. *Psychiatric Quarterly, 17*(3), 3–19, 246–257, 470–487.

Ferenczi, S. (1920). The further development of an active therapy in psychoanalysis. In J. Richman (Ed.) (1960), *Further contributions to the theory and techniques of psychoanalysis* (pp. 198–216). London: Hogarth.

———. (1927). *Further contributions to the theory and technique of psychoanalysis*. New York: Boni & Liveright.

Fisch, R., Weakland, J., & Segal, L. (1982). *The tactics of change: Doing therapy briefly*. San Francisco: Jossey-Bass.

Fleuridas, C., Nelson, T.S., & Rosenthal, D.M. (1986). The evolution of circular questions: Training family therapists. *Journal of Marital and Family Therapy, 12*(2), 113–128.

Foerster, H. von. (1981). *Observing systems.* Seaside, CA: Intersystems.

Foley, V.D. (1974). *An introduction to family therapy.* New York: Grune & Stratton.

———. (1989). Family Therapy. In R.J. Corsini & D. Wedding (Eds.), *Current psychotherapies* (4th ed.) (pp. 455–500). Itasca, IL: Peacock.

Foucault, M. (1980). Power/knowledge: Selected interviews and other writings. New York: Pantheon.

———. (1982). The subject and power. In H. Dreyfus & P. Rabinow (Eds.), *Michel Foucault: Beyond structuralism and hermeneutics.* Chicago: University of Chicago Press.

———. (1984). *The history of sexuality.* Great Britain: Peregrine Books.

Frankl, Viktor. (1963). *Man's search for meaning: An introduction to logotherapy.* New York: Washington Square Press.

Freud, S. (1900). *The interpretation of dreams.* In J. Strachey (Ed. & Trans.). Standard edition of the complete psychological works of Sigmund Freud, Vol. IV. London: Hogarth.

———. (1950). *Totem and taboo.* (J. Strachey Trans.). New York: Norton. (Original work published in 1913).

———. (1937). *Analysis terminable and interminable.* In J. Strachey (Ed.) (1950), *Collected Papers*, Vol. V. London: Hogarth.

Fromm-Reichmann, F. (1948). Notes on the development of treatment of schizophrenics by psychoanalytic psychotherapy. *Psychiatry, 11*, 263–274.

———. (1950). *Principles of intensive psychotherapy.* Chicago: University of Chicago Press.

Garfield, S.L. (1989). *The practice of brief psychotherapy.* New York: Pergamon Press.

Goldenberg, I., & Goldenberg, H. (1991). *Family therapy: An overview* (3rd ed.). Pacific Grove, CA: Brooks/Cole.

Gingerich, W., de Shazer, S., & Weiner-Davis, M. (1988). Constructing change: A research view of interviewing. In E. Lipchik (Ed.), *Interviewing* (pp. 21–31). Rockville, MD: Aspen.

Glasersfeld, E. von. (1984). An introduction to radical constructivism. In P. Watzlawick (Ed.), *The invented reality* (pp. 17–40). New York: Norton.

Guerin, P.J., Jr. (1976). Family therapy: The first twenty-five years. In P.J. Guerin, Jr. (Ed.), *Family therapy: Theory and practice.* New York: Gardner Press.

Haley, J. (1963). *Strategies of psychotherapy.* New York: Grune & Stratton.

———. (Ed.). (1967*). Advanced techniques of hypnosis and therapy: Selected papers of Milton H. Erickson.* New York: Grune & Stratton.

———. (1971). Family therapy: A radical change. In J. Haley (Ed.), *Changing families: A family therapy reader.* New York: Grune & Stratton.

———. (1973). *Uncommon therapy: The psychiatric techniques of Milton H. Erickson, M.D.* New York: Norton.

———. (Ed.). (1985). *Conversations with Milton H. Erickson, M.D.* (3 Volumes). New York: Triangle.

Harré, R., & Lamb, R. (1983). *The encyclopedic dictionary of psychology.* Cambridge: MIT Press.

Heims, S.P. (1977). Gregory Bateson and the mathematicians: From interdisciplinary interaction to societal functions. *Journal of the History of the Behavioral Sciences, 13,* 141–159.

Heisenberg, Werner. (1930). *The physical principles of the quantum theory.* Chicago: University of Chicago Press.

Hoffman, L. (1981). *Foundations of family therapy.* New York: Basic Books.

318 • *Breakthroughs in Six Brief Psychotherapies*

Horney, K. (1937). *The neurotic personality of our time.* New York: Norton.

———. (1939). *New ways in psychoanalysis.* New York: Norton.

———. (1945). *Our inner conflicts, a constructive theory of neurosis.* New York: Norton.

Hothersall, D. (1984). *History of psychology.* Philadelphia: Temple University Press.

Jackson, D.D. (Ed.). (1960). *The etiology of schizophrenia.* New York: Basic Books.

———. (1965a). Family rules: Marital quid pro quo. *Archives of General Psychiatry, 12,* 589–594.

———. (1965b). The study of the family. *Family Process, 4,* 1–20.

Kant, I. (1961). *Critique of pure reason.* Garden City, NY: Doubleday. (Original work published in 1781).

Karpel, M.A. (1986). Questions, obstacles, contributions. In M.A. Karpel (Ed.), *Family resources: The hidden partner in family therapy.* New York: Guilford.

Keeney, B.P. (1983). *Aesthetics of change.* New York: Guilford.

Keeney, B.P., & Ross, J.M. (1985). *Mind in therapy: Constructing systemic family therapies.* New York: Basic Books.

Keeney, B.P., & Sprenkle, D. (1982). Ecosystemic epistemology: Critical implications for the aesthetics and pragmatics of family therapy *Family Process, 21,* 1–19.

Kelly, G. (1963). *A theory of personality: The psychology of personal constructs.* New York: Norton.

Kempler, W. (1965). Experiential family therapy. *International Journal of Group Psychotherapy, 15*(1), 57–71.

———. (1966). The moving finger writes. *Voices, 2,* 107–11.

———. (1967). The experiential therapeutic encounter. *Psychotherapy: Theory, Research and Practice, 4*(4), 166–172.

———. (1968). Experiential psychotherapy with families. *Family Process, 7*(1), 88–99.

———. (1969). The therapist's merchandise. *Voices, 5*, 57–60.

Keyser, C. J. (1922). *Mathematical philosophy: A study of fate and freedom.* New York: Dutton.

Kuhn, T. (1970). *The structure of scientific revolutions.* Chicago: University of Chicago Press.

Lambert, M.J., & Bergin, A.E. (1994). The effectiveness of psychotherapy. In A.E. Bergin & S.L. Garfield (Eds.), *Handbook of psychotherapy and behavior change* (4th ed.) (pp. 143–190). New York: Wiley.

Lanham, R.A. (1969). *A handlist of rhetorical terms.* Berkeley: University of California Press.

Lidz, R.W., & Lidz, T. (1949). The family environment of schizophrenic patients. *American Journal of Psychiatry, 106*, 332–345.

Lipchik, E. (1988). Interviewing with a constructive ear. *Dulwich Centre Newsletter,* Winter, pp. 3–7.

Lipchik, E., & de Shazer, S. (1986). The purposeful interview. *Journal of Strategic and Systemic Therapies, 5*, 88–99.

MacKinnon, L. (1983). Contrasting strategic and Milan therapies. *Family Process, 22*, 425–440.

Mahoney, M.J. (1991). *Human change processes.* New York: Basic Books.

———. (1993). The theoretical developments in the cognitive psychotherapies. *Journal of Consulting and Clinical Psychology, 61*, 187–193.

Mahoney, M.J., & Lyddon, W.J. (1988). Recent developments in cognitive approaches to counseling and psychotherapy. *Counseling Psychologists, 16*, 190–234.

Malan, D.H. (1963). *A study of brief psychotherapy.* London: Tavistock.

Maruyama, M. (1974). The second cybernetics: Deviation-amplifying mutual causative processes. *American Scientist, 51*, 164–179.

Maturana, H.R., & Varela, F.J. (1987). *The tree of knowledge: The biological roots to human understanding.* Boston: New Science Library.

320 • *Breakthroughs in Six Brief Psychotherapies*

Maslow, A.H. (1962). *Toward a psychology of being.* Princeton, NJ: Van Nostrand.

Menaker, E. (1982). *Otto Rank: A rediscovered legacy.* New York: Columbia University Press.

Midelfort, C.F. (1957). *The family in psychotherapy.* New York: Blakiston.

Molnar, A., & de Shazer, S. (1987). Solution-focused therapy: Toward the identification of therapeutic tasks. *Journal of Marital and Family Therapy, 13*(4), 349–358.

Naisbitt, J. (1982). *Megatrends.* New York: Warner Books.

Napier, A.Y. (1988). *The fragile bond.* New York: Harper & Row.

Neill, J.R., & Kniskern, D.P. (Eds.). (1982). *From psyche to system: The evolving therapy of Carl Whitaker.* New York: Guilford.

Neimeyer, G.J. (Ed.). (1993). *Constructivist assessment: A casebook.* Newbury Park, CA: Sage.

Neimeyer, R.A., & Neimeyer, G.J. (Eds.). (1987). *Personal construct therapy casebook.* New York: Springer.

Nichols, M.P. (1984). *Family therapy: Concepts and methods.* New York: Gardner Press.

O'Hanlon, W.H. (1987*). Taproots: Underlying principles of Milton H. Erickson's therapy and hypnosis.* New York: Norton.

———. (1990). *An uncommon casebook: The complete clinical work of Milton H. Erickson.* New York: Norton.

———. (1993). Possibility therapy: From iatrogenic injury to iatrogenic healing. In S. Gilligan & R. Price (Eds.), *Therapeutic conversations* (pp. 3–17). New York: Norton.

O'Hanlon, W.H., & Weiner-Davis, M. (1989). *In search of solutions: A new direction in psychotherapy.* New York: Norton.

O'Hanlon, W.H., & Wilk, J. (1987). *Shifting contexts: The generation of effective psychotherapy.* New York: Guilford.

Papp, P. (1983). *The process of change.* New York: Guilford.

Penn, P. (1982). Circular questioning. *Family Process, 21,* 267–280.

———. (1985). Feed-forward: Future questions, future maps. *Family Process, 24*(3), 299–310.

Pentony, P. (1981). *Models of influence in psychotherapy.* New York: Free Press.

Peters, T., & Waterman, R. (1982). *In search of excellence: Lessons from America's best-run companies.* New York: Harper & Row.

Phillips, E.L., & Wiener, D.N. (1966). *Short-term psychotherapy and structured behavior change.* New York: McGraw-Hill.

Rank, O. (1932). *Art and artist.* New York: Knopf.

Real, Terry. (1990). The therapeutic use of self in constructionist /systemic therapy. *Family Process, 29,* 255–272.

Roback, A.A. (1961). *History of psychology and psychiatry.* New York: Citadel Press.

Rogers, C. (1942). *Counseling and psychotherapy.* Boston: Houghton Mifflin.

———. (1951). *Client-centered therapy.* Boston: Houghton Mifflin.

Rosen, S. (Ed.). (1982). *My voice will go with you: The teaching tales of Milton H. Erickson.* New York: Norton.

Rosenthal, R. (1966). *Experimenter effects in behavioral research.* New York: Appleton-Century-Crofts.

Rossi, E. (1980). *Collected papers of Milton Erickson on hypnosis* (4 Volumes). New York: Irvington.

Rossi, E., & Ryan, M. (1986). *Mind-body communication in hypnosis.* New York: Irvington.

Ruesch, J., & Bateson, G. (1951). *Communication: The social matrix of psychiatry.* New York: Norton.

Satir, V. (1976). *Making contact.* Berkeley: Celestial Arts.

Segal, L. (1982). Brief family therapy. In A.M. Horne & M.M. Ohlsen (Eds.), *Family counseling and therapy.* Itasca, IL: Peacock.

———. (1987). What is a problem? A brief family therapist's view. *Family Therapy Today, 2*(7), 1–7.

Selvini-Palazzoli, M. (1986). Towards a general model of psychotic family games. *Journal of Marital and Family Therapy, 12,* 339–349.

Selvini-Palazzoli, M., Boscolo, L., Cecchin, G.F., & Prata, G. (1978). *Paradox and counterparadox: A new model in the therapy of the family in schizophrenic transaction.* New York: Aronson.

———. (1980).HypothesizingCcircularityCneutrality: Three guidelines for the conductor of the session. *Family Process, 19*(1), 3–13.

Sheinberg, M. (1985). The debate: A strategic technique. *Family Process, 24,* 259–271.

Sheinberg, M., & Penn, P. (1991). Gender dilemmas, gender questions and the gender mantra. *Journal of Marital and Family Therapy, 17,* 33–44.

Sheridan, A. (1980). *Michel Foucault: The will to truth.* London: Tavistock.

Shklar, J. (1976*). Freedom and independence: A study of the political ideas of Hegel's phenomenology of mind.* Cambridge: Cambridge University Press.

Simon, F.B., Stierlin, H., & Wynne, L.C. (1985). *The language of family therapy: A systemic vocabulary and source book.* New York: Family Process Press.

Simon, R. (1982). Behind the one-way mirror. *The Family Therapy Networker, 6*(1), 18–59.

———. (1987). Good-bye paradox, hello invariant prescription: An interview with Mara Selvini-Palazzoli. *The Family Therapy Networker, 11*(5), 16–33.

Sluzki, C. (1985). Families, networks, and other strange shapes. *AFTA Newsletter, 19,* 1–2.

Snyder, M., & White, P. (1982). Moods and memories: Elation, depression, and the remembering of the events of one's life. *Journal of Personality, 50*(2), 149–167.

Stone, M. (1997). *Healing the mind*. New York: Norton.

Sullivan, H.S. (1953). *The interpersonal theory of psychiatry*. New York: Norton.

Szasz, T. (1961). *The myth of mental illness: Foundations of a theory of personal conduct*. New York: Hoeber-Harper.

———. (1980). *Sex by prescription*. New York: Penguin.

———. (1993). *A lexicon of lunacy: Metaphoric malady, moral responsibility, and psychiatry*. New Brunswick: Transaction Publishers.

Terry, L.L. (1989). Systemic assessment of families through individual treatment: A teaching module. *Journal of Marital and Family Therapy, 15*(4), 379–385.

Thompson, K.F. (1990). Metaphor: A myth with a method. In J.K. Zeig & S.G. Gillian (Eds.), *Brief therapy: Myths, methods, and metaphors*. New York: Brunner/Mazel.

Tomm, K.M. (1984a). One perspective on the Milan systemic approach: Part I. Overview of development, theory and practice. *Journal of Marital and Family Therapy, 10*(2), 113–125.

———. (1984b). One perspective on the Milan systemic approach: Part II. Description of session format, interviewing style, and interventions. *Journal of Marital and Family Therapy, 10*(3), 253–271.

———. (1987a). Interventive interviewing: Part I. Strategizing as a fourth guideline for the therapist. *Family Process, 26*(1), 3–13.

———. (1987b). Interventive interviewing: Part II. Reflexive questioning as a means to enable self-healing. *Family Process, 26*(2), 167–183.

———. (1993). The courage to protest: A commentary on Michael White's work. In S. Gilligan & R. Price (Eds.), *Therapeutic conversations*. New York: Norton.

Tomm, K.M., Lipchik, E. (1987). Interviewing. Presentation at the American Association of Marriage and Family Therapists National Conference.

324 • Breakthroughs in Six Brief Psychotherapies

Vico, Giambattista. (1961). *The new science of Giambattista Vico* (T.G. Bergin & M.H. Fisch, Trans.). Garden City, NY: Anchor Books. (3rd edition published in 1744).

Walter, J.L., & Peller, J.E. (1992). *Becoming solution-focused in brief therapy*. New York: Brunner/Mazel.

Watzlawick, P. (1978). *The language of change: Elements of therapeutic communication*. New York: Basic Books.

————. (1990). *Münchhausen's pigtail*. New York: Norton.

Watzlawick, P., Beavin, J.H., & Jackson, D.D. (1967). *Pragmatics of human communication: A study of interactional patterns, pathologies and paradoxes*. New York: Norton.

Watzlawick, P., Weakland, J., & Fisch, R. (1974). *Change: Principles of problem formation and problem resolution*. New York: Norton.

Waxler, N. (1975). The normality of deviance: An alternative explanation of schizophrenia in the family. *Schizophrenia Bulletin, 14,* 38–47.

Weiner-Davis, M. (1992). *Divorce busting*. New York: Simon & Schuster.

Weiner-Davis, M., de Shazer, S., & Gingerich, W. (1987). Building on pretreatment change to construct the therapeutic solution: An exploratory study. *Journal of Marital and Family Therapy, 13,*(4), 359–363.

Weingarten, K. (1987). On language-based systemic therapy. Presentation in *Advanced program in systemic therapy*, Family Institute of Cambridge.

Well, R.A. (1993). Clinical strategies in brief psychotherapy. In R.A. Wells & V.J. Giannetti (Eds.), *Casebook of the brief psychotherapies* (pp. 3–17). New York: Plenum.

Whitaker, C.A. (1976). The hindrance of theory in clinical work. In P.J. Guerin, Jr. (Ed.), *Family therapy: Theory and practice* (pp. 154–164). New York: Gardner Press.

Whitaker, C.A., & Malone, T. (1953). *The roots of psychotherapy*. New York: Blakiston.

White, M. (1984). Pseudo-encopresis: From avalanche to victory, from vicious to virtuous cycles. *Family Systems Medicine, 2*(2), 150–160.

————. (1985). Fear-busting and monster taming: An approach to the fears of young children. *Dulwich Centre Review,* 29–33.

————. (1986a). Negative explanation, restraint and double description: A template for family therapy. *Family Process, 25*(2), 169–184.

————. (1986b). Anorexia nervosa: A cybernetic perspective. In J. Elka-Harkaway (Ed.), *Eating disorders and family therapy.* New York: Aspen.

————. (1986c). Family escape from trouble. *Case Studies, 1*(1).

————. (1988). The process of questioning: A therapy of literary merit? *Dulwich Centre Newsletter,* Winter, pp. 37–46.

————. (1993). Deconstruction and theory. In S. Gilligan and R. Price (Eds.), *Therapeutic conversations* (pp. 22–61). New York: Norton.

White, M., & Epston, D. (1990). *Narrative means to therapeutic ends.* New York: Norton.

Whitehead, A.N., & Russell, B. (1910–1913). *Principia mathematica.* Cambridge (U.K.): Cambridge University Press.

Wittgenstein, L. (1968). *Philosophical investigations.* New York: Macmillan.

Wolberg, L.R. (1965). *Short-term psychotherapy.* New York: Grune & Stratton.

————. (1980). *Handbook of short-term psychotherapy.* New York: Thieme-Stratton.

Zeig, J.K., & Gilligan, S.G. (Eds.). (1990). *Brief therapy: Myths, methods, and metaphors.* New York: Brunner/Mazel.

Zuk, G.H., & Rubenstein, D. (1965). A review of concepts in the study and treatment of families with schizophrenics. In I. Boszormenyi-Nagy & J.L. Framo (Eds.), *Intensive family therapy: Theoretical and practical aspects*. New York: Harper & Row.

Index

A

amplification, 15, 121, 133, 165, 173, 176, 186, 197-198, 207, 268, 270-271, 273, 275-276, 278-282, 291, 308, 327, 333

amplifying, 82, 165, 176, 197, 210, 224, 248, 251, 267-268, 270, 275, 281-282, 327

autopoiesis, 293, 327

Andersen, T., 311, 327

Anderson, H., 311, 327

Aristotle, 188, 327

Ackerman, N.W., 311, 327

Adler, A., 311, 327

Ahola, T., 327

Ashby, W.R., 311, 327

Auerswald, E.H., 311, 327

B

both-and position, 246, 327

brief therapy project, 7, 17, 21-22, 38, 49, 59, 69, 71, 73, 75, 77, 79, 87, 89, 91, 93, 105-106, 327

Bandler, R., 311, 327

Bateson, G., 311-312, 321, 327

Becvar, D.S., 312, 327

Becvar, R.J., 312, 327

Berg, I.K., 312, 327

Bergson, H., 312, 327

Bertalanffy, L. von, 313, 327

Bloom, B.L., 313, 327

Bodin, A.M., 313, 327

Boscolo, L., 313, 322, 327

328 • *Breakthroughs in Six Brief Psychotherapies*

Bowen, M., 313, 327

Bowlby, J.P., 313, 327

Brammer, L.M., 313, 327

Brief Family Therapy Center, 0, 151, 153-154, 158, 172, 312, 327

Bromberg, W., 314, 328

Bruner, J., 314, 328

Burnham, J.R., 314, 328

C

change talk, 209, 328

channeling, 217-222, 224, 328

circular questioning, 6, 44-45, 109-110, 112-115, 119, 121, 123, 125-126, 130-131, 134-139, 145, 147, 150, 156, 239-240, 258, 289-290, 320, 328

circular causality, 54, 63, 328

circular interview, 0, 112-115, 125, 130, 137, 146, 328

co-constructed, 217, 328

co-creation, 204, 252, 289, 304, 328

coalition, 121-122, 124, 276, 328

compliment, 101, 156-157, 159, 166, 172, 250, 253, 328

conjoint therapy, 14, 21, 30, 49-50, 52, 328

construct, 218-220, 227-230, 233, 235, 241, 320, 324, 328, 332

constructivism, 0, 180, 187, 200, 229-230, 241, 317, 328

contextualization, 138-139, 263, 273, 328

counterparadox, 44, 111, 118, 124, 126, 132, 322, 328

crystal ball technique, 19, 328

cybernetics, 0, 25-27, 29-33, 41, 50-51, 54-55, 57, 59, 61-63, 67, 70, 73-75, 78, 90-91, 109, 111, 143, 145, 150, 235, 311, 319, 328

Cecchin, G.F., 322, 328

Collingwood, R.G., 314, 328

Cooper, J.F., 314, 328

Corsini, R.J., 314, 328

D

depression, 35, 38, 56, 63, 77, 96, 101-102, 127-129, 134, 138, 174-175, 211, 236, 256-257, 260-263, 271, 301-302, 304-305, 322, 328

de Shazer, S., 0, 19, 143, 145, 161, 163, 165, 179, 184, 186, 191, 193, 314, 317, 319-320, 324, 328

deconstruction, 217, 220, 222, 297, 325, 328

depathologize, 0, 28, 183, 201, 223, 328

dialectic, 0, 121, 138, 148, 228-229, 239, 328

double description, 0, 113, 240, 298, 303-304, 325, 328

double-bind hypothesis, 28, 30, 60-61, 81-82, 328

dyadic questions, 328

E

ecological, 0, 4, 11, 33, 36, 236, 311, 329

eliciting, 0, 9, 35-36, 76, 78, 82, 112, 133, 145-146, 165, 168, 176, 198, 235, 245-251, 255, 257, 267, 270, 329

empowerment, 0, 6, 10, 12, 20, 33, 35, 152, 168-169, 191, 194, 198, 204, 250, 289, 291, 310, 329

enthymeme, 77-78, 329

erudite knowledge, 297, 329

exception-finding questions, 160, 162, 164, 329

experimenter influence, 195, 329

externalization of the problem, 0, 287-288, 290-291, 299-301, 305, 308, 329

E.A.R.S., 159, 167-168, 176, 328

Epston, D., 325, 329

Erickson, M.H., 315, 329

Eysenck, H., 315, 329

F

family games, 113, 122, 132, 322, 329

feedback, 26, 29, 52, 54-55, 74-76, 84-86, 119, 251, 253, 282, 307, 329

Family Process, 23-24, 43, 62, 150, 311, 314-315, 318-323, 325, 329

Ferenczi, S., 0, 9, 17, 315, 329

Fisch, R., 315, 324, 329

330 • *Breakthroughs in Six Brief Psychotherapies*

Fleuridas, C., 316, 329

Foerster, H. von, 316, 329

Foley, V.D., 316, 329

Foucault, M., 316, 329

Freud, S., 8-10, 17-18, 40, 54, 171, 316, 329

Fry, W., 329

G

gender issues, 329

Galois, E., 329

Gingerich, W., 317, 324, 329

Glasersfeld, E. von, 317, 329

Goldenberg, H., 317, 329

Goldenberg, I., 317, 329

Goolishian, H.A., 311, 329

Greek chorus, 116, 155, 329

Grinder, J., 311, 329

Guerin, P.J., 317, 329

H

helpful certainties, 224, 330

history as interpretation, 227, 230-231, 330

hologram, 129, 139, 330

homeostasis, 24, 27, 42, 63, 66, 95, 111, 114, 118, 121, 330

homework assignment, 167, 172, 330

hypothesizing, 119-120, 330

Haley, J., 312, 317, 330

Heims, S.P., 317, 330

Heisenberg, W., 330

Hoffman, L., 313, 317, 330

Horney, K., 318, 330

Houston-Galveston School, 36, 172, 330

I

insight, 10, 12, 19, 28, 37, 40, 53, 57, 79-80, 131, 182, 190, 330

Index • 331

intrapsychic, 12-13, 22-24, 37, 40, 53, 61, 80, 119, 192-193, 330

invariance, 92-93, 330

invariant prescription, 132, 322, 330

I-thou, 237-238, 243, 282, 330

J

joining, 26, 83-84, 121, 154-155, 161, 205-206, 212, 214, 223, 264-265, 275, 330

Jackson, D.D., 312, 318, 324, 330

K

Kant, I., 318, 330

Karpel, M.A., 318, 330

Keeney, B.P., 318, 330

Kelly, G., 318, 330

Kempler, W., 318, 330

Keyser, C.J., 319, 330

Kniskern, D., 320, 330

Kuhn, T., 319, 330

L

logical paradoxes, 56, 58, 100, 330

labeling, 0, 33, 35, 126, 129, 217-218, 314, 330

languaging, 0, 126, 130, 133, 175, 205, 211, 215, 221-223, 241, 330

linguistic sensitivity, 119, 126-127, 130, 137, 207, 241, 330

Lipchik, E., 319, 323, 330

M

matching, 15 16, 205, 207, 211-217, 220, 245, 263-267, 270, 275-276, 278-279, 281, 331

metacommunication, 42, 64-66, 331

metaphor, 11, 15, 19, 75, 169, 183, 198, 213, 323, 331

miracle question, 19, 160-164, 167, 169, 175-176, 205, 208, 211, 331

monadic questions, 136, 331

multiple engagement, 237-238, 243, 282, 331

multiverse, 239, 299, 310, 331

MacKinnon, L., 319, 331

332 • *Breakthroughs in Six Brief Psychotherapies*

Madanes, C., 331

Mahoney, M.J., 319, 331

Maruyama, M., 319, 331

Maslow, A.H., 320, 331

Maturana, H., 319, 331

Menaker, E., 320, 331

Midelfort, C.F., 320, 331

Milan school, 0, 6, 42, 44-45, 109-111, 113, 115-117, 119, 121-127, 129, 131, 133, 135, 137, 139, 146, 150, 156, 240, 259, 331

Milan group, 0, 6, 110-114, 116-117, 119, 121, 124, 129, 131-133, 137, 139, 145-146, 148, 150, 156, 172, 331

MRI, 0, 6-7, 23, 38-39, 41-45, 49, 51, 53-55, 57, 59, 61-65, 67-83, 85-87, 89-93, 95-97, 99, 101, 103, 105-106, 109-112, 115, 131, 133, 143-146, 148, 150-154, 156-157, 159, 171-172, 179, 184, 198, 204, 238, 287, 292, 331

N

naive knowledge, 331

narrative techniques, 0, 33, 268, 287-297, 299, 301, 303, 305, 307, 309, 331

negentropy, 114, 121, 126, 129, 289, 331

negotiable reality, 331

neutrality, 119, 122-124, 133, 137, 331

normalization, 217, 295, 331

not-knowing, 331

Naisbitt, J., 320, 331

Napier, A.Y., 320, 331

Neill, J.R., 320, 331

Nichols, M.P., 320, 331

O

O'Hanlon, W.H., 320

P

paradigm shift, 37, 40, 61, 149, 332

paradoxical intervention, 80, 84-85, 102, 105, 126, 332

pathology, 0, 79, 181-183, 185, 194-195, 197, 204-205, 221, 252, 332 positive connotation, 45, 114, 119, 124-126, 137, 147, 173, 176, 191, 239, 332

preemptive construct, 219-220, 332

prescribing the symptom, 78, 80, 82-87, 89, 102, 105, 152, 332

presuppositional questions, 168, 191, 207-211, 216, 220, 332

pretreatment change, 207, 324, 332

probing, 18, 236, 245, 250, 252-255, 257, 263, 267, 270-271, 332

problem-focused model, 0, 67-68, 73-74, 81, 106, 109, 153, 332

pseudo-orientation in time, 17, 19-20, 152, 185-187, 315, 332

pseudosolutions, 103-104, 332

Palo Alto Project, 55, 331

Papp, P., 320, 331

Penn, P., 313, 320, 322, 332

Pentony, P., 321, 332

Peters, T., 321, 332

Prata, G., 322, 332

R

reauthoring, 0, 287, 290-292, 296-297, 299, 303, 308-309, 332

reciprocal influence, 24, 202, 228, 332

reframing, 0, 42, 45, 74, 76, 78, 82, 101-102, 105-106, 113-114, 125, 135, 147, 151, 185, 191, 222, 233, 235-236, 254, 271, 289-290, 332

relationship questions, 160, 162, 164-166, 168, 332

relative certainty, 60, 221-222, 229, 332

relative influence questioning, 0, 287-288, 290, 303-308, 332

resistance, 15, 43, 70, 83-84, 154, 171-172, 193-194, 297, 315, 332

rituals, 45, 114, 119, 131, 147, 332

rules, 18, 58, 63, 65-66, 70, 78, 80, 85, 87, 89, 93, 96, 103-104, 113, 118, 131, 198, 318, 333

Rank, O., 321, 332

Real, T., 332

Riskin, J., 332

Roback, A.A., 321, 332

Rogers, C., 321, 332

334 • Breakthroughs in Six Brief Psychotherapies

Rosen, S., 321, 332

Rosenthal, R., 321, 332

Ross, J.M., 318, 332

Rossi, E., 315, 321, 333

Russell, B., 325, 333

S

scaling questions, 160-163, 165-166, 168, 214, 333

schizophrenia, 0, 21-23, 27-30, 38, 49, 51-52, 54-55, 59-60, 62-64, 82, 312, 318, 324, 333

second-order change, 6, 41, 57, 70, 72, 76, 79, 85, 87, 89, 91, 96, 98-99, 101-103, 105-106, 113, 153, 238, 243, 333

semantics, 143, 145, 173-175, 190, 249, 333

sensory data, 216, 233, 333

skeleton keys, 169-170, 333

solution-focused model, 0, 153, 167, 175, 187, 205, 268, 333

solution-oriented model, 198, 205-206, 333

symptom, 45, 68, 78, 80, 82-89, 102, 105, 120, 125, 137, 144-145, 152, 192-193, 201, 260, 332-333

symptom-maintenance, 184, 333

systemic/family, 3, 5, 7, 13-14, 21, 23, 31

Satir, V., 321, 333

Segal, L., 315, 321, 333

Selvini-Palazzoli, M., 110, 322, 333

Sheinberg, M., 322, 333

Sheridan, A., 322, 333

Silverstein, O., 333

Simon, F.B., 322, 333

Simon, R., 322, 333

Sluzki, C., 322, 333

Snyder, M., 322, 333

Sprenkle, D., 318, 333

Sullivan, H.S., 323, 333

Szasz, T., 323, 333

T

thematic amplification, 270, 333

theory of groups, 91-92, 333

theory of logical types, 55, 58-59, 91, 97-98, 333

therapeutic double bind, 81, 85-86, 105-106, 118, 126, 334

therapeutic flexibility, 34-35, 195, 237, 278, 334

tolerable discrepancy, 252, 254, 263, 334

triadic questions, 155, 164, 334

trigger words, 126, 174, 334

Tavistock Clinic, 50, 333

Terry, L.L., 323, 333

Thompson, K.F., 323, 334

Tomm, K.M., 323, 334

U

uncertainty principle, 180, 235, 334

unhelpful certainty, 221-222, 334

unilateral truths, 292, 334

unique possibilities, 297, 303-304, 306-307, 309, 334

unique redescription, 290, 303-304, 306, 334

unique account, 290, 304, 306, 334

unique outcomes, 268, 270, 288, 290-292, 297, 303-306, 308-309, 334

utilization strategy, 17, 20, 155, 164-165, 167, 171, 185, 187, 214, 334

V

verum et certum convertuntur, 228, 334

Varela, F., 319, 334

Vico, G., 334

W

word salad, 212, 334

Waterman, R., 321, 334

Watzlawick, P., 324, 334

Weakland, J., 312, 315, 324, 334

Weiner-Davis, M., 317, 320, 324, 334

Weingarten, K., 324, 334

Whitaker, C.A., 324, 334

White, M., 325, 334

Whitehead, A.N., 325, 334

Wilk, J., 320, 334

Wittgenstein, L., 325, 334

About the Author

Degreed in Renaissance literature (Rutgers, 1973), Dr. Carpetto has published many articles and books including poetry, fiction, and literary analysis in Italian Humanism. He recently edited *Italian Americans of the Twentieth Century* (1999). With a masters degree in mental health (Nova, 1993), he teaches counseling at St. Leo University.

Printed in the United States
46709LVS00003B/91